Mixing Musics

STANFORD STUDIES IN JEWISH HISTORY AND CULTURE

EDITED BY *Aron Rodrigue and Steven J. Zipperstein*

Mixing Musics
Turkish Jewry and the
Urban Landscape of a Sacred Song

Maureen Jackson

STANFORD UNIVERSITY PRESS
STANFORD, CALIFORNIA

Stanford University Press
Stanford, California

©2013 by the Board of Trustees of the Leland Stanford Junior University.
All rights reserved.

No part of this book may be reproduced or transmitted in any form or by any means, electronic or mechanical, including photocopying and recording, or in any information storage or retrieval system without the prior written permission of Stanford University Press.

Printed in the United States of America on acid-free, archival-quality paper

Library of Congress Cataloging-in-Publication Data

Jackson, Maureen (Maureen Barbara), author.
  Mixing musics : Turkish Jewry and the urban landscape of a sacred song / Maureen Jackson.
        pages ; cm.--(Stanford studies in Jewish history and culture)
  Originally presented as the author's thesis (doctoral)--University of Washington, 2008.
  Includes bibliographical references and index.
  ISBN 978-0-8047-8015-5 (cloth : alk. paper)
  ISBN 978-0-8047-9726-9 (pbk. : alk. paper)
  1. Synagogue music--Turkey--Istanbul--History and criticism. 2. Jews--Turkey--Istanbul--Music--History and criticism. 3. Sacred music--Turkey--Istanbul--20th century--History and criticism. 4. Sacred music--Turkey--Istanbul--21st century--History and criticism. I. Title. II. Series: Stanford studies in Jewish history and culture.
  ML3195.J33 2013
    782.3'600949618--dc23   2013005336

    ISBN 978-0-8047-8566-2 (electronic)

Typeset by Bruce Lundquist in 10.5/14 Galliard.

*Dedicated to my mother, Barbara Jackson—
your aesthetic sensibility delights and resilience inspires*

Contents

Acknowledgments ix
A Note on Terminology, Transcription, and Translation xiii

Introduction 1
1. Mapping Ottoman Music-Making 17
2. Into the Nation: A Musical Landscape in Flux 49
3. The Girl in the Tree: Gender and Sacred Song 87
4. Staging Harmony, Guarding Community 117
5. Into the Future: Texts, Technologies, and Tradition 141
   Epilogue 169

Notes 179
Glossary 225
Discography 231
References 235
Index 249

Acknowledgments

Countless individuals and institutions supported the completion of this book. Ethnographic and archival materials gleaned from interviews, conversations, participant observation, and personal collections on both sides of the Atlantic form the foundation of the study. In Seattle, I am indebted to Judith Amiel and Isaac Azose, who generously offered their memories, knowledge, and encouragement throughout the course of the project. Thanks are also due Lilly De Jaen, Al and Isaac Maimon, and Rabbi Solomon Maimon. In Istanbul, musicians, scholars, and others made crucial contributions during the research, especially Cem Behar, Mehmet Güntekin, and David Sevi, together with Hayim and Victoria Abravanel, Rav Leon Yeuda Adoni, Nevzat Atlığ, Yusuf Altıntaş, Rıfat Bali, İzzet Bana, David Behar, Viki and Janti Behar, Victor Beruhiel, Rıfat Dana, Menahem Eskenazi, Jak Esim, Father Gaspar, Karen Gerson Şarhon, Moşe Grossman, Ahmet Gürsel, Selin Maçoro, Oral Onur, A. Nevzat Tırışkan, Necdet Yaşar, Alaeddin Yavaşça, and Yavuz Yekta. Credit also goes to the Maftirim singers at Şişli synagogue and in the Sinagog Maftirim Korosu.

The Fulbright Foundation supported research in Istanbul in 2005–2006 through a Fulbright-Hays International Dissertation Research Fellowship. At the University of Washington, fellowships from the Walter Chapin Simpson Center for the Humanities, the Textual Studies program, and the Samuel and Althea Stroum Jewish Studies program contributed to additional research, writing, and analysis. An ACLS Mellon New Faculty Fellowship in 2010–2012 supported completion of the book manuscript. Subventions from the AMS 75 PAYS Endowment of the American Musicological Association and the

Lucius N. Littauer Foundation have enriched the illustrative material of the final publication.

Academic mentorship and training at the University of Washington prepared me for my work. Sarah Abrevaya Stein is unmatched for cultivating an intellectually rigorous and empowering relationship, interwoven with kindness. Raimonda Modiano offered early and unconditional support for the project, and a theoretical home in her innovative Textual Studies program. Reşat Kasaba encourages the highest standards of scholarship and humanity, and Münir Beken exemplifies how an artist and scholar can thrive within the same human being. I also thank Kathie Friedman, Martin Jaffee, Paul Remley, and Philip Schuyler for their early encouragement; Biff and Jane Keyes for their loyal friendship; and the interdisciplinary Turkish Studies Research Group, led by Reşat Kasaba, for its companionship and commentary, especially Senem Aslan, Arda İbikoğlu, Ali İğmen, Turan Kayaoğlu, Sevim Kebeli, Selim Kuru, and Tuna Kuyucu. For reading and commenting on book chapters and incorporated articles, I am grateful to Cem Behar, Walter Feldman, Ian Jackson, Amy Mills, and Sarah Abrevaya Stein, and the anonymous readers of the original manuscript. I am indebted to Edwin Seroussi for his foundational research and generosity.

My research in Istanbul depended upon many acts of kindness and logistical support. I particularly thank Işık and Ferruh of Pan Yayıncılık; Lina Filiba, former Executive Vice President of the Hahambaşlığı offices, and her staff; Karen Gerson Şarhon, Coordinator of the Ottoman-Turkish Sephardic Culture Research Center; Gila Erbes of Gözlem Press; and Bensi Elmas, coordinator of the Sinagog Maftirim Korosu. The American Research Institute in Turkey (ARIT) not only provided library and living space, but also friendships and resources through its staff, Tony Greenwood, Gülden Güneri, and Semrin Korkmaz with Sündüz Gürses and Gazel Kayhan, and co-residents in 2005–2006, especially, Gábor Ágoston, Jane Hathaway, Başak Kuş, and Davidson MacLaren. For ongoing musical learning I am grateful to the teachers at Üsküdar Musıki Cemiyeti, conductor Atilla Gündüz and the Kasdav Korosu, and Robert Reigle, ethnomusicologist at Istanbul Technical University. I appreciate the translation assistance of Kai Herklotz, Shira Jaret, Hila Lenz, and Arzu Sekirden.

At numerous conferences and symposia I received valuable feedback on diverse aspects of this study. I especially thank the participants in the "Sacred Spaces, Sacred Sounds" conference in the Sawyer Seminar series, Diversity and Conformity in Muslim Societies: Historical Coexistence and Contemporary Struggles (University of North Carolina, at Chapel Hill, April 2010); "Creative Expressions of the Sephardic Experience" symposium (Indiana University, March 2009); "Integrating Sephardi and Mizrachi Studies: Research and Practice" conference (UCLA, November 2008); and "Entangled Lives: Social Encounters in the Mediterranean and Beyond" (Stanford University, Sephardi Studies Project and Mediterranean Studies Forum, May 2008). Invitations to speak at Yale University, the Hrank Dink Foundation, and the American Research Institute in Turkey, together with presentations at conferences of the Middle East Studies Association, the Society for Ethnomusicology, the Association for Jewish Studies, and the Society for Textual Scholarship have brought my work into fruitful and ongoing dialogue with a wide range of interdisciplinary scholars too numerous to thank individually.

Those working with me at Stanford University Press gracefully facilitated all aspects of the book's publication. I especially thank Aron Rodrigue, Norris Pope, Mariana Raykov, Emma Harper, Richard Gunde, Rob Ehle, and David Stein. Credit is also due to independent cartographer Bill Nelson.

I am grateful for the constancy and encouragement of my family—my parents, Barbara and David Jackson; my sister, Nan, and brothers Mark and Ian; and my sister-in-law Ann and brother-in-law Vern. Beth Harris, Alix Huff, and Rie Nakamura offered the sweetness of aged-in-wood friendships, and Lynda Misher and Keith Snodgrass a second family as well. Finally, I owe a tribute to my late friend Hüseyin Özbek, with whom I first encountered Turkey and without whom this project might never have been conceived.

Portions of this study have been published previously as journal articles and are reproduced by permission of Duke University Press and Indiana University Press: "Crossing Musical Worlds: Ottoman Jewry, Music Making and the Rise of the Nation," in *Comparative Studies of South Asia, Africa and the Middle East*, vol. 31, issue 3, pp. 569–587 (©Duke University Press, 2011), and "The Girl in the Tree: Gender,

Istanbul Soundscapes, and Synagogue Song," in *Jewish Social Studies: History, Culture, Society*, vol. 17, no. 1, pp. 31–66 (© Indiana University Press, 2010).

A Note on Terminology, Transcription, and Translation

Transcription and Translation

In transliterating Turkish and Hebrew I have sought to make vocabulary accessible to a scholarly and general readership. I preserve original Turkish words as used by Turkish writers and speakers, unless they represent commonly understood terms in English (for example, Jewish holidays: Roş Aşana becomes Rosh Hashanah). In transliterating Hebrew I use the Library of Congress system without diacritical marks, unless a cited source utilizes an alternate transcription (for example, community spellings of the title of a Hebrew composition, name of a synagogue, or holidays). All translations of texts into English are my own, unless otherwise noted. Out of the numerous terms referring to the language of Sephardi Jews (for example, İspanyolca, Judezmo, Judeo-Spanish, Ladino), I have chosen to use the term Ladino for the written, spoken, or sung forms of the language.

Tangling with Musical Terminology

One of the challenges of the project is employing terms for the Ottoman music under discussion, and its Jewish or Hebrew forms. Practicing musicians, scholars, and contemporary listeners utilize a variety of terms, depending upon scholarly, political, or popular perspective. My overarching goal for choice of terminology has been to highlight the focus of the book, that is, changing musical interactivity, and to avoid cumbersome verbiage. With that in mind, I generally use the term "Ottoman music" (or "Ottoman court music") to refer to the distinctive, defining music of the imperial state and urban society, that is, the art music patronized by the court, developed by multiethnic composers, and cultivated in a variety of urban settings. This usage reflects a narrow definition that does not include diverse musical cultures of the empire. For music related to Ottoman court music and performed in the twentieth- and twenty-first-century Turkish Republic, I use the terms "classical Turkish music" (*klasik Türk müziği*) and "Turkish art music" (*Türk sanat müziği*), as used loosely by general listeners in Turkey. When referring to more specific historical developments, the former connotes an offshoot of Ottoman music developed by traditionalist musicians in the early Republic to protect Ottoman practices from commercialization and elevate the music's status in a Europeanizing era. "Turkish art music" will generally mean lighter classical forms progressively developing in Turkish society and entertainment venues since the early twentieth century.

It is similarly a challenge to label Jewish or Hebrew forms of Ottoman music. "Maftirim" represents only a paraliturgical subset of musical forms found in the synagogue that are related to Ottoman court music practices, such as the use of makams and vocal improvisations during prayer services. I generally use the terms "Ottoman synagogue music" and "Turkish synagogue music" to refer to the in-synagogue practices that include the Maftirim, span the empire and republican periods, and foreground the urban contexts and circulations emphasized in the study. Specific discussions may require more specific terms, such as the Maftirim repertoire, and Hebrew forms of Ottoman music, among others. "Ottoman (or Turkish) synagogue music" refers specifically to historical court music practices (most commonly Hebrew-language forms), not the whole of music performed in the synagogue or on Turkish Jewish religious occasions over time (which may include music of European origin or Ladino song).

Note on Terminology, Transcription, and Translation   xv

Turkish Pronunciation Guide

Several vowels and consonants in the Turkish alphabet do not appear in English or have a different pronunciation:

- ç   *ch*imes
- c   *j*angle
- ş   *sh*eet music
- ö   f*oo*t
- ü   m*u*sic
- ı   op*e*n string
- i   1) p*i*tch   2) tr*i*o
- ğ   (silent; lengthens preceding vowel)

Mixing Musics

Introduction

It is Saturday afternoon in a bustling, traffic-filled neighborhood of central Istanbul. Off a narrow side street, in a synagogue, a group of men gather between prayer services to sing together—deep, strong voices in chorus. They sing five Hebrew songs that parallel the Ottoman court suite, a chamber music style that, beginning in the seventeenth century, was performed and cultivated in the palace and Ottoman homes, and later popularized on stages of entertainment venues into the Turkish Republic. As the only woman, I sit outside the circle of men singing in the small upstairs room of the synagogue. Today, surprisingly, a female visitor joins me. "This is just like Zeki Müren—the music of my childhood here!" she exclaims to me in a whisper. Hers is high praise for the group, as Zeki Müren is considered one of the great vocalists of Turkish art music, performing on disc, radio, TV, film, and stage, particularly in the decades before 1980. After the singing is over, the visitor and I descend to the street, as the men go into the main body of the synagogue for the final prayer services of the day. In order to leave the synagogue, we enter a secured vestibule unlocked for us by pressing a buzzer. Within the vestibule a tinted, one-way mirror obscures security personnel, and once outside the building, surveillance cameras track us walking away, as we pass two or three plainclothes guards near the synagogue. "I've missed this music since I left Turkey," the woman says wistfully. "I hear someone may be starting a Maftirim group of expats abroad," I respond. "Really?" She turns toward me. "That's wonderful!"

Maftirim songs, sung on Saturday afternoons in this central Istanbul synagogue, share diverse musical elements with Ottoman court music, forming a paraliturgical "sacred suite" of pieces composed in

2   Introduction

the same *makam* (mode). Historically performed in the early hours before Saturday prayer services, the suite is currently sung mid-day to attract more listeners and singers from the numerically reduced Jewish community of Istanbul. Like the woman visitor, I experienced frequent musical epiphanies when I attended Maftirim gatherings in the city: here, a melody I had heard with Turkish lyrics on the radio, there, a vocal improvisation recalling Muslim religious singers. How exactly did this sacred suite develop, I wondered, its musical forms so intertwined with those of a broader Ottoman and Turkish artistic culture? What can its musical mixtures tell us about the place of Jews and other minorities in Ottoman and Turkish society? In a century of nationalisms, which included the Turkish Republic, how do we explain the unexpected survival of Ottoman-era Jewish religious music? And what do present circumstances—men singing within a high-security synagogue—reflect about social change, contemporary politics, and intercultural relations in Turkey and the broader Middle East today?

The current Jewish community of which the Maftirim singers are a part is relatively stable and non-emigrating, having a central religious administration, the Hahambaşlığı (chief rabbinate), and supporting institutions, such as a weekly newspaper, school, hospital and community centers, and a number of active neighborhood synagogues. However, emigration has greatly reduced a minority that once constituted a significant ethno-religious group in Ottoman cities such as the capital Istanbul, provincial centers of Edirne, Salonika, Izmir, and Bursa, as well as numerous smaller towns across the empire. An integral part of a multiethnic urban fabric of the past, Ottoman Jewry participated in diverse ways in economic, social, and cultural life, their histories shaped by Jewish communal institutions, as well as the broader crosscurrents of Ottoman, Turkish, and European history. The present-day Turkish Jewish population (approximately 18,000–20,000) residing primarily in Istanbul amounts to 25 percent of the population in the 1920s (approximately 82,000) and 15 percent of late Ottoman Jewry in 1911–1912 (approximately 122,000).[1] Waves of internal and external migration throughout the century explain these figures, largely correlating with early twentieth-century wars, anti-minority political events in Turkey, and the establishment of the State of Israel in 1948–1949.[2] Once administered by the Ottoman government as one of the relatively autonomously self-governed *dhimmi* ("protected people") populations, Turkish Jewry today share a more contentious urban landscape in their Muslim-majority country, representing those who have chosen to remain through the sociopolitical upheavals of the twentieth century.

While I lived and conducted research in Istanbul in 2005 and 2006, signs of this more contentious urban landscape continually greeted me. Like the story about the Maftirim session and female visitor, my frequent synagogue visits involved security guards, surveillance technology, and fortified vestibules, as well as an initial approval process through the Hahambaşlığı for permission to visit. These precautions had been taken after attacks on Istanbul synagogues in 1986, 1992, and 2003. Other community institutions I visited, such as the weekly newspaper *Şalom* and Hahambaşlığı, initially had been difficult to locate, in part because of the lack of identifying signs as a security precaution. During a year of research in the city, I became accustomed to visible and invisible marks of social division, and as security personnel likewise grew accustomed to my presence, I moved around community spaces with greater ease. Furthermore, I was first surprised, then grew unsurprised, by the aural resonances I experienced in the secured synagogues—sounds connecting inside with outside, echoing something shared before and now walled off. Once the call to prayer from the mosque behind the synagogue interrupted and responded in Arabic to the free-form vocal style just heard in Hebrew inside the synagogue during prayer services. Another time I took a cab after Yom Kippur services, only to hear Qu'ranic chant for Ramazan on the radio, and the driver chat about fasting, without his knowing Turkish Jews were fasting that day too. Such impressionistic experiences across walls heightened my sense of living in a city ethnically and religiously divided in specific ways, stimulating questions about current sociopolitical relations in Turkey, the nature of past intercommunality, and the extent to which shared histories might be steadily lost behind secured doors.

These real-life experiences in Istanbul of the twenty-first century motivated the present study of Ottoman and Turkish synagogue music in its native urban environment of multireligious music-making. In contrast to post-Holocaust scholarly interests in documenting Turkish Jewish cultural forms, especially those lost or feared to be lost, by representing Jewish particularity or communities in isolation, this project joins Ottoman and ethnomusicological research engaging with the blending and blurring potential of an intercommunal focus. The inclusion of the contemporary community, moreover, challenges a priori assumptions about what constitutes authenticity in threatened cultural forms, often represented by "older" and "pure"—rather than "newer" and "diluted"—music. In the case of Turkish Jewry as a whole, their reduced size and relatively hidden institutional life has contributed to scholarly inattention until recently, falling under the conceptual category of a Jewish enclave in decline or socially assimilated owing to twentieth-century anti-Semitisms, nationalisms, and emigration.[3] As a result of a greater focus on Ottoman Jews in Sephardic studies of the past, scholars in the field of music history know significantly more about the Ottoman period of Jewish religious music, early twentieth-century singers considered to be the last "masters," and the musicological links to court music than about the contemporary community and the sociological dimensions of musical interchange.

This study addresses lacunae in scholarship by prioritizing the broader social history and relationships underpinning musical links on paper, in addition to focusing on the understudied span of the twentieth and twenty-first centuries—the late Ottoman decades across the Turkish Republic today. Exploring the intersection of musical and historical studies, it engages with Jewish-Ottoman-Turkish music-making as a cultural thread for tracing intercommunal artistic relations and their transformations in the course of imperial endings and the building of a nation. As such, the study joins a nascent body of scholarship seeking ways for the fields of music and history to enrich each other, with the potential to recover lost voices, social relations, daily life, and art worlds. By encompassing the contemporary, culturally active community, moreover, the historical narrative avoids a simple story of decline, but rather engages with signs of social loss and division, such as high-security Istanbul synagogues and cultural preservation efforts, for the new historical stories they tell us.[4] In foregrounding underrecognized social continuities and contemporary musical resonances, we can replace the well-worn statistical and musicological story of degeneration with the perspective of Turkish Jewry today—that is, arguably surprising cultural legacies with real-life meanings to a community, however numerically diminished, living in the present.

A single musical form—the parallel suites of the court and the synagogue—provides a rich case study to explore the intercommunal dimension of imperial and postimperial sociocultural life. The study aims to interweave the sacred suite of the Maftirim repertoire with a number of linked histories—the Turkish Jewish community, an emerging nation, and the urban landscape of Istanbul—to illuminate multiethnic Ottoman music-making and its transformations in the course of the twentieth and twenty-first centuries. In order to tell this multilayered cultural history across a period of intense social change, the present work draws on the interdisciplinary spacial turn in Middle East studies by foregrounding the urban environment of Ottoman music-making and its national reconfiguration.[5] By focusing on music as a social, collective process, rather than a series of artistic products, and by incorporating particular urban spaces, the resulting sociomusical analysis enables an appreciation of the social ethos and economy implied in musicological textual sources, while complicating undifferentiated notions of Ottoman urban "cosmopolitanism."[6] The general concept of art-making contextualized in urban space places the empirical evidence in the framework of a historical music world in which Jewish composers and their non-Jewish counterparts interacted through specific roles and intermediaries, places and activities, to generate a common musical culture. While artists of other regions may share in conceptual categories of artistic collectivities, such as aesthetic understandings, patronage patterns, divisions of musical labor, and learning methods, specific elements in the Ottoman case, such as long-standing oral transmission, contribute to a more complex understanding of unique aspects of Jewish-Turkish-Ottoman musical interchange.

By articulating how music and musicians moved in city life, we are able to fill lacunae remaining from past assumptions of ethno-religious isolation in the empire: that is, a distinct *millet* system isolating communities from each other through demarcated neighborhoods and communal self-governance.[7] The more recent acknowledgment of Ottoman cosmopolitanism has elicited more complex studies of intercommunal contact, but also poses the danger of leaving the complexity of Ottoman social relations unexplored, especially in the sphere of music, often assumed to naturally unify linguistically diverse peoples under a common musical language. Even as an Ottoman social sphere intermixed musicians, at times in opposition to communal identifications, geographic, ethno-religious, and historical contingencies often shaped, curtailed, or expanded musical encounters. A focus on the urban landscape of music, then, helps us map Ottoman music-making, nuancing our perspectives on urban cosmopolitanism in the empire and contextualizing isolated evidence of employment and meetings within a broader social and economic arena. Such an enriched portrait of historical musical life, moreover, provides a sufficiently detailed basis for investigating transformations of the art world and its urban space arising from political developments in the twentieth and twenty-first centuries in the Turkish Republic.

In exploring cultural history from within a specific musical and social milieu, conventional historical markers in Ottoman and Turkish history may or may not be particularly relevant. On the one hand, because past ethnomusicological scholarship has prioritized the musicological over imperial social history, Ottoman historical contextualization can contribute further insight into musical developments. For example, scholars have recognized the city of Edirne as the place where Maftirim music flourished beginning in the seventeenth century, becoming the capital of Hebrew religious music. The missing piece of Ottoman history—that Edirne served as the second Ottoman capital before the taking of Constantinople and continued as a default capital for the sultan's residency and military campaigns until 1700—explains Hebrew musical flourishing in the fertility of an imperial court culture (as we shall see below) cultivating Ottoman arts. On the other hand, political events considered watershed moments in Ottoman and Turkish historiography include major wars, legal reforms, and revolutions that may, in fact, obscure our understanding of cultural currents in daily life and the specific historical experiences of minorities. A well-established late Ottoman entertainment industry, for example, as well as war-related migrations, help to explain a burgeoning Jewish musical scene in Istanbul in the 1920s that laid the foundation for subsequent intercommunal and musical continuities in the twentieth and twenty-first centuries—developments overlooked in past histories demarcating the founding of the Turkish Republic and its reforms after 1923 as a moment of rupture in the area of law, culture, and religion. In the ensuing pages, then, we will periodize Ottoman, Jewish, and Turkish history to illuminate minority and musical worlds not easily chronologized by top-down imperial or national political events.

New historical sources and ethnographic methods support revising cultural history toward a fuller understanding of the changing urban landscape of Turkish Jews and intercommunal music-making. Specifically, oral histories among Jews and non-Jews, musicians and non-musicians, capture life stories, memories, and empirical material absent from textual or national historical records. The ethnographic methods engaged here join a growing trend in historical scholarship to incorporate oral methodologies, especially for researching under-recognized or under-historicized populations, such as religious and ethnic minorities, women and children, among others, with limited textual traces in specific areas or eras. This study draws productively on personal interviews in Istanbul and its environs for new insights from Muslim friends of Jewish musicians, students of deceased cantorial masters, and women singing Maftirim songs, to expand on scholarship based primarily in Hebrew, Ladino, and musical texts. Such sources provide valuable material concerning, for instance, intercommunal relations, their continuities and discontinuities, Jewish musical biographies, and the participation of women and children in a male performance practice—material enriching, and often complicating or challenging, received wisdom about minority musical cultures of so-called Orthodox religious communities or nationalizing states.[8] Participant observation in a variety of Jewish and non-Jewish venues, including synagogues, concert halls, state and community choruses, and social gathering places, contribute in particular to understandings of contemporary musical and social life linked to extant Maftirim music. In addition, Turkish-language scholarship and memoirs as well as critical readings of Ottoman and republican histories, serve to contextualize Ottoman and Turkish Jewry in ambient social and cultural currents, thereby resisting a narrow ethno-religious focus while elucidating the place of Jewish musicians in the wider society, across significant social change.

A note about appropriate language to refer to Jews living in the late Ottoman empire and Turkish Republic is in order. Well-represented in Sephardic culture areas (the Balkans and Levant), the Jewish musicians, religious leaders, composers, students, and diverse others that fill this study might be referred to as "Sephardi," a term used in the past to categorize descendents of Iberian Jews exiled by the Spanish Inquisition in the fifteenth century, and currently to define Ladino-speaking Ottoman and post-Ottoman worlds. Scholars have also debated the utility of "Sephardi" as a broad category of identification in Jewish history today.[9] Despite the term's usefulness for a variety of scholarly foci, the intercommunal and musical dimension of the present study begs for language reflecting the ethno-religious breadth and interactivity of Ottoman and Turkish music-making, however contentious and changing over time. Indeed, this varied, shifting collectivity included a wide swath of Jewish individuals, not only so-called Sephardi composers, for example, but also Arabic-speaking instrumentalists from Ottoman Arab territories, Jewish gramophone entrepreneurs from Eastern Europe and Russia, *dönme* composers from Salonika, and Jewish émigrés from Nazi Germany, Austria, and Hungary.[10] These Jewish musicians and businesspeople also interacted closely with Greeks, Armenians, and diverse Muslims straddling the worlds of their coreligionists and the surrounding urban musical spheres. Whereas highlighting the ethno-religious distinctiveness of any one of these musicians risks over-accenting Ottoman religious communities or retroactively imposing contemporary ethnic boundaries, language reflecting the interactive cultural realm of music-making elucidates aspects of individual and communal identifications transcending the so-called millet system and at times opposing it.[11] By speaking of "Ottoman Jews" we can capture the social and musical milieu of which musicians were a part, and "Turkish Jews" follows them into the Republic, reflecting new national identifications and citizenship as well as the disjunctions and transitions from what might be called their Ottoman culture area.

Let us briefly survey Ottoman court music as the historical foundation for the Maftirim repertoire at the core of this cultural history.[12] Based on compelling and well-documented *textual* analysis by music historians,[13] the current study investigates the social and urban *contexts* of this historical record. Patronized by the palace and cultivated in a variety of urban settings over time, Ottoman court music shares musical structures—compositional, rhythmic, melodic, poetic—with historical liturgical practices of Muslims and non-Muslims worshipping in Sufi lodges, churches, and synagogues of the empire, including gatherings of Maftirim groups. The Ottoman court suite, or *fasıl*, arose within a longtime regional environment of suite forms in the Near East, Persia, and North Africa, developing a specific Ottoman style, distinctive from Arab and Persian predecessors, by at least the seventeenth century. As a chamber music form, the court suite was generally performed in intimate settings (palace, homes) by an ensemble of instrumentalists and singers, showcasing a series of compositions of distinct genres in the same makam. Similar and contrasting, the sacred suite of Maftirim pieces translated court musical forms into Jewish religious space through Hebrew-language pieces performed a capella by a male choral ensemble in synagogues on Shabbat.[14] This vocal ensemble presented original compositions by Jewish composers, as well as adaptations from non-Jewish Ottoman pieces with Hebrew poems or scriptural passages as lyrics. Historically, Maftirim singers performed one suite in one makam before weekly prayer services, and by the nineteenth century established a tradition of early morning performances in Ottoman cities with significant Jewish populations (Edirne, Salonika, Izmir, and Istanbul).

Textual sources point to a measure of interaction between Jewish and Mevlevi ("whirling dervish") musicians, suggesting clear avenues of musical contact and confluence. Originating in Konya in the thirteenth century, the Mevlevi gradually became the most prominent Muslim Sufi order connected to the sultan and Ottoman ruling class, establishing lodges in 1436 in the second Ottoman capital of Edirne and in 1494 in the third capital of Constantinople. Developing a distinctive musical form, the *ayin*, to accompany their religious choreography, the order played a central role in court music culture through the presence of Mevlevi musicians at the palace, the significant role of Mevlevi lodges in music education, and the further development of the ayin as some of the most complex compositions related to Ottoman court music. Meetings between Mevlevi and Jewish musicians are reported from the early empire in biographical accounts of sixteenth-century Edirne religious scholar R. Joseph Caro and composer R. Avtalyion ben Mordechai, and in contemporary times in life stories from Jewish urban centers. For example, Mevlevi musicians attended synagogues in

Izmir and Salonika to hear renowned *hazanim* (prayer leaders, or cantors) like İsak Algazi (1889–1950), and Samuel Benaroya (1908–2003) visited the Mevlevi lodge in Edirne as a boy to learn Ottoman music.[15] As mentioned earlier, it is significant that the city of Edirne figures in these reports since it was the Ottoman capital (1402–1453) before the taking of Constantinople and a default royal residence at least until the eighteenth century. Given the Mevlevis' historical linkages with the Ottoman ruling class and musical education, interactions with Jewish musicians—especially in Edirne and Istanbul—would effectively spell the latter's active participation near or at the very center of religious and musical crosscurrents in Ottoman imperial culture. Ongoing visitations until the end of the twentieth century, moreover, suggest a historically multifunctional dimension to Ottoman and Turkish synagogues for learning, making music, and socializing—a dimension that has progressively narrowed and been reduced exclusively to Jewish religious practice today.[16]

According to the textual source of the *güfte mecmuası* (song-text collection), Jewish composers documented music in ways similar to their non-Jewish counterparts and participated in contemporaneous developments in court music. From an early Ottoman Jewish güfte mecmuası (Israel Najara, 1587) to later collections starting in the seventeenth century, Jewish composition and documentation of religious pieces correlated more and more with pervasive Ottoman practices, incorporating lyrics, makam, *usul* (rhythmic patterns), and genres in use in the Ottoman court suite.[17] Developing into the Maftirim repertoire, the non-notated compositions confirm performance and educational practices in common with Ottoman musical culture. Until the twentieth century, oral learning through master-pupil apprenticeship relationships (*meşk*) predominated in the empire, taking place within such venues as the palace music school (Enderun), Mevlevi lodges, private homes, and later music schools and societies of the early twentieth century. The well-documented historical employment of Jewish, Armenian, and Greek Orthodox composers at court suggests another avenue for the sharing of such musical practices through active involvement of Jews in palace culture.

Far from being a static tradition, Ottoman court music changed and developed over the centuries, and as it did so participating Jews and other minority composers infused such developments into their own religious music. Ottoman innovations included new instrumentation, complex or new makams and usuls, development of the vocal and instrumental *taksim* (improvisation), and changes in fasıl genres, such as the nineteenth-century light classical *şarkı* (literally, "song") that popularized the fasıl cycle in the twentieth century.[18] European genres and instruments, as well as notational systems, presented further musical choices to Ottoman composers, especially by the nineteenth century; however, oral transmission and performance dominated the musical scene through the early twentieth century. With the advent of records and growth of *gazino*s (nightclubs) at the turn of the century, fasıl music found a popular, commercial stage—an early entertainment industry often owned and operated by minorities, including Jews, and showcasing vocalists who may have also sung religious songs in synagogues. Maftirim music shared in such musical crosscurrents of the time, and by the early Republic boasted big audiences and a repertoire that included contemporary composers and topical subjects. In the 1920s, as Turkish Jews from the provinces increasingly congregated in Istanbul, local Maftirim singers joined Edirne émigrés to perform at numerous synagogues in the city, providing a popular, weekly venue to hear Ottoman court music forms in an era of political and cultural reform.

In the course of the twentieth century, as Jews gradually vacated their neighborhoods in Istanbul, whether through emigration or upward mobility, the historical practice of Maftirim gatherings on Shabbat diminished into today's single secured session, together with one public performance group. By the 1990s, three male vocalists were considered the last remaining masters of the genre in Istanbul: David Behar, İsak Maçoro, and David Sevi. Recently, the Ottoman-Turkish Sephardic Culture Research Center completed a major project remastering their recordings together with notation and historical background of extant Maftirim compositions. Taken as a whole, the evidence of the century appears to match a story of increasing cultural reduction, isolation and, ultimately, preservation. As we shall see, however, behind this apparent decline lies a more complex history of music-making across the twentieth and twenty-first centuries, as Jewish and non-Jewish musicians continued to network together to protect endangered Ottoman musical forms in a republican era of cultural reform. More recently, amid diverse sociopolitical tensions, synagogue security and enclosed Maftirim sessions resemble a kind of second-stage, internal emigration of the religiously observant—a departure from the street into secured space. As such, Maftirim performance today continues to have much to tell us about the urban landscape of music-making, intercommunal relations and tensions, and the place of Jews in contemporary Turkish society.

※

The thematically based chapters of the book interpret music-making in Ottoman-Turkish synagogues, with particular reference to the Maftirim repertoire, as a part of a shared imperial and national history, even as the Jewish population in Turkey significantly decreased over the course of the twentieth century. Understudied in comparison with Ottoman Jewry and locally settled and self-sustaining today, the Turkish Jewish community, though small, is worthy of scholarly attention. In order to do justice to contemporary life and write against the grain of a narrative of decline, each chapter begins with ethnographic historical traces located in the present. The traces not only serve as a springboard for the historical discussion of the chapters, but also suggest a contemporary mixture of tenses more aligned than linear decline to a lived experience of an Ottoman-Turkish-Jewish musical culture today. To hear the historical and contemporary music behind the lines of this cultural history, a discography is provided at the end of the book.

Taken as a whole, the five chapters move chronologically from the turn of the twentieth century to the present day. At the same time, each chapter focuses on a specific theme significant to this changing historical period. Through the life stories of four Ottoman-born Jewish composers living in the early twentieth century, Chapter One explores how Jews in linked roles of religious vocalist and leader (from hazan to congregation head to chief rabbi) as well as popular artists facilitated cultural flows by circulating in musical urban spaces of which synagogues were a part. Framing music-making within the urban environment assists in examining the precise places and people participating in common patterns of patronage, aesthetic conventions, and apprenticeships to cultivate changing, multiethnic Ottoman music-making. Through attention to Jews of differing positions and their compositional output, the chapter teases out a heterogeneous intercommunality, as well as makes visible Jewish composers who were socially active, but absent from past and present Ottoman and Turkish sources because of their Hebrew-only music. A finer articulation of urban music-making provides the basis for the investigation in Chapter Two of transformations associated with the dissolution of the empire and the establishment of the nation. The chapter proposes minority-focused historicization of the early Republic to foreground late Ottoman factors, particularly developments in the recording and entertainment industries, that initially provided new musical spaces and patronage for Jews, despite their imperial and republican political losses after 1923. In the course of a secularizing reform movement promoting European musical values—a trend reflected in immigrant German and Austrian Jewish musicians and emigrant Turkish Jewish hazanim—remaining Jews engaged with traditionalist non-Jewish performers in alternative venues and patronage patterns to sustain Ottoman court music forms in a nation-building era, and to continue to perform them in Turkish synagogues.

The Maftirim repertoire, with its close ties to court music forms, provides a fruitful locus in Ottoman and Turkish synagogue music to probe such intercommunal changes from empire to nation. At the same time, republican Jewish memoirs and oral histories challenge the conceptual exclusion of women from this male-only performance practice and extend recent ethnomusicological moves to complicate gendered dichotomies in Sephardic musical scholarship, that is, the association of Hebrew, religious, and textual forms with males, and Ladino, folk, and oral forms with females. By exploring fasıl music entertainment and education at the level of home and neighborhood, Chapter Three examines the under-recognized participation of Jewish women in popular classical Turkish music as a platform for some to learn Hebrew religious music in general and the Maftirim repertoire in particular. Through incorporating the concept of urban "soundscapes" that sonically include those excluded from formal performance venues, the chapter focuses on how one woman learned in direct and less direct ways, negotiating the space between gendered community musical expectations and a changing Turkish society.

After the mid-1980s we witness a shift from ongoing visitations and networking between Turkish Jewish and Muslim musicians to Jewish religious music-making in increasingly security-conscious synagogues regulating the entry of visitors. Currently, a multiethnic Ottoman music world is reconstructed annually on stage through "tolerance" concerts shaped by Islamist party politics and including a Maftirim ensemble among its multireligious choirs. By analyzing new divisions in Maftirim performance today—participation in official concerts on the one hand, and on the other, historical practices in secured synagogues—Chapter Four engages the political and historiographical uses of both inventing traditions and hiding community among Turkish Jews seeking national belonging and communal protection after three attacks on Istanbul synagogues at the turn of the twenty-first century. Finally, the recent textualization of the Maftirim repertoire, a major preservationist project of the community produced in 2009, is the subject of Chapter Five. In the absence of those considered living masters of an orally transmitted music, the publication may be the sole representation of the legacy of the Maftirim for today and tomorrow. The Turkish Jewish historical record testifies to a striking persistence of Ottoman oral methods of transmission and performance across the twentieth century. With the massive, recently produced Maftirim publication important questions emerge about the preservation of so-called traditional forms, a subject of global cross-cultural discussions among ethnomusicologists and others around recording, notating, and distributing oral musical forms perceived to be at risk: what constitutes musical authorship and authenticity, originals and versions, masters and non-masters within new texts and technologies, new locales and audiences? Since the project effectively constructs the Maftirim of the future, we may ask how the music will be perceived, received, and used by scholars and musicians, congregants and listeners. To what extent will its Ottoman and Turkish oral foundations persist in a European-oriented academic and musical culture? What clues, if any, about its social and intercommunal history will remain between the lines of printed notes and lyrics?

Broad and blurred shifts between oral and textual patterns in Maftirim music-making across the last two centuries suggest viewing its story through the lens of multilayered and changing modes of transmission.

The following five chapters weave an Ottoman-Turkish-Jewish social history of cultural flows, actualized through city spaces and facilitated by individuals, reconfigured by political change and documented for posterity. The thread of musical transmission runs throughout changing sociopolitical contexts, tracing the variety of pathways, however divergent, overlapping, or diminishing over time, that represent the core of a process of mixing musics. There is an apparent broad shift from oral to textual transmission as one moves through the twentieth to the early twenty-first century. However, the oral and textual dimensions of urban transmission are never far apart: late Ottoman meşk sessions, musical scores, song-text collections, and records coexisted. Even as cassettes, compact discs, and scholarly editions appeared, real-life use of new technologies has determined how the music is passed on. Long-standing patterns of Ottoman and Turkish oral learning form the basis for the longevity of Maftirim music, reflecting, until relatively recently, musical relationships and enduring engagement with Turkish art music.

The voices of the Maftirim group continue to be heard in the unobtrusive synagogue in central Istanbul. Their songs echo wider practices of Ottoman-Turkish composing, performing, and learning, even as secured walls effectively reduce and hide the historical interchange evident in their performance. How did people, places, and music mix in the urban landscape of the city to cultivate such music-making in Ottoman society? Why have musical strands survived, and what stories do they tell us about intercultural life of the past century and the present day? Such puzzles are among those motivating this ethnographic investigation into the artistic and social life interpenetrating late Ottoman and Turkish synagogues, mixing (and unmixing) musics, and shaping the urban landscape of a sacred song.

One Mapping Ottoman Music-Making

Necdet Yaşar (b. 1930), Turkish classical musician and renowned master of the *tanbur* (long-necked lute), came to the United States from Istanbul in the early 1970s to teach in the ethnomusicology program at the University of Washington in Seattle. There he met the late Reverend Samuel Benaroya, who was born and raised in Ottoman Edirne in the early twentieth century, emigrated to Seattle through Switzerland in 1952, and was serving as hazan (prayer leader, or cantor) at one of the two Sephardic synagogues in the city. Thirty-four years after their first meeting in Seattle, Necdet Yaşar sits at his print shop in the central neighborhood of Unkapanı in Istanbul, and remembers first meeting Benaroya:

> He came to the university and introduced himself. . . . Later I saw him beat a long *usul* [rhythm pattern]. He beat devir kebir. I was surprised. He beat long usuls on his knees, Ottoman-style, meşk usuls,[1] and he recited a piece for me. He really surprised me. He beat usuls incredibly well. . . .
>
> He knew [the old makams, or musical modes]. For example, when I gave my class at the University of Washington, he came to watch. . . . I was teaching Rast makam to the students; rather, makams from that family. I was explaining makams that were like Rast. I'd say this is Rehavi, the difference is so and so, this is Sazkar, this is Suzidil Ara. He knew the Rast family, that is, the whole family of makams. He was a good musician, an excellent musician. . . .
>
> [He said] while in Tekirdağ [*sic*] he learned classical Turkish music—long usuls, makams—but I have no idea whom he learned from. Maybe a teacher lived in Istanbul. Maybe he learned in Istanbul and went back to Tekirdağ [*sic*] from there, I don't know.[2]

Necdet Yaşar goes on to describe how "Ottoman culture has a language. It has a particular old language" that Benaroya also knew. "There are a lot of fine musicians, a lot of talented instrumentalists. But they use only the new language, they use today's language." Using the linguistic analogy of the Turkish word "to go," he explains that in the past, speakers drew from a colorful palate of vocabulary with shades of meaning, such as to go hurriedly, to go and reach a destination, to go by car, train or ferry, to set off early:

> To describe something there are five, six, seven, maybe eight different words, ten words. This is the richness of a language, but a person could describe their emotions with one word. They could describe them, but the richness would be lost. . . .
>
> Music is the same. . . . In the musical and makam system, as well as in improvisation, there is such a thing. There is the same richness. . . .
>
> [Benaroya and I] spoke the same language. He loved me and I also loved him. I respected him highly, and he also highly respected me.[3]

According to Necdet Yaşar, he and Benaroya shared an Ottoman musical language, even though Necdet was twenty-two years his junior, was separated for years by geographical distance, and had grown up musically among the Turkish Muslim majority of Istanbul rather than within a provincial minority. Strikingly, based on the memories of Benaroya's daughter, Benaroya recalled Necdet with high esteem throughout the years since their first meeting, conveying an intimacy unfamiliar to her in his other relationships.[4] It may not be surprising that two musicians growing up in the same home country (Turkey) and meeting abroad (Seattle) would be drawn to each other. We can also effectively bridge their musical age gap by placing both musicians within the same late Ottoman musical aesthetics: a student of Mes'ud Cemil in the 1950s, Necdet nonetheless considers the father, tanbur player and composer Tanburi Cemil Bey (1871–1916), his "spiritual teacher," as he assiduously listened to, and strove to understand, his innovative style in his youth from recordings of the early twentieth century.[5] Tanburi Cemil Bey was also among the most popular instrumentalists performing and recording at the time of Benaroya's youth in Edirne.

Even if trained, figuratively speaking, in the same musical period, Necdet Yaşar, Samuel Benaroya, and their relationship raise questions

Mapping Ottoman Music-Making 19

Tanburi Cemil Bey on the cover of the musical score of his composition "Şedd-i Araban Peşrevi." According to the text, the composition was taken from and corrected by his son Mes'ud Cemil and was published after his death by Chamlı Iskender (Tr, Şamlı İskender, a music publisher in Istanbul circa 1910–1950). Reproduced by permission from the collection of Mehmet Güntekin.

that bear closer examination: how did two musicians, separated by community, mother tongue, and city of origin, share the same musical language? Whereas Necdet gave public concerts of classical Turkish music, locally and internationally, on the tanbur, Benaroya sang only in Hebrew for Jewish religious services in synagogues in Edirne, Geneva, and Seattle. As Necdet Yaşar himself asks, how exactly did a young Jewish man like Benaroya, growing up in a provincial city at a distance from the imperial center of the arts and performing exclusively in the synagogue, learn a broader Ottoman musical theory, complete with specialized terminology, at the advanced and comprehensive level that Necdet observed? Indeed, Necdet Yaşar, recognized in Turkey today as a living master of historical Ottoman makams, musical aesthetics, and the tanbur, is unquestionably a highly credentialed judge of Benaroya's high-level musical skills.

It is common knowledge among ethnomusicologists today that, based on the musicological evidence, Ottoman court music forms interpenetrated the religious services of non-Muslim Ottoman houses of worship—Jewish synagogues, and Armenian and Greek Orthodox churches. Moreover, a measure of published archival evidence testifies to interreligious contact and palace employment, suggesting pathways of cross-cultural flows. A number of sources, centuries apart, related to Ottoman Hebrew religious singing, confirm reciprocal meetings between Jewish and Mevlevi ("whirling dervish") musicians.[6] Recordings and publications about Jewish, Greek, and Armenian musicians reveal musical lives lived as musicians and composers at the court as well as cantors and religious leaders in their own synagogues or churches.[7] One term for such individuals is *haham-bestekar* (haham-composer), alluding to the Jewish and wider realms that such composers sometimes worked within.[8]

Drawing on the rich Ottoman-Jewish musical scholarship of the past, we can enrich our understanding of Necdet Yaşar and Samuel Benaroya's shared musicality by investigating Ottoman music-making through the prism of the historical urban landscape of the music and its practitioners. Among Istanbul's streets and structures are the precise places, people, and activities involved in artistic cross-fertilization in the late Ottoman period. In the city, well-documented but isolated evidence of musical encounters enlarges into patterns of urban circulations, making visible and detailing our commonplace but under-articulated knowledge of multiethnicity in Ottoman music. Moreover, by tracing both structural and demographic changes in the urban landscape of Istanbul, we can track the migrations of music and its makers generally, and specifically among Ottoman and Turkish Jewry, to elucidate both the ruptures and continuities, however altered, in multiethnic music-making in a postimperial, nation-building era. Through bringing together discipline-specific source material—the ethnomusicological with urban and migration studies—we can "urbanize" the music-making under consideration and "musicalize" the urban landscape across a period of intense social change.

Questions arising from the particular musical friendship of Yaşar and Benaroya in the late twentieth century motivate this investigation into the details of Ottoman musical history in order to conceptualize the social ethos, economy, and urban configuration—and reconfiguration—of their world. How were artistic and social relationships cultivated between local Jews and musicians of other ethno-linguistic communities in the late empire? By extension, how did the well-documented musicological linkages between the respective repertoires develop within these diverse communities? What stories does the changing urban landscape of Istanbul have to tell us about distinctive residential soundscapes, patterns of music-making, Jewish practitioners and their migrations within and out of the city across the twentieth and twenty-first centuries?

Focusing on music as a social, collective process, rather than a series of artistic products, we will follow a selection of understudied Jews working as composers, commercial performers, religious leaders, and hazanim as they circulated in a variety of inclusive urban spaces, some composing or performing exclusively for their own communities, others participating in both Ottoman synagogue and court music, including its popularized forms. The life stories of such late Ottoman Jewish musicians—some of whom were religious leaders—who composed court music forms, be they instrumentals, or Hebrew and Ottoman-Turkish song, provide valuable evidence from daily life in Ottoman cities to delineate how court music circulated among Jews and their synagogues, and the ways in which Jews circulated among the music of the court. By analyzing Jewish biographical data in terms of how musicians moved within urban space, individual life details cohere into a fuller understanding of interactive urban music-making based in common patterns of musical activity, such as patronage, professional specialization, and apprenticeship. As we encounter distinctive examples of performing, composing, and teaching, we will contextualize particular activities in wider Ottoman music practices, to specify the contemporaneous nature of Jewish musical involvement. A focus on patterns of transmission will illuminate the pathways of the musical interactivity around such repertoires as the Maftirim. As a whole, the individuality of the biographies takes us beneath the surface of a seemingly amorphous imperial cosmopolitanism as the apparent source of cultural confluences, expanding on evidence from previous periods toward an understanding of the late Ottoman era. Our musicians' shifting patterns of residency, moreover, together with the changing musical cityscape of Istanbul will lay the foundation for investigating the upheavals and survivals in their musical culture across the Turkish Republic.

A vibrant Ottoman studies scholarship is enriching our understanding of the empire's social complexities in different locales at different historical junctures. Several studies spanning the empire, from the eighteenth to the twentieth centuries, challenge past assumptions of ethnic divisions of labor and residence, suggesting groupings that include and cut across ethno-religious communities, such as networks of migrants, shopkeepers, workers, and café-goers.[9] From the outset the Ottoman court employed teachers, performers, composers, and theoreticians from a wide swath of the population, cultivating musical forms held in common and an Ottoman artistic identity at times separate from or opposing one's religious community.[10] To the growing body of intercommunal research this chapter contributes a case study of late Ottoman musicians and their quotidian encounters, activities, and relationships within and beyond the palace.

This is not to say that the musical world or other social and economic relationships were without ethnic tension, conflict, or even violence in the course of the empire's history. Those making music moved within multiple other worlds as well, and were thus affected by wider sociopolitical currents beyond their particular artistic milieu. As we shall see in Chapter Two, in times of social and political crisis, such as the violent shift from empire to nation, a musician's affiliation with the Jewish community became increasingly significant to his social experience and life choices. As we follow Jewish composers interacting in shared urban spaces among diverse personages, then, we will see that these same musicians lived amidst distinctively Jewish spaces as well, and their lives, in the end, were shaped by their status as Jews as much as by their multireligious artistic relationships. It required specific musical, personal, and political advantages, as the following pages will show, to succeed as a Jewish musician in the Turkish Republic.

Musicians Circulating in the City

The life stories of four late Ottoman Jewish musicians—Hayim Moşe Becerano, Samuel Benaroya, Nesim Sevilya, and Mısırlı İbrahim Efendi—provide clues about the musical activity and urban ambulations that constituted interreligious music-making in the late Ottoman period. Two of these musicians composed or performed solely for liturgical settings (Becerano and Benaroya), whereas the other two composed a largely nonreligious repertoire (Sevilya and Mısırlı İbrahim Efendi). Three of them were religious functionaries at various levels (Becerano, Benaroya, and Sevilya), and one (Mısırlı İbrahim Efendi) worked only in the "secular" music marketplace (*piyasa*) outside the synagogue.[11] All four musicians, nonetheless, moved among urban spaces, both far-reaching and more closely communal, that facilitated musical flows between their religious communities and the Ottoman public sphere as a whole. On the one hand, individuals performing both musical and religious roles, such as Hahambaşı (chief rabbi) Hayim Becerano, Hazan Samuel Benaroya, and Haham Nesim Sevilya, would have most effectively composed and directly transmitted the court-related musical practices of their time for the benefit of paraliturgical and liturgical synagogue music.[12] The skills necessary for composing imply knowledge of music theory, shared with non-Jewish Ottoman musicians, such as usuls, makams, and compositional genres—skills that, combined with their authoritative religious positions, enabled them to teach contemporaneous court music practices to young men in the synagogue. A Jewish composer and performer of nonreligious music, on the other hand, did not directly teach Maftirim singers or hazanim-to-be, but arguably transmitted music for liturgical use as effectively as musicians with religious positions. Ud-player (*udi*) and vocalist Mısırlı İbrahim Efendi was a prolific composer of songs popular in the Ottoman art music repertoire of the time.[13] By performing and recording this genre for mixed urban audiences that included Jews, he contributed to the musical exposures that informed the songs and performance practices of Maftirim singers. For singers performing a repertoire such as the Maftirim, which included *contrafacta* (adaptations) and pieces by contemporary Jewish composers, the world of entertainment offered valuable learning opportunities, even if less traceable by the historian than documented teachers, pupils, and lessons.[14] The varied involvement of these four musicians in Ottoman music-making and Jewish religious institutions, then, promotes a greater understanding of the shared social ethos that embraced the synagogue and the pathways of transmission through both religiously and less religiously involved musical practitioners.

Taken together, the lives of these late-Ottoman musicians offer individual detail to foreground city spaces structuring and animating their art worlds. By sketching out these distinctive and overlapping spaces, we bring into view the people, places, and activities of Ottoman music-making in the late empire and contextualize the less abundant Jewish source material within the more extensive record of Ottoman musical practices in which Jews were involved. Read alongside each other, the life stories highlight trends significant to Ottoman and Jewish music-making as well as to dynamics in the lives of Jewish musicians residing, moving, emigrating, or remaining in the postimperial national city. In the case of Becerano and Benaroya, both musicians composed or performed exclusively religious repertoires in different positions: one as the chief rabbi of the late empire and early Turkish Republic, the other as hazan at his local provincial synagogue in Edirne and subsequent immigrant congregations in Europe and the United States. Their comparable and relatively high level of musical competence by standards of the time, however, testifies not only to their central positioning in a wider music world, but also to the significance of musical merit within a wider music-making sphere. Through this pragmatic ethic supporting the success of a labor-intensive orally transmitted repertoire, an economically disadvantaged Jewish boy, for example, was not excluded from but rather was enabled to excel in Ottoman musical and Jewish liturgical learning, becoming a teacher and transmitter himself. By contrast, the lives and compositions of Nesim Sevilya and Mısırlı İbrahim Efendi, both composers of a largely nonreligious repertoire, reflect a common, changing Ottoman music scene at the turn of the twentieth century with its growing commercialization and documentation of historically oral learning and transmission practices. At the same time, their increasingly religious commitments (Sevilya) and commercial activities (Mısırlı İbrahim Efendi) spell out divergent life trajectories exemplifying larger trends among Istanbul Jewry in the

Republic: dispossessed Jews emigrating from the country, on the one hand, and on the other, upwardly mobile individuals choosing to remain. In the following chapter we will explore how it was that one of our musicians, Mısırlı İbrahim Efendi, not only survived but thrived as a musician during the first decades of the Republic.

Making Religious Music

The musical lives and works of Hayim Becerano and Samuel Benaroya generally do not appear in state archives of compositions, encyclopedias about music, and biographical dictionaries of composers in Turkey today.[15] Rather, their names are recorded nearly exclusively in Jewish communal and diasporic historical records and publications. These musicians did not compose or perform outside the synagogue, and their musical legacy—Hebrew-only religious works and liturgical leadership—as well as their textual invisibility in current Turkish music history has relegated them to a particularistic communal historiography not in keeping with the actual record of their lives. Despite their religious-only music, the urban musical activities reflected in their life stories place them each at the center of Ottoman music-making of the period. Like the composer Sevilya, their religious positions facilitated high standards of interaction between secular and Jewish liturgical music. At the same time, the hierarchical gap between them—one a chief rabbi, the other a hazan—furthers our understanding of the primacy of talent in Ottoman music: musical ability trumped status or wealth in an oral art world sustained by specific competencies.

Hayim Moşe Becerano (1846–1931) spent most of his life in the Balkans, moving for reasons of employment and security, before arriving in Istanbul at the age of seventy-four to serve as the last Ottoman and first republican hahambaşı.[16] Born in Eski Zağra (today Stara Zagora, Bulgaria), Becerano acquired extensive religious, musical, pedagogical, and political experience by holding increasingly higher institutional positions in Rusçuk (today Ruse, Bulgaria) and in Bucharest, Romania. In 1873 he joined the teaching staff of the new Alliance Israélite school in Rusçuk, fleeing the city after the Ottoman-Russian War of 1877–1878 to work as a Jewish school principal, governmental translator-in-chief, and Sephardic chief rabbi in Bucharest (1878).[17] As chief rabbi of Edirne (1910–1920), Becerano interacted with political and religious leaders during the upheavals of World War I and the empire's demise, befriending Atatürk when he was military attaché in Sofia and hosting him regularly in Edirne. During these visits Atatürk reportedly debated political issues in meetings with the hahambaşı and two other community leaders, Mevlevi leader Şeyh Selahaddin Efendi and educator Rıdvah Nafiz Bey.[18] Clearly, the hahambaşı's reputation as a high-level religious leader, developed during his Balkan years, placed him in an advantageous position to succeed Hahambaşı Hayim Nahum in Istanbul in 1920, and his friendship with Atatürk assured the continuity of his position after the establishment of the Turkish Republic in 1923.

In a life story remembered for its religious and political leadership, it is important to emphasize the centrality of music for Becerano, who spent his early years apprenticing in Ottoman music and its Hebrew forms by serving as hazan in Bulgarian synagogues. According to Şemtov Kohen (1924–1986), as hahambaşı of Turkey, Becerano revealed his strong musical focus in a sermon to the congregation:

> One day on Shabbat,[19] Becerano Efendi went up to the teva [hazan's lectern] in Keneset [Israel] synagogue in Şişhane . . . [and] as part of his talk, Hahambaşı Hayim Ben Moşe Becerano addressed this question to the crowd of worshippers who had come to listen to him: "Dear friends, have you ever considered, who is the one and only loyal friend in a person's life?" Complete silence fell over the synagogue. Hahambaşı Becerano Efendi continued to speak in an easy, fluent way: "Who is the one and only friend who purifies a person from their problems throughout his life; whom a person takes refuge in during the sad times without showing any hesitation; who stands by him even in his most lonely moments? In short, who is the one and only true friend who lives with a person from birth to death?" he asked and immediately answered himself: "This true friend is music. Turkish music."[20]

Becerano's speech, delivered not informally to a group of friends or students, but rather to a full congregation in a major Istanbul synagogue on the Jewish holy day, reflects the personal and collective importance he placed on music, specifically the heritage of Ottoman music. Rather than elevating scriptural texts, religious law, or even God to the status of ultimate, lifelong companion, Becerano instead speaks of music in spiritual, almost divine, terms: a friend of the heart, who transcends any human relationship, and has the power to purify and heal, offering an abiding fidelity removed from the everyday vicissitudes of life. Moreover, it is significant that in his speech, Becerano refers not specifically to Hebrew scriptural songs, but to the broader classical music of Ottoman and Turkish society. In this way, despite his own Hebrew-only compositions, Becerano shows himself to be deeply embedded in the ambient music culture, and its national representation, as his primary, generative musical foundation. His public reference to Turkish music may project national commitments of a Jewish leader and his community; however, his contemporaneous writings confirm a cosmic understanding of music related to that of Islamic philosophers.[21] It is the music itself, set to whatever language or poetic form, that forges a lifelong and transformative spiritual friendship.

Thus, within his demanding work as Jewish religious leader, Becerano prioritized music consistently enough to make such public declarations late in life, as chief rabbi of the Republic. Although he composed only religious pieces, including at least one Maftirim composition,[22] Becerano clearly participated in a broader Ottoman music culture, receiving foundational training as hazan in the Balkans and coming into contact with a multireligious pool of leaders, musicians, and music. At times these contacts enabled him to advance music performed in the synagogue. As hahambaşı of Turkey, for example, Becerano sponsored a project to notate the Maftirim repertoire that, beginning in Edirne, had been transmitted exclusively orally over the course of three hundred years. In 1926 he employed the Armenian composer, teacher, and notator Kirkor Çulhayan (1868–1938) to transcribe the Maftirim repertoire into European notation.[23] It was through the Jewish composers İzak Varon, Moşe Kordova, and İzak Algazi that Becerano and Çulhayan were first introduced at the chief rabbinate offices in Galata, which doubled as Becerano's home, and in turn, it was likely at Kirkor's music store and/or commercial recording studios that the three Jewish composers and Çulhayan first became friends years earlier.[24] The story of these introductions and friendships highlights how, through his status as hahambaşı, Becerano networked with a range of recording artists, bringing institutional support to bear on a significant documentary project of his community, which, as we shall see in the case of Nesim Sevilya, reflected his engagement with the shifting musical values of his day, that is, European modes of musical transmission.

Becerano's broad multireligious relationships can also be discerned in news reports of his funeral in Istanbul in August 1931, conveying his popularity across the city. Moiz dal Mediko, journalist for the Ladino paper *La Voz de Oriente*, wrote that he could not report on the funeral, because a crowd of thousands, at times falling on top of each other, separated him from the synagogue in Galata.[25] Another reporter wrote that representatives from all minority religious institutions attended the funeral: Armenian Gregorian, Greek Orthodox, Christian missionaries, Syrian Christian, Armenian Catholic, and others, as well as officers of European consulates and the Turkish state.[26] Even if such official and religious representation would be expected at the funeral of a national Jewish leader, the obituaries in minority newspapers confirm religious and musical relationships beyond the mere official. According to *Nor Lur gazetesi*, an Armenian daily, "[Becerano] was loved not only by the Jews, but by everyone. Among those loving and respecting him are the Armenians. Hahambaşı Becerano knew the Armenian religion and Armenian religious music very well."[27] The daily Armenian paper *Jamanak gazetesi* confirmed and specified his musical knowledge and participation:

> Becerano possessed a soft and sweet character. He was an aficionado of Armenian religious services. When he was hahambaşı in Edirne, on several occasions he joined religious services at Armenian churches. He learned many Armenian prayers flawlessly. When he was the hahambaşı of Turkey, he maintained respect for our religion, just as he did for all religions.[28]

Beyond the mere panegyric, these reports reflect a musical dimension to Becerano's official ecumenical role as hahambaşı. It is probable that his relationship with the notator of the Maftirim collection, Kirkor Çulhayan, who after 1893 served as cantor in Armenian churches across Istanbul, personalized his engagement with Ottoman Armenian church music.[29] The life story of Becerano, then, reveals how a religious figure devoted to Ottoman music could generate cross-communal cultural interactions when occupying a high-ranking provincial or national position. Through particular relationships cultivated in his spheres of circulation as hahambaşı, Becerano brought rich social relationships to bear on Jewish community projects and liturgies. By artistic output (religious Hebrew compositions) he is not hailed in mainstream Turkish music history, but by his socioreligious relationships Becerano clearly and uniquely participated fully in Ottoman and Turkish music-making through his distinctive official status.

In contrast to Becerano, Samuel Benaroya (1908–2003) exemplifies how an economically disadvantaged Jewish boy, who was musically inclined and eventually worked solely as prayer leader in numerous synagogues, nonetheless circulated in an interactive, cross-communal musical culture in the former Ottoman capital of Edirne. A highly skilled practitioner of Ottoman synagogue music, he performed and taught exclusively religious music for his community, and is therefore remembered today primarily outside Turkey by his congregants and listeners or scholars.[30] Later in life, nonetheless, he exhibited the musical expertise to attract an intense, mutually respectful friendship with someone renowned as a contemporary master of Ottoman music, Necdet Yaşar. "Finally he had met somebody who understood what the essence of his being was. He *was* Turkish classical music," his daughter later recalled.[31] In particular, his visits to the Mevlevi lodge in his city confirm the longevity of historical relationships between lodge and synagogue, and the opportunities open to a youth with musical aptitude and family connections.[32]

In Edirne, Samuel Benaroya showed an early interest and skill in music, often singing as the youngest member in religious musical performances or gatherings.[33] He received an extensive religious education through the synagogue and communal schools, and a secular education at the Alliance school in Edirne, where he acquired French and other nonreligious subjects.[34] Despite coming from a poor family, his musical talent opened up early learning opportunities and subsequent recognition as a musical authority in the community. Ottoman music apprenticeships, in fact, placed a high value on a fine ear and memory, while masters did not traditionally accept money as payment—educational patterns that allowed a musically adept but poor student to excel.[35] Hayim Becerano, hahambaşı of Edirne during Benaroya's childhood, taught him in some fashion, as did the Jewish composer, and his maternal uncle, Haribi Avram Behor Menahem.[36] Moreover, although he did learn synagogue music from his father, Haham İsak Benaroya, who was hazan for sixty years at the Catalanes synagogue, it was his uncle Haribi Avram Behor who became his musical mentor.[37] Further, his uncle's position with the Beit Din (religious court) undoubtedly facilitated contact with the musically cosmopolitan Hahambaşı Becerano.[38]

Benaroya's uncle also took him as a young boy to the Mevlevi lodge every Friday night. Throughout Ottoman history, the Mevlevi order maintained close ties to the Ottoman court as the *tarikat* of the ruling classes, influential in musical, religious, and political spheres.[39] Their own lodges in Ottoman cities, including the former capital of Edirne, became central to music (and other) education, with Mevlevi composers considered musical masters in Ottoman court music culture. As Benaroya remembers:

> In this period of twelve, thirteen, fourteen years we get acquainted with the people who used to sing in the Mevlane. Mevlane was the gathering in the mosque every Friday that the dervish people used to have their services by turning and performing and dancing and playing some instruments, which were very appreciated by us because we wanted to learn also from them. . . .[40]
>
> Now with the time we got well-acquainted with some of these people. We invited them in our synagogue to listen [to] what we are singing and also vice versa they invited us to listen or to take advantage of their knowledge of what they were singing. . . . [We] used to sing in Hebrew from *Shire Yisrael*[41] and they sang their own liturgical [songs]. . . . Their melody we interpreted with our Hebrew words and we were singing [it] in our synagogue. . . . They didn't need to [learn our songs] because they were much more up-to-date, much more learned than we were.[42]

Benaroya and his companions were thus able to hear the Mevlevi *ayin*, an instrumental and vocal cycle accompanying the *sema* and representing some of the most complex forms in Ottoman music.[43] That they seemed more "up-to-date" in Benaroya's eyes reflects his understanding of the Mevlevi lodge's historical role as a center of Ottoman music education, as well as the nineteenth-century flourishing of new ayin compositions far beyond the output of previous centuries.[44]

Benaroya and his uncle, as far as we know, entered the lodge by invitation, advantaged by personal relationships to visit a space attended by religiously diverse guests.[45] Benaroya also remembers the Maftirim sessions that the Mevlevi dervishes, in turn, attended in the synagogue. He was the youngest in a group of twenty to twenty-five Jewish singers, mostly older and married, who would meet in El Kahal Grande (the Great Synagogue) in Edirne on Saturday morning, one hour before prayer services.[46] A number of professional singers, composers, "teachers of this kind of singing from Istanbul,"[47] and Mevlevi dervishes joined the Maftirim session. Up to eighty or more congregants came to listen "because they were amateurs . . . they loved to hear Maftirim."[48] Through such mutual visitations to relatively open musical-religious venues Benaroya came into contact with a wide range of Jewish and Mevlevi composers. Benaroya's memories and the intertextual Maftirim repertoire through contrafacta testify to the endurance of well-documented long-lasting relationships over the centuries between *mevlevihane* (Mevlevi *tekke* or lodge) and synagogue in Edirne, supporting Jewish musical education, composition, and performance practice.

Through such learning, Benaroya sang in the synagogue as a youth, organized and conducted a boys' choir when he was a teenager, and led services as a young adult.[49] After anti-minority events in Thrace, he emigrated from Turkey to Geneva (1934), where he led a small, struggling congregation of Edirne refugees, and from there to Seattle (1952), where he served as hazan at Sephardic Bikur Holim synagogue until 1984.[50] There, he made a priority of orally teaching religious music and recitation to boys in his home, maintaining the high value he placed on oral, in-context learning: "These [vocal and musical skills] should come by tradition. . . . No school, only tradition."[51] Benaroya also adapted pieces prolifically: he would "tap continually this odd beat" on the dining room table, his daughter remembers, setting a scriptural text to a known melody, then recorded it, after which he listened to it and revised it in an oral process of adaptation.[52] "We knew he was serious when he began to tap," she recalls, not realizing at the time that her father was beating the usul and creating a musical adaptation or piece using the oral methods of Ottoman composers before the prevalence of notation in the twentieth century.[53] His criticisms of the performance of some Sephardic-American hazanim in the same way confirm a well-learned Ottoman Turkish aesthetic: he deplored the random mixing of makams in one song ("you can't mix oil and water") and not singing a *taksim* (improvisation) before a piece ("you can't go to Mercer Island without a bridge").[54] Both these critiques reflect Benaroya's own careful adherence to makam norms, as well as the general practice of introducing the makam through an improvised prelude. Indeed, moving primarily between local confessional communities (Mevlevi lodge and synagogue), he had learned Ottoman music as a youth from key historical centers of imperial musical activity in Edirne. By interacting with local Jewish composers and leaders, moreover, he gained knowledge from their activities and contacts beyond his immediate communal sphere. Benaroya embodies the extensive knowledge of Ottoman court music practices acquirable by a talented son of a poor hazan, valued for liturgical expertise and musical skills central to Ottoman learning and transmission. Though devoting his musical career and output solely to his own congregations, Benaroya gleaned experience and expertise from interactive spaces and composers interacting in worlds within and beyond his own.

Composing and Performing on Stage

In contrast to Becerano and Benaroya, Haham Nesim Sevilya and Mısırlı İbrahim Efendi appear in publications on Turkish music history, active as they were in the urban world of secular music in late nineteenth- and early twentieth-century Istanbul.[55] Compositions of both composers can be found in the music archives of Turkish Radio and Television. Both musicians composed, taught, and performed nonreligious music in an environment of commonplace imperial practices, such as invitations for prestigious artists to perform at the palace, as well as changing musical practices and production, such as the commercialization of music education (through private schools), the mass production of sound recordings (through local and international record companies), and the rising publication of notated fasıl music. Their musical activities reveal details about Jewish participation in a wider music world at the turn of the twentieth century, and the diverging currents of their lives over time narrate a larger story of Jews remaining in, leaving, or adapting to a nationalizing culture in the Turkish Republic.

Nesim Sevilya (1856–1949), unlike Mısırlı İbrahim Efendi, wrote secular compositions in the Ottoman court music tradition as well as Hebrew religious music. Known as an Ottoman composer, as well as haham and hazan, respectively, of Turkish-Jewish congregations in Istanbul and Sofia, Sevilya was born in Hasköy ("Imperial Village"), a neighborhood on the Golden Horn comprising primarily Sephardic and Karaite Jews; acquired foundational religious, liturgical, and secular knowledge there; and, like Benaroya, began to serve as hazan in his teenage years (age fifteen), and later as Maftirim şef (conductor) at Hasköy synagogues.[56] His biography confirms the high level of his musical knowledge, gained not only through an early liturgical education in the synagogue, but also through movements between diverse social venues in the city. According to his former student Rav Leon Yeuda Adoni, Sevilya took lessons from the Ottoman composer, teacher, and performer İsmail Hakkı Bey (1866–1927), who grew up in the neighborhood of Balat (across the Golden Horn from Hasköy) and was muezzin (caller to prayer) at age thirteen in the neighborhood mosque in Molla Aşkı, and later lead singer and teacher at the palace.[57] Known simply as "Muallim" (teacher), İsmail Hakkı Bey reportedly taught numerous hazanim in addition to Sevilya, possibly because he lived in Jewish-majority Balat.[58] Though we lack information on how Sevilya met this prolific teacher, because of his age it is likely that he took lessons before İsmail Hakkı Bey founded his own music school in 1908 (Musıki-yi Osmani Mektebi) or taught at Darülelhan (1917–1926), a school where both Turkish and European-style music was taught.[59] Nonetheless, his lessons explain at least some of Sevilya's musical expertise, including his ability to compose *and notate* compositions during his mature years.[60] The mixed characteristics of his education reflect his participation in developments in Ottoman music and learning: especially after 1826 and the appointment of European composers at court, music instruction increasingly adopted certain European musical values, such as solfège and notation, while maintaining the foundations of an oral Ottoman musical pedagogy— and all these Sevilya likely acquired through İsmail Hakkı Bey's up-to-date teaching.[61]

İsmail Hakkı Bey (*seated, center of third row from the top*) with musicians and students of his school, Musıki-yi Osmani Mektebi, including udi and composer Mehmet Fahri Kopuz (1882–1968) (*seated, far left, third row from the top*), Kanuni Ama Nazım Bey (1884–1920) (*far right, third row from the top*), and vocalist Avram Karakaş (*far right, top row*). Photograph from *Şehbal Mecmuası*, a journal of politics and culture published 1909–1914. Reproduced by permission from the collection of Mehmet Güntekin.

Sevilya received palace invitations from two sultans (Abdülaziz, r. 1861–1876, and Abdülhamid II, r. 1876–1909), royal gestures that reflected the historical role of the palace as patron of the arts and Sevilya's status as a high-ranking musician. Community sources report that the invitations were facilitated by the chief rabbis of the time and institutional connections between the palace and Istanbul's Jews.[62] For the second performance, Sevilya reportedly presented a program consisting not only of Ottoman language but also Hebrew pieces.[63] A composer of both religious and nonreligious music, Sevilya's extant compositions include Maftirim compositions as well as at least nineteen nonreligious pieces in fourteen makams, encompassing a diversity of Ottoman forms.[64] After returning from serving as hazan in Sofia (1916–1926), Sevilya established a children's Maftirim group at the Kasturiya synagogue on the outskirts of Balat. One of his students, Moşe Niyego, remembers him as a devoted teacher of the Jewish boys there:

> I was seven years old then. The year was 1928. At that time, Haribi Sevilya was the hazan at Kasturiya synagogue. He served at that synagogue for seven years straight. He had a very beautiful voice. He put a lot of importance on children—he passed on his wealth of knowledge to them.
>
> In 1928, for Friday evenings and Shabbat, Ribi Sevilya established a Maftirim group composed of up to ten children, ages eight to thirteen, a group which I also joined. Encouraging us, instilling in us "beautiful singing," and the love of music, giving us children the chance [to lead prayers] at the teva: these were the important qualities of R. Nesim Sevilya. In the years 1928 to 1930, on Saturdays, a Maftirim group met at Ahrida synagogue, the biggest and most popular synagogue of the Balat neighborhood. Members of the congregation filled the synagogue to listen to this religious singing group. R. Nesim Sevilya preferred to stay at Kasturiya synagogue. He placed a great deal of importance on us children.[65]

A teacher of boys at Kasturiya synagogue, Sevilya rotated the products of his reputation and high musical activity between the synagogue and wider society. In this way, Jewish boys, who may or may not have eventually made music that was nonreligious, benefited from the extensive knowledge of a master of Ottoman music. By valuing youth in the synagogue—their musical education and opportunities to perform in a youth Maftirim group—over his own participation in major musical and religious activities in Balat, Nesim Sevilya made a priority of transmitting his extensive expertise in Ottoman music to a younger generation. Over time his commitment to religious life and culture appears to have intensified, exemplified in teaching boys at Hemdat Israel synagogue in Haydarpaşa in the 1940s. Rav Leon Yeuda Adoni remembers the lessons of this teacher as a student of age eleven or twelve:

> When he gave us lessons he was ninety or ninety-five years old. He had a cane and beard. He was very old.... He would sing, we would listen. There was no notation or anything. For example, he would sing Mizmor le David five or ten times, and the children would learn quickly.... He spoke in Judeo-Spanish. He would beat the usul with

this cane. . . . He'd sing together with us. If there were mistakes, he'd correct them. We learned in this way.[66]

Clearly, Sevilya was teaching metrical compositional forms through Ottoman methods of oral learning: a master modeled an entire piece and/or its sections to the beat of the usul, while students listened, imitated, and were corrected. Called *meşk*, this form of oral transmission was notably long-lasting throughout the Ottoman period, promoting close master-pupil relationships and relational values in order to successfully transmit entire repertoires of compositions held in memory. Sevilya undoubtedly learned Jewish religious music orally, simply by being present at synagogue services; however, his other musical endeavors, particularly composition, performance, notation, and meşk learning and teaching, required knowledge of Ottoman music theory, performance practice, and the European notational system. As a composer circulating in an Ottoman world within which synagogues were active, Sevilya cultivated his musicianship through cross-communal, upper-level musical and political contacts, probable access to the court through the chief rabbi, and a meşk relationship with the major Ottoman-Turkish composer and teacher İsmail Hakkı Bey. In this way, he expanded his artistic reputation, transmitting its musical fruits to a younger generation of hazanim not only indirectly through leading prayer services, but also in a concerted manner, through prioritizing group lessons and Maftirim sessions for Jewish boys. Synagogue music itself, both liturgies and paraliturgical Maftirim performances, engaged in contemporaneous musical flows between the synagogue and the court, and the newer venue of the private music school, in part, through the person of Nesim Sevilya.

Unlike Nesim Sevilya, an Ottoman Jewish composer whose religious rank of haham facilitated direct musical transmission in the synagogue, Mısırlı İbrahim Efendi (1878–1948), became known for his ud-playing, popular *şarkı* (literally, "song") compositions, *gazino* (nightclub) performances, and audio recordings. Although a vocalist as well as an udi, Mısırlı İbrahim Efendi did not perform in synagogues, but rather in the urban entertainment world of the early twentieth century, which was an integral part of Jewish daily life. His biography is valuable for understanding crosscurrents not only in the late empire, but also, as we will witness later, during the Republic, between Jewish liturgical performance and popular recorded and live broadcasted Turkish art music. As a successful practicing musician in the first decades of the Republic, moreover, his life story helps to distinguish the factors that led some Jewish musicians to emigrate and others to lead successful musical careers in the new nation. Born in Aleppo as Avram Hayat Levi, Mısırlı İbrahim Efendi acquired a professional nickname, a common historical practice among Ottoman musicians. To be sure, musicians' nicknames typically referred to birthplace or residence, in addition to profession and title; in this case the name uniquely associated him with Egypt (presumably from touring there) and Islamicized his Jewish first name, in a manner that, as we shall see, served him well in a later era of rising nationalism.[67] Mısırlı İbrahim Efendi was reportedly self-taught from an early age, moving to Istanbul and the neighborhood of Balat around 1900 with his new wife and son. In Istanbul he learned from Sevilya's teacher, İsmail Hakkı Bey, as well as Kirami Efendi (1840–1908) and Üsküdarlı Bestenigar Hoca Ziya Bey (1877–1923).[68] He resided in the Lonca section of Balat, a district known for its 'Gypsy' (*çingene*) musicians and vibrant musical entertainment, and later joined the ensemble of Kemani Memduh (1869–1939), a Lonca Gypsy violinist considered one of the most successful piyasa musicians of the period.[69] His extant opus primarily includes the genre *şarkı*, which entered the fasıl beginning in the mid-nineteenth century and became increasingly prevalent and popular in gazino programs.

In the first decades of the twentieth century Mısırlı İbrahim Efendi performed in art music ensembles (*ince saz takımı*) for sultans and their families, in aristocratic Ottoman homes, and in gazinos throughout the city. Historically a range of social venues offered a variety of services (such as alcoholic or nonalcoholic beverages) and activities (such as card-playing or musical entertainment), as, in the course of the nineteenth century, certain old and new spaces progressively showcased the ince saz takımı related to subsequent musical programs of gazinos.[70] Such ensembles generally presented a fasıl of compositions related to the historical Ottoman court suite: typically, a group of instrumentalists with singer would present a multi-genre set of pieces, historically in a single makam and later in mixed makams.[71] The *meyhane* (tavern) and

Udi Mısırlı İbrahim Efendi on the cover of the musical score of his composition "Şen gözlerine neş'e veren" in Kürdilihicazkar makam. This piece was published by Şamlı İskender in Istanbul. Reproduced by permission from the collection of Mehmet Güntekin.

çalgılı kahvesi (instrumental café), in particular, began to accommodate such Ottoman music ensembles toward the end of the nineteenth century, antedating the establishment of large gazinos in Istanbul combining a Turkish-style (*alaturka*) music program and European-style (*alafranga*) space with its elite clientele, formal program, and alcoholic beverages.[72] In the twentieth century, "fasıl music" increasingly meant not the historical Ottoman court suite, but rather the light classical music programs of gazinos.[73]

Like the minority representatives of early recording companies in the empire, most owners of gazinos were non-Muslims until 1928.[74] Mısırlı İbrahim Efendi worked in the burgeoning gazino scene that established itself through venues in the imperial center (Arif Gazinosu and Sultan Ahmet Belediye Bahçesi), the suburbs of Galata (İptaloğos and Aynalı Gazinosu), and along the Bosphorus (Çubuklu Hasan Bey and Artaki'nin Gazinosu).[75] Catering to Muslim bureaucrats and diverse others working in the old city, gazino performances generally thrived in central neighborhoods, like the theater and café district of Şehzadebaşı (or Direklerarası) during the winter months, whereas in the summer they provided entertainment, often in open-air spaces, to a mixed population of means in Bosphorus villages such as Arnavutköy, Bebek, Büyükdere, Sarıyer, and İçeri Göksu.[76] Indeed, new modes of transport, particularly steam ferries, progressively increased mobility for the city's residents from the mid-nineteenth century forward, connecting workplace, permanent residences, and summer homes, and allowing easy access to often waterside gazinos, at times located conveniently near ferry landings.[77]

Frequently playing alongside his brother udi Selim, Mısırlı İbrahim Efendi performed art music programs for general entertainment as well as during Ramazan for festivities after the daily fast. In 1910 the Aynalı Gazinosu in Beyoğlu-Taksim, for instance, advertised his ensemble as appearing every evening during the holiday and three evenings a week after the holiday.[78] In the nineteenth century Ramazan celebrations generally included music, storytelling, and *karagöz* (shadow puppetry), historically presented at a *semai kahvehanesi*, and by the turn of the twentieth century upscale gazinos offered holiday entertainment for mixed, wealthy audiences.[79] At times Mısırlı İbrahim Efendi was joined for Ramazan programs by other prominent Jewish vocalists (for example, Avram Karakaş and Salomon Efendi); the Jewish majority on stage reflected a pattern of non-Muslim commercial activity during a holiday for which Muslims were more often celebrants than employees.[80] As with gazinos, the exploding transportation networks of ferries and streetcars in the city after the mid-nineteenth century promoted non-Muslim participation in such pervasive celebrations as Ramazan.[81] The udi also performed in groups represented as "Arab art music ensembles" (*arap ince saz takımı*) that generally included Istanbul musicians, although the city hosted singers and players from Ottoman Arab provinces as well. His musical activities included performing for two sultans

Neighborhoods of the Golden Horn and Bosphorus in the late Ottoman era. By the early twentieth century the commercial center had shifted from the old city to Galata, the European and non-Muslim banking district to which upwardly mobile Jews and others moved from Balat. With the construction of new imperial palaces (Dolmabahçe Sarayı and Yıldız Sarayı) on the Bosphorus, the waterway's villages became popular sites for summer homes and gazinos.

(Abdülhamid II, and Mehmed Reşad, r. 1909–1918) as well as private concerts for Ottoman family members, statesmen, and aristocratic residents of Istanbul's *yalılar* and *konaklar* (mansions).[82] Indeed, the musician's success in the piyasa music world is reflected in part by his move from the less expensive neighborhood of Balat after a fire in 1912 to upscale Şişhane in the Galata area. By this time the fine neighborhoods just outside the walls of Galata were dominated by non-Muslim and European residents and had become a common destination for upwardly mobile Jews from the historical Golden Horn core.

Mısırlı İbrahim Efendi, like numerous other composers of the time, devoted a significant amount of time to teaching. He taught privately as well as at the Mehterhane, the Ottoman institution for military band music that had been revived during a decade of wars (1914 to 1923) after its closure early in the nineteenth century.[83] He reportedly received an award, most probably for teaching, from the Sanayi-i Nefise Mektebi, a school of fine arts founded in 1882.[84] These positions reflect his integration into the secular Ottoman school system expanding since the mid-nineteenth century, a phenomenon witnessed in the lives of certain other Jewish composers of the period, such as Santo Şikari in Izmir.[85] As far as we know, unlike Sevilya, Mısırlı İbrahim Efendi did not teach or perform in Istanbul's synagogues; however, as noted earlier, his performances and lessons in Ottoman music schools nonetheless transmitted nonreligious Ottoman music that constituted the basis of Hebrew song, such as the Maftirim repertoire. Although we can only make historical inferences for the late Ottoman period, testimonies of mid-century Turkish hazanim, discussed in later chapters, elucidate the importance of such popular music-making to live liturgical and paraliturgical performance in the synagogue. In the Republic, the performance of popular art songs like his own on state radio and television, as well as his recorded taksims would expose a range of musical material to practicing hazanim, cultivating makam usage and improvisatory technique. Thus, a popular instrumentalist like Mısırlı İbrahim Efendi, most probably in his own day and most certainly after his death, provided theoretical and melodic material central to both free-form singing within liturgies and performance practices for the paraliturgical sacred suites of the Maftirim.

Mapping Ottoman Music-Making

The musical lives of four late Ottoman Jewish musicians present overlapping and distinctive activities that assist us in visualizing Ottoman music-making in Istanbul in the early twentieth century. Through tracing music as a social and collective process, rather than focusing solely on artistic output, we can begin to imagine such a culture and avoid filtering out participants who may have composed or performed only for their own communities. By the late nineteenth and early twentieth centuries, with Ottoman music practices well established in urban society and alternative modes emerging, Jewish musicians interacted in a variety of urban spaces, depending on their position in Ottoman music and society, generating multiethnic musical activity and communal cross-fertilization, and contributing to both a common Ottoman repertoire and particular religious liturgies and intra-communal learning. In late Ottoman Istanbul and Balkan cities, well-established spaces included the palace, Mevlevi lodges, synagogues, churches, and institutional offices, with newer spaces developing by the turn of the twentieth century—gazinos as well as recording studios, private music schools, and music shops, such as those of İsmail Hakkı Bey and Kirkor Çulhayan. In this framework, traces of cross-communal meetings, such as mevlevihane-synagogue visits in Edirne, or Jewish-Muslim apprenticeships, such as that of Sevilya and İsmail Hakkı Bey, take their place, despite gaps in national music history, as integral threads in a fabric of music-making within and between Ottoman cities.[86]

Furthermore, opportunities for such meetings generally arose not so much through personal initiation on a level playing field of students, masters, and musical opportunities, but rather from connections with specific, well-positioned individuals. As we have seen in the lives of Jewish composers and singers, connections with personages of status frequently opened the way to artistic accomplishment. Samuel Benaroya's musicianship benefited not only from generations of hazanim in his family, but also from his uncle's role as a local composer and official in the religious court, which facilitated meeting the composer and provincial chief rabbi of Edirne Hayim Becerano, as well as visiting the Mevlevi lodge during ceremonies. Becerano himself attained increasingly higher religious positions through political contacts, ultimately becoming, as chief rabbi of cities (Bucharest and Edirne) and nation (the Turkish Republic), the person sought out by youth such as Benaroya and enabled by rank to achieve wide ecumenical relationships and community projects. For the latter he relied on friendships of musicians such as those who introduced him to Kirkor Çulhayan, who, unlike himself, worked in the burgeoning, multi-genre recording industry. Nesim Sevilya likely came to the attention of the palace through his relationship with the chief rabbi of the empire, thus increasing his own status in the Jewish community, as well as his wider musical recognition.[87] And, it goes without saying that, gaining recognition at the palace and in the piyasa music world of entertainment, Mısırlı İbrahim Efendi worked within a web of musical and political relationships that, particularly in a later period, would have an impact on his music career. Thus, intersecting with musical meeting places were hierarchical positions and intermediaries easing upwardly mobile movement, musically speaking, among our four Jewish musicians. Crucially, as is clear in the stories of Sevilya and Benaroya, high musical merit—more valued than wealth by Ottoman teachers—was important in such movement, through the support of synagogue and well-positioned members encouraging the development of musical talent.

By contextualizing individual Jewish biographies such as these within larger patterns of Ottoman music-making, well-documented in historical sources, we can foreground the shared nature of a social and musical economy: specific biographical elements represent examples of larger cultural currents, albeit with community-specific significance to Ottoman and Turkish Jews as Jews. Key among socioeconomic dynamics promoting meetings in such a mixed and migrating music world was musical patronage by the palace, and later by the urban aristocracy, which included non-Muslim musicians and gave legitimacy and status to Ottoman court genres.[88] Through this legitimation, a pervasive musical aesthetics established itself, however transformable, over time, and was articulated in theoretical treatises, performance practices, and critical understandings of musical mastery.[89] In addition, the division of musical labor reflected in the Maftirim notation project brought together people of varying skill in the art-making marketplace: in some cases these services may have divided up along ethno-religious lines (for example, notators), in others, such as the overlapping positions of teacher, composer, and performer, ethnic or religious divisions were less distinct. More research needs to be done to include artists such as lyric-writers and artisans such as instrument-makers and binders of song-text collections, as well as nineteenth- and twentieth-century music-related businesses (for example, printers of lyrics and notation, and recording companies). Suffice it to say that such patterns of Ottoman music-making—changing over time through the interplay of convention and innovation—structured a music world that enabled diverse people to meet regularly, however spontaneous, unforeseeable, and individualized the meetings may have been. Such encounters provide expression to a longtime music world under continual construction, looping the generative effects of such relationships back into that world.

A particularly significant dimension to the ethnically and religiously interactive Ottoman music world is meşk and its apprenticeship relations. Whereas patterns of patronage, aesthetic convention, and division of labor correlate, albeit distinctively, with art music in other regions (for example, Europe), the oral transmission of Ottoman music brings uniquely intensive relations of reciprocity into the musical scene, melding people together in more intimate ways than relations of buyer to seller, performer to audience, or even artist to patron. The method of meşk can be described as the *harç* (mortar) binding together masters and pupils in relationships of great respect, loyalty, merit, and service.[90] Because of the massive task of orally transmitting complex Ottoman pieces—both instrumental and vocal—to successive generations, Ottoman social codes of conduct developed to support this key relationship. For example, for the success of the time-consuming process of meşk, a master's generosity of time and knowledge was valued, as was a pupil's loyalty and sense of responsibility to learn pieces well for posterity.[91] Moreover, master musicians provided pupils with their musical pedigree,[92] while students legitimized specific versions of compositions—a variability inevitable in the process of oral transmission—through claims to particular teachers.[93] In fact, a discourse against notation, deemed an inadequate form of learning, reflects the high value placed on meşk in the service of Ottoman musical aesthetics and transmission, if not the careers of oral-based teachers.[94]

This Ottoman code of ethics supported the more or less successful transmission, over centuries, of a large repertoire through historical chains of masters and pupils that were essentially multiethnic. Among our four musicians, apprenticeships involved Ottoman teachers who were prominent in the period (for example, İsmail Hakkı Bey) as well as Jews teaching in the synagogue in ostensibly Jewish-only chains of hazanim (for example, Becerano, Sevilya, and Benaroya). Although mixed chains of apprenticeships are common in Turkish music history, the national literature on the subject tends to privilege early Ottoman Jewish teachers and those residing in the capital, such as Tanburi İsak (1745?–1814), over those who lived in the provinces or during the politically contentious environment of the late empire and early Republic.[95] At the turn of the twentieth century, for example, Jewish composer and teacher Şemtov (Santo) Şikari (1840–1920) taught Neyzen (ney player) Hoca Mehmed Rakım Elkutlu (1872–1948) for ten years in Izmir.[96] Although not highlighted in Turkish music sources, Şemtov (Santo) Şikari was a master in the musical pedigree of Neyzen Elkutlu and his students in the latter's capacity as imam of Hisar Cami and head of the Turkish music society in Izmir, as well as singer, ney player, and prolific composer of diverse musical genres, including at least one Mevlevi ayin.[97] Şikari also taught the famed republican composer and ney player Şükrü Şenozan (1874–1954), and, as music teacher at the Izmir Hamidiye Sanayi Mektebi (Hamidian Trade School), likely belongs to innumerable meşk chains of lesser-known musicians and composers.[98] Over the course of five years, another Jewish composer, İsak Varon (1884–1962), studied with Refik Bey (1854–1909), both of whom were composers and practicing lawyers in Salonika. In 1908, when Refik Bey was appointed to the Second Constitutional cabinet, Varon moved from Salonika to Istanbul to continue to study with him.[99] Such long-term apprenticeships as those of Şikari (as master) and Varon (as pupil) confirm significant cross-cutting meşk relations in Ottoman music, cultivating closely woven loyalties and commitments, including among ordinary students absent from the historical record, and generating valorized chains of masters and pupils that were inextricably ethnically and religiously mixed.

Such an interactive musical activity—sharing patrons, aesthetic conventions, artistic skills, masters, and pupils—may lead us to assume a standard, specialized knowledge across Ottoman composers of different backgrounds. However, because meeting places, performance venues, and intermediaries differed among musicians, their personal circulations in the music world not only determined the nature of their participation and contribution, but also their particular window on the music world itself. Together with a social and textual impression of universal, nonethnic ownership of Ottoman music, specific circulations of composers simultaneously served to expand or contract their own musical perspectives, shaping, for example, how inclusive or exclusive they imagined their own repertoires to be. For example, because Samuel Benaroya made music primarily within his own religious community, he was shocked to hear Necdet Yaşar perform a familiar Maftirim melody at a concert in Seattle, assuming the piece was a Hebrew original adapted by Yaşar from the Jewish religious repertoire: "It was an extremely pleasant surprise for me to hear exactly what we sing ourselves in our synagogue in Turkey. I was going crazy. How can they sing that?!. . . . My excitement . . . I couldn't wait, not one minute, until they finish the first part, the intermission, to approach them and talk with them."[100]

In fact, Necdet Yaşar was performing Yusuf Paşa's *peşrev* (instrumental introduction) in Segah, a piece well-known by aficionados of the Ottoman repertoire, which a Jewish composer had adapted to a text by Israel Najara for the Maftirim repertoire.[101] What is significant about Benaroya's reaction is, despite his advanced musical knowledge, he wasn't aware of a widely known nineteenth-century Ottoman composer, Yusuf Paşa (1821–1884), and his compositions—a composer Becerano, Sevilya, and Mısırlı İbrahim Efendi, in view of their milieu, most certainly would have known, if not met, and an original composition they would have recognized.[102] Depending on whom one met where, one's consciousness of Ottoman music developed, creating the imagined definitional borders of one's community's repertoire and practices. As we shall see, over the course of the twentieth century, as knowledge of classical Turkish music, the presence of minority communities, and interreligious interactions diminished in Turkey, the groundwork was laid for more sharply defined communal traditions, the hiding of shared histories, and fewer and fewer social opportunities for musical surprise.

For now, however, by tracing the urban musical lives of late Ottoman Jewish composers, we can envision in a fine-grained way the social ethos and economy of late Ottoman music-making. In their distinctive and multiple lives each musician sheds light on Jewish involvement in intercommunal musical flows, as they made music, depending upon position and intermediaries, on their liturgical or commercial musical stages, in older inclusive spaces (palaces, Mevlevi lodges, synagogues, churches), and newer commercial ones (music schools, shops, recording studios, gazinos). Sharing patterns of patronage, aesthetic understandings, apprentice relations, and professional specialization, each focused attention on teaching, allowing music in synagogues to stay current with court music forms composed and performed in the public sphere. Among Jews, religious positions of higher or lower rank, as in the case of Becerano and Benaroya, determined whether or not one could contribute funds and professional resources to congregational music, whereas extensive musical training, despite differences in wealth, testifies to the leveling role of native musicality, valued for the smooth functioning of an oral Ottoman music world both inside and outside the synagogue. Sevilya, by both religious rank and wider musical reputation, promoted the practice of contemporaneous music at a high level within the synagogue, whereas the commercial fame and prolific nonreligious music-making of Mısırlı İbrahim Efendi transmitted musical knowledge as effectively, albeit less traceable in tangible ways, to interested Jews on the street, among them synagogue singers present or future. Thus, by the late Ottoman empire Jewish composers were integrally involved in Ottoman music-making, circling in ever wider or more communally intimate spheres, participating in and reinforcing relatively stable artistic practices, and establishing reputations within Ottoman musical lineages and repertoires. By framing Ottoman music-making as a collective art world, we can not only foreground the historically recognized, prolific musical activity of Nesim Sevilya and Mısırlı İbrahim Efendi, but also revise insular assumptions about composers of Hebrew-only synagogue music, such as Hayim Becerano and Samuel Benaroya, excluded from the Turkish music record based on compositional output, but active in the urban music-making spaces of their day. In the early years of the Republic two of the musicians—Sevilya and Benaroya—would leave the country, at least one under duress, whereas the remaining two—Becerano and Mısırlı İbrahim Efendi—would successfully complete their careers in Turkey. Understanding the dense, ethnically mixed fabric of Ottoman music-making, as elucidated in their life stories, provides the necessary foundation for tracing subsequent individual and collective national developments, and the transformations of their music world in the transition from empire to Republic.

Two Into the Nation:
A Musical Landscape in Flux

Ascending the narrow stairway inside Şişli (Bet Israel) synagogue, located in the central district of Osmanbey/Şişli in Istanbul, I enter the women's balcony, where a male congregant bustles around preparing paper plates of fruits, nuts, and small pastries.[1] He carries them into a side room and arranges them on a long table together with bottles of water and Coke. A few men sit chatting at the table, while others gradually enter the room, filling the available seats at the table, as well as the chairs lined up along the wall. A relaxed, sociable atmosphere pervades the room, as the men talk, laugh, and whisper, gradually quieting and coming to attention as David Sevi (b. 1953), a hazan at the synagogue, comes in and sits at the head of the table. David Behar (b. 1918), a well-respected kanun player in his eighties and student of famed hazan İsak Algazi (1889–1950), occasionally joins him, as he often does during his visits to Istanbul from his current home in Israel.[2] This is the weekly Maftirim gathering at Şişli synagogue, one of two groups performing the Maftirim repertoire in Istanbul today. After the *kiddush* (a prayer over wine) Sevi delivers a vocal taksim introducing the makam he has chosen for that day, in order to aurally establish the mode for the singers.[3] Over the next hour, everyone sings four or five pieces in a single makam together. In the course of several weeks, they will sing compositions by Jewish composers, as well as non-Jewish Ottoman pieces adapted to Hebrew texts.[4]

From my very first visit to the Maftirim gathering, I was reminded of my classes at the Üsküdar Musıki Cemiyeti in Istanbul, a music society founded in 1917 and known for its meşk style of learning. Both the *cemiyet* (society) and synagogue mixed the oral and textual in similar ways, reflecting Ottoman practices as well as engagement with European music, particularly in the twentieth century in the area of notation. In both the *cemiyet* classes and the Maftirim sessions, the leaders held sheets of notation as guides in front of them, while students and singers had only notebooks of lyrics without notation, which required them to learn the song by ear.[5] Though not a class, the Maftirim sessions I attended included familiar aspects of oral learning at the *cemiyet*: sometimes David Behar, the older teacher, beat the usul in the air, pointing to emphasize a beat. Sometimes he corrected the singers' pronunciation, or, leaning toward David Sevi, held a mini-meşk lesson with him—singing phrases solo or in unison, so that Sevi could then teach the group. Touching Sevi's face, smiling and whispering in Ladino, Behar exuded the affection, encouragement, and appreciation of a master with his best apprentice, or an affectionate father with a favored son. Amid the intimacy of their close personal and teaching relationship, the diverse, multigenerational group around the table learned songs from the two leaders, as well as, in time, from each other, the more experienced attendees taking the lead in singing and the relative newcomers learning by listening every week.

David Sevi's gathering strives to maintain the historical nature of Maftirim sessions among Ottoman-Turkish Jewry.[6] Although it now aims to attract more participants by meeting in the afternoon, rather than in the early morning as was traditional, the group continues to gather weekly and sing a collection of pieces in a single makam that parallels the Ottoman court suite. Paraliturgical in nature, the session is held before the last two prayer services of Shabbat and includes religious observances, such as the opening prayer, a concluding rabbinical homily and discussion, and the recitation of the kaddish, all of which distinguish it from a public performance. It is significant that, despite the intensified promotion of European music under the Republic, not simply notational, but also oral learning methods of transmission take place at Bet Israel synagogue. More to the point, a chain of transmission survives through David Behar and David Sevi from the late Ottoman/early republican master hazan İsak Algazi.

Given significant social and cultural upheavals of the Turkish Republic, we may ask how practices so embedded in Ottoman social structures were maintained during the republican decades, particularly within an emigrating religious minority. Not only did a broad modernizing and secularizing state agenda, as we will see, militate against Ottoman practices through the curtailment of public Turkish music programs, so too did the closure of Sufi lodges and the establishment of European-style music programs and conservatories beginning in the 1930s. Jewish communities also grew smaller in the decades following 1923, owing to a variety of legal, social, and economic pressures targeting ethno-religious minorities in a nationalizing state. What is the history behind Maftirim sessions at Bet Israel synagogue today, particularly in view of the changes in Mevlevi-Jewish relations and spaces that transpired during the Republic? As the Jewish population, in addition to patronage for court and religious music, significantly decreased, how did the Maftirim repertoire survive? Was it primarily a devotion to cultural preservation, ongoing interethnic relationships, or other factors that facilitated continuity? That is, what exactly happened to the Ottoman music-making ethos of Becerano and Benaroya, Sevilya and Mısırlı İbrahim Efendi, with its circulations of composers, religious leaders, piyasa performers, teachers and students of diverse backgrounds—people meeting people in places in the city, participating in a common art?

The story of Turkish synagogue music in cross-communal perspective in the twentieth and twenty-first centuries is a tale of complex, tumultuous social, cultural, and political change—a story of a shrinking minority community and of musical losses, but also of striking continuities. By revising the common historical periodization for twentieth-century Turkey, we gain a more complex understanding of these processes than national histories often convey.[7] If we overemphasize the changes that occurred with the establishment of the Republic in 1923 and subsequent social reforms as the key watershed moments of the new nation, we risk losing the historical thread linking today's Maftirim performances to their Ottoman precursors. Instead, by focusing on daily musical and community life in the decades before the founding of the Republic, it becomes clear that late Ottoman social, cultural, and commercial currents shaped public life and music worlds of the early nation in ways obscured by historiographies overemphasizing national origins and reform. Specifically, war-related movements of peoples, together with new modes of musical production, complicated the impact of later top-down state policies by actually intensifying Ottoman-style musical activity in the postimperial capital during the Republic's early years. The recording and entertainment industries, well established during the three decades before 1923 and so integral to the careers of musicians like Mısırlı İbrahim Efendi, initially sustained and popularized Ottoman court music forms, whether Hebrew or Turkish, in the early Republic, particularly for musicians and audiences concentrated in Istanbul through migrations related to late Ottoman wars. Indeed, in the first decade of the Republic David Behar and İsak Maçoro, teachers of the current Maftirim leader David Sevi, acquired their foundational music education from İsak Algazi as youth in the synagogue and from the ambient music culture on Istanbul's streets.

It is in the second decade of the new Republic that we witness increased cultural and economic nationalism, developing in a global context of rising fascist regimes and national xenophobias resulting in part from the late 1920s economic crash and ensuing depression. In periodizing a cultural history of Turkish Jewry, it is important to highlight the shift from the 1920s to the 1930s, because, while various state policies touched the lives of Turkish citizens as a whole, this period ushered in a series of anti-minority laws and sometimes violent events that led to losses of communal life in non-Muslim populations, and unleashed a trend of progressive emigration among Turkish Jews. In addition to these adverse sociopolitical conditions, within the lives of Jewish religious singers, performers, and composers increased state funding for European-style programs, and in the commercial world, changing tastes in classical Turkish music negatively affected musical careers. Indeed, as part of the debates in Turkish society between alaturka and alafranga tendencies, a contentious cultural division was opened up between long-term Turkish and new European Jewish artists through the eclipsing of one and employment of the other by the state in this period.[8] In the context of the significant social, cultural, and political losses to the Turkish-Jewish community in the course of the twentieth century, it was primarily alternative urban spaces and patterns of patronage, and not communal insularity or intraethnic preservationism, that ultimately helped to sustain classical music-making among non-emigrating Turkish Jews, both within and outside the synagogue. Culturally endangered themselves, non-emigrating Turkish Jewish religious musicians are testimony to historical musical continuities in Ottoman practices in synagogues today, as well as to the ongoing multiethnicity of a broader, unofficial (that is, not officially state-supported) music world. Exploring the cultural shift from the 1920s to the 1930s reveals the fertile musical activity of the first decade of the Republic generated by late Ottoman sociocultural developments and significant to communal culture in the late twentieth century. The intensified nationalism of the early 1930s marks the beginning of a progressive demographic decline among minorities that, important as it was for these communities and Turkish society at large, has motivated parallel cultural historiographies of decline masking musical continuities among Turkish Jews and their compatriots. However depleted musically and intercommunally, today's Maftirim performance evidences a chain of transmission cultivated through unofficial channels beginning in the first decade of the Turkish Republic.

Cultivating Imperial Music in an Era of Reform

Commercial and technological music developments—so influential in early republican music culture—took place in Ottoman urban centers within an environment of interurban migration in the late nineteenth century. Migration motivated by economic and wartime pressures combined with these commercial and technological trends to make Istanbul a significant place for Jewish music-making in the 1920s both in and outside the synagogue. Before turning to new musical developments in the late nineteenth century, let us examine their context—population movements throughout the empire—and their role in intensifying musical life, specifically Turkish synagogue music and Maftirim performance, in the first decade of the Republic.

The movement of provincial Ottoman Jews to Istanbul, which bolstered both religious and nonreligious music-making there in the 1920s, parallels a general rural-to-urban migration in the empire beginning in the last decades of the nineteenth century as European investment in the capital increased and as refugees, fleeing from Ottoman wars and the empire's shrinking territories, arrived in the city.[9] Such population movements intensified after 1900, as, like their Muslim counterparts, Jews migrated as Ottoman subjects from lands lost to lands still in Ottoman hands.[10] During the Balkan Wars (1912–1913), residents of Edirne fled to Istanbul, even as refugees from other regions of the Balkans arrived in their city. By the end of World War I, more residents of Edirne had left, as had many Jewish residents of Izmir, where only a third of its prewar Jewish population remained after the social upheavals of the War of Independence (1921–1922).[11] The demand for synagogue space in Istanbul rose with the dramatic increases in population in the first two decades of the twentieth century, and in response synagogues were made available, or newly constructed, for Balkan Jews.[12]

In the end, these migrations under duress enriched the musical life of Jews, and others, in Istanbul in the nascent Republic. Among the new residents of Istanbul was the prominent vocalist İsak Algazi (who immigrated from Izmir in 1923), as well as religious singers who came from Edirne, the historical center of Maftirim activity, and who, once they were settled in Istanbul, activated, led, and participated in Maftirim singing in the city. These musical migrations stimulated Hebrew religious singing in Istanbul, although Edirne did maintain a considerable Jewish population, including valued hazanim like Samuel Benaroya, as religious activity continued into the early 1930s. In 1923, after a new synagogue (Knesset Israel) was hastily established in a former cinema (the Apollon) to accommodate the growing Jewish population of Galata,[13] a refurbished Maftirim society officially performed at the opening ceremonies, and continued as the main gathering, led by Edirne immigrants, in the city for at least a decade.[14] The Maftirim group, led by Behor Papo, at Knesset Israel raised the status and importance of the gathering through the attendance of such respected hazanim as Nesim Sevilya and İsak Algazi. In 1926–1927 (and possibly at other times), the group presented concerts in all the main Jewish communities of the city.[15] A prominent musician from Edirne, Moşe Kordova, began to lead the group in the early 1930s.[16]

Significantly, two major projects to document the music and texts of the Maftirim repertoire also took place during the 1920s. In 1925, as we have seen, Chief Rabbi Hayim Becerano befriended the Armenian composer, teacher, and notator Kirkor Çulhayan and sponsored his notation of the orally transmitted Maftirim repertoire. A second project—the publication of the song-text collection *Shire Yisrael be-Erets ha-kedem*, which today provides the lyrics for David Sevi's group—was undertaken by publisher Benjamin Rafael B. Joseph, circa 1921.[17] These initiatives reflect Jewish participation in broader musical trends in the society, as well as particular communal interests. The publication of songbooks and sheet music had increased since the early part of the century, generating and responding to public demand in a period of growing amateur music activity.[18] At the same time, Jewish leaders sought to document a tradition perceived to be threatened by political upheavals, particularly in the Balkans.[19] Parallel developments in Salonika reflect a shared concern for Ottoman Hebrew liturgical continuities across regional Jewish congregations in the period.[20] The songbook *Shire Yisrael* contains topical pieces departing from strictly religious themes, suggesting an increasing entertainment role for the weekly performances for the congregation.[21] Compositions by familiar republican Jewish composers (e.g., İsak Varon and Hayim Becerano) and adaptations of popular non-Jewish compositions (e.g., by Yusuf Paşa and İsmail Hakkı Bey) similarly blurred and blended with musics enjoyed outside the synagogue, attracting large audiences on Saturdays.[22] Thus, through unequivocal institutional support, popularity among congregants, regularity of performance on Shabbat, and new song-text publications, Maftirim gatherings flourished in Istanbul in the 1920s, providing predictable opportunities for Jewish, and sometimes non-Jewish, residents of the city to hear an Ottoman fasıl in a Jewish religious register.

The entertainment value of Maftirim gatherings developed in part because of the rise of the record industry and gazino culture in the early twentieth-century Ottoman empire. Recording studios and gazinos helped musicians build careers, as seen in the case of Mısırlı İbrahim Efendi as well as of Algazi, Çulhayan, and Varon. The major record labels, which were European and American at the time, typically favored the recording and dissemination of richly diverse local genres, including those of various ethno-religious communities, since selling their main product, record players, depended upon satisfying local musical tastes.[23] As in their other regional markets, record companies employed local representatives in Istanbul to engage the most promising artists, commonly networking with minority or foreign businessmen in the city.[24] Blumenthal Brothers, for example, who were German-origin

Advertisement for a sound recording of Tanburi Cemil Bey and a phonograph in the newspaper *Ahenk* (August 28, 1907). Cylinders of the kind shown in the illustration were eventually eclipsed by discs or records. Collection of the author.

Jewish immigrants to Istanbul from the Caucasus, acted as agents for Zonophone, Odeon, and Columbia, in addition to manufacturing records locally after 1911 on their own Orfeon label.[25] Likewise, Sigmund Weinberg of Polish Jewish heritage served as a representative of Gramophone Records, running a number of stores in the district of Beyoğlu.[26] In fact, numerous non-Muslim composers, including İsak Varon and Antaki Candan, worked as record company representatives or studio directors during the first half of the twentieth century.[27] Thus, local businesspeople—from the Jewish community as well as other minority communities—who at times were musicians themselves, profited both their respective companies and local artists through their knowledge of the contemporary, regional musical terrain.

In the early twentieth century, among the most recorded Jewish musicians were vocalists İsak Algazi, Avram Karakaş Kohen Efendi (active 1890–1914), and Edirneli Hayim Efendi (or Edirneli R. Hayim Apacık, 1864–1937), as well as instrumentalists İsak Varon (1884–1962) and Mısırlı İbrahim Efendi. Algazi, for example, recorded for twenty years (c. 1909–1929) with Columbia, Odeon, and Orfeon, among others,[28] companies that had established themselves globally soon after the development of recording technology in the late nineteenth century. Mısırlı İbrahim Efendi recorded with Columbia as well as performed with the studio ensemble of the company.²⁹ The volume of recordings produced and the testimony of contemporary informants confirm the growing popularity of records among Ottoman and Turkish Jewry. According to one Istanbul resident, Algazi's records sold "in the thousands," and were found in almost all Jewish homes equipped with a gramophone in the 1930s.³⁰ It is most likely that non-Jews also purchased recordings of Jewish artists owing to the wide distribution of big-company labels such as Columbia, the artists' frequent public appearances, their multilingual recordings, and the sometime custom of producing religiously or ethnically mixed albums. Blumenthal Brothers, for example, produced an album with Hayim Efendi on one side and Derviş Abdullah Efendi on the other.³¹ Vocalists like Algazi, who recorded multi-genre (liturgical, folk, classical) and multilingual (Hebrew, Ladino, Turkish) music, were often accompanied by ethnically diverse instrumentalists: though the names of these musicians did not generally appear on record labels, we know, for example, that Algazi was regularly accompanied by udis Yorgo Bacanos, Aleko Efendi, and Abraham Daniel, and therefore most likely recorded with them as well.³²

Avram Karakaş recorded on Favorite Record, one of the labels competing for the Istanbul market before World War I. The song is "Bir Meleksin," by Armenian composer Arşak Çömlekciyan (1880–1930), who studied with Kirkor Çulhayan and Tatyos Efendi (1858–1913) and was known for his *piyasa* ud-playing. Reproduced by permission from the collection of Mehmet Güntekin.

Thus, recording studios reflected the ongoing multiethnic composition of Ottoman and republican music-making, and became alternate avenues of commercial patronage for musicians. By seeking to maximize profits, the recording industry responded to, and generated through sales, widespread musical tastes among the general population, not those of a reforming minority. Though participating in changing tastes and styles, the industry nonetheless helped to partially finance Ottoman-style musicians—particularly after 1923, when official support from the new state began to dry up—and thus contributed to a musical environment in which Jewish performers continued to be active. Jewish composers, musicians, and religious vocalists now passed between synagogue and a diversifying musical cityscape. For example, İsak Algazi served as hazan at the İtalyan sinogog (Italian synagogue) in Galata, teaching masters-to-be İsak Maçoro and David Behar, while simultaneously making albums, participating in Maftirim sessions, facilitating such projects as the Maftirim notations by Çulhayan, publishing a notated Maftirim fasıl, and reportedly giving music lessons to non-Jewish women students.[33] Avram Karakaş similarly moved between more and less religious worlds, worshipping at Etz Ahayim synagogue in Ortaköy and becoming renowned as a gazino performer, recording artist, and vocalist at the court of Abdülhamid II.[34] Such composer-instrumentalists as İsak Varon and Mısırlı İbrahim Efendi, while not holding religious positions, also crossed between Hebrew and Ottoman-Turkish music spheres in their capacity as recording artists, studio directors, ensemble members, and Maftirim participants.[35] These wide-ranging musical activities kept synagogue music culture in the loop of contemporary musical developments, teaching its fruits to future prayer leaders, Maftirim participants, and congregants in a manner not unlike that of the Jewish musicians of the late nineteenth century.

A second major commercial arena for musicians in Istanbul and other Ottoman-Turkish cities was live performance venues.[36] As we saw in the life of Mısırlı İbrahim Efendi, gazinos rapidly expanded in Istanbul and its environs on the foundation of nineteenth-century coffeehouse culture, the rise of a Muslim bureaucratic class, new modes of waterway transport, and historic shifts in commercial activity from the imperial core to Galata and beyond. After 1917 an influx of White Russian immigrants was responsible for a rise in venues owned by entrepreneur-refugees fleeing the Russian Revolution.[37] According to one source, in 1925 there were 1,656 coffeehouses and 227 gazinos in Istanbul.[38] Although Algazi reportedly did not sing publicly for pay, Mısırlı İbrahim Efendi and Avram Karakaş (often together) as well as other Jewish vocalists and instrumentalists did perform on commercial stages. As Istanbul resident Sermet Muhtar Alus remembers of the music entertainment scene of around 1900, early recording cylinders had become as popular as radio was forty years later; gazinos and coffeehouses abounded in Istanbul's neighborhoods; and performing singers and instrumentalists drew from a multiethnic pool of musicians.[39] Clearly, a lively and widespread entertainment scene complemented the nascent record industry—primarily minority-owned enterprises employing musicians of diverse backgrounds—as early as two decades before the founding of the Republic.

Through the centralization of Maftirim performance in Istanbul, the rise of the recording industry, and the proliferation of nightlife entertainment, the Jewish community as well as society at large enjoyed a flourishing of art music in the city over the first thirty years of the twentieth century, into the first decade of the Turkish Republic. Commercial and religious channels of patronage supported both individual musicians and multiethnic music-making as a whole, operating within newly developing (recording studio and gazino) and well-established (synagogue) urban spaces. Despite this vibrant Jewish music-making and an expanding marketplace for musical entertainment in Istanbul, the Republic's secularizing and Europeanizing cultural reforms, as we will detail later, began to encroach financially and spacially on the art music world of the 1920s. In addition, the marketplace laid the groundwork for popularization and hybridization of styles in Turkish music that eventually marginalized traditionalist musicians.[40] However, by the time of the establishment of the Turkish Republic and its reforms, Jewish migration had already swelled the number of musicians in Istanbul, while commercial musical enterprises had already become firmly established enough to provide alternative remunerative and performance venues for art music. As new sources of patronage and artistic interaction, these businesses offset, to a certain degree, the deleterious effects of official withdrawal of support, generating and sustaining musical activity relatively independent of official policies.

The closure of dervish orders and lodges (1925), which followed the earlier dismantling of Ottoman religious legal/administrative structures, represented a serious loss to multireligious performers of Ottoman music, who attended, learned, and performed at the lodges. Given the long-standing historical interchange between Jewish and Mevlevi musicians, as can be seen in Samuel Benaroya's biography, how did the closure of dervish lodges and orders affect their relationships? This question is especially important since, in the early nineteenth century, Mevlevi lodges grew increasingly central to Ottoman music education, after the palace began to patronize and teach both European and Turkish music through refashioning the palace school (1826) and appointing Giuseppe Donizetti as director.[41] In fact, in the late nineteenth century, leading Mevlevi *şeyh*s were responsible for promoting modernist approaches to music theory, encouraging the composition of new pieces, musical publications (song-text collections, scores, and articles), and even the use of new technology to accurately measure intervals.[42] Again, after the Second Constitutional period (1908), palace education diminished even further with the closing of the palace music school and the rise of private music societies (*cemiyet*s).[43] Thus, the closing of dervish lodges in 1925 followed their growing importance to music education, as well as the gradual establishment of alternative learning settings outside both tekke and palace. The unemployment of tekke leaders and musicians after 1925 led some to emigrate, while others remained in Turkey as either preservationist or commercial practitioners of Ottoman musical genres.

Despite few textual sources, there is evidence that Mevlevi and Jewish musicians sustained a musical relationship after 1925. In fact, some Sufi lodges never completely shut down, operating beyond government oversight and evading police raids.[44] It is unlikely that Mevlevi musicians from either underground or closed lodges stopped attending synagogue performances, which they had frequented before 1925.[45] In addition, republican musicians, composers, and theorists, such as Rauf Yekta (1871–1935), Ruşen Kam (1902–1981), Zekâizade Ahmet Efendi (1869–1943), and İsmail Hakkı Bey with his students visited the synagogue to hear Algazi sing.[46] Muslim religious singers, moreover, circulated in the same commercial venues (recording studios and gazinos) as Jewish performers such as Algazi, Karakaş, and Edirneli Hayim

Efendi, thus maintaining social and musical contact. David Behar, student of Algazi and Maftirim şef (conductor), reported historical and ongoing Mevlevi-Jewish relationships in his lifetime.[47] It is in Edirne, the historical center of Maftirim music-making, that we witness a significant sign of ongoing Mevlevi-Jewish interchange. The synagogue leadership, which had maintained an active religious culture despite losses to migration, invited Mevlevi dervishes to perform their ceremony (*sema*) in the main synagogue of the city for a number of years after the mid-1920s:[48]

> Atatürk prohibited classical music. What could the Mevlevi do? . . . [The tekke] was closed. They came to the synagogue. They performed there. In the synagogue, the Big Synagogue. The old Jews said this, they remembered. The Edirne community head, Yeuda Romano, related this to me. . . . Yes, it's true, they did the *sema* in the synagogue. . . . They wanted to perform. . . . Because their *sema*, their instruments, everything [that was musical was the same as with the Jews]. [Romano] didn't know what day [of the week they performed]. You see, this was in the past, in the 1930s, long ago.[49]

At least in Edirne, there is concrete evidence of the historic musical relationships between Jewish hazanim and Mevlevi dervishes prevailing, and even intensifying, in response to anti-religious legislation, effectively doubling the religious role of the synagogue for at least five years, and sustaining the activities of Muslim dervishes and musicians against the efforts of the state to shut them down. It is possible that such goodwill gestures were more likely in a provincial city, at a distance from the oversight of governmental authorities; however, on a metaphoric level, the Edirne story crystallizes the fluctuating patterns of musical space usage in the changing music world of the early Republic. As some inclusive spaces closed (tekkes and Turkish music programs), others had already opened (gazinos and recording studios) or increased their activity (synagogues), being sufficiently well-established to take up the slack in patronage and places to meet, perform, teach, and learn. New commercial or old religious centers thus accommodated historically established intercommunal relationships in an era of secularizing reforms. As in the late Ottoman period, the synagogue continued to serve multiple functions of socializing, music-making, and learning through ongoing visits by Mevlevi dervishes and republican musicians, alone or with their students, further expanding its historical usage in the late 1920s to accommodate the practice of the Mevlevi ceremony in Edirne. Circulations between communities thus continued to operate under the official radar, rechanneling Ottoman music activity, transmitting it liturgically to a younger generation, and protecting for a time multifunctional and intercommunal synagogues, though not Mevlevi lodges, in the Turkish Republic.

Departing Turkish Jews, Arriving European Jews

In the early 1930s, following a decade of musical florescence, some Jewish hazanim, highly valued by their communities, began to leave Turkey. İsak Algazi emigrated to Uruguay through Paris (1933); Samuel Benaroya to Switzerland, then Seattle, Washington (1934); and Moşe Kordova to Palestine (before 1935).[50] Given the lively musical culture in which they participated in the 1920s—active and interactive, despite state curtailments—why did these musicians choose to leave their country? Indeed, new channels of patronage, as well as performance and religious space, enabled the continuance of Ottoman and synagogue music in this period, even as heated debates about an appropriate music for the new Republic called such music into question. Through examining the political shifts between the first and second decades of the Republic we can contextualize these departures in intensified practices of nation-building that created national outsiders, including particular Jewish musicians. Such sub-periodization of the early Republic and presidency of Atatürk (1923–1938) guards against a linear or teleological history privileging the 1930s over an initial transitional decade significant to social and cultural continuities among Turkish Jewry.

Political threats to the status of diverse ethnic and religious populations began in the 1920s, laying the foundation for increasing antiminority measures in the following decade. For example, foreign companies, nationalized industries, and civil service employers were expected to hire Turkish citizens, conceived of as Muslim, and such campaigns as "Citizen, Speak Turkish!" put pressure on ethnic and religious minorities to speak Turkish in public.[51] By the 1930s, in line with global trends, economic and cultural nationalism intensified in Turkey. Pressure on foreign companies to hire Muslim citizens was codified into law (1932), even as the discourse about who was a "Turk" was increasingly linked to race more than religion.[52] Pre-Islamic Turkic tribes as the original race formed the basis for nationalizing history, language, and civilization through the Turkish Historical Society (1931) and Turkish Language Society (1932), and "national" music, as discussed below, was increasingly imagined in terms of ethnic authenticity (Turkish folk music) and the art of the future (Western classical music). The events surrounding İsak Algazi's emigration from Turkey help to explain the motivations of one Jewish vocalist and prayer leader for leaving the country—motivations inextricably interwoven with the artistic, the political, and the economic. Algazi exemplifies a non-Muslim musician and intellectual moving among high-level republican circles, while never achieving insider status within a nationalizing Turkish state. Official connections that benefited Jewish musicians in their profession and community status one decade earlier, now just as easily destabilized one's career and position in the political culture. In addition to facing a weakening of his political relationships, Algazi experienced a cultural demotion through the increasing aesthetic polarization between European-secular music ("new," "modern," "Turkish-to-be," and valued) and Ottoman-religious music ("old," "imperial," ethnically mixed, and devalued), which, in the end, ideologically embraced European Jewish émigrés over their Turkish Jewish counterparts, however "European," within a changing national music world. By contrast, the career of piyasa performer and composer Mısırlı İbrahim Efendi arguably rose even further in the early Republic and in the presence of new European arrivals in Turkey. His life provides a counterpoint to Algazi's that elucidates the advantages and adaptations underpinning one Jewish musician's artistic and political success in the new state.

To Stay or To Leave?

A highly respected hazan and Ottoman music expert, İsak Algazi, like Chief Rabbi Hayim Becerano, supported the reformative direction of the Republic, perhaps in part because he had been educated at the Alliance Israélite Universelle school in Izmir, which inculcated European civilizational values underpinning the new state's policies. Evidence of his political and philosophical support for the Turkish nation appears in his published articles on religion, history, and politics, in addition to his co-founding of *La Voz de Oriente*, a progressive weekly Ladino newspaper, in Istanbul in 1930.[53] Moreover, Algazi wrote the "Türk Hava Kuvvetleri Marşı" (Turkish Air Force March),[54] and performed for Atatürk (1932).[55] In the 1920s he participated in performances in wealthy republican homes, in recording Hebrew, Ladino, and Turkish language song, and in teaching Jewish and non-Jewish students.[56]

A precipitating reason for Algazi to leave his country, according to those close to him, was his exclusion from national radio. In 1928 he appeared on early broadcasts of the infant Istanbul Radio station.[57] Already by 1930, debates erupted in Turkey over the appropriate role of radio in public life—whether it should be for market-driven musical entertainment or for social engineering through state cultural programming.[58] Turkish radio in the 1930s, moreover, faced competition from political and cultural programming accessible to Turkish listeners from neighboring countries.[59] In the end, nationalized Turkish stations included popular alaturka music programs to attract citizens to listen, but excluded exponents of Ottoman musical forms such as Algazi. More than that, based on oral testimonies, Algazi was denied an appointment to the Board of Ankara Radio (established in 1927), apparently motivating him to emigrate from Turkey.[60]

Whatever the immediate causes, it is the broader social, political, economic, and artistic environment, progressively developing since the first decade of the Republic, that more fully accounts for Algazi's departure. Despite the European educational and cultural milieu of his Jewish community in Istanbul, which would presumably advantage him within a Europeanizing nation, Algazi remained an outsider insofar as the state was concerned. No matter how European-leaning, the state apparatus progressively privileged Muslim over non-Muslim Turkish citizens in diverse legislation. It is thus possible that a growing ethos of a Muslim Turkish civil service affected Algazi's exclusion from a position with Ankara Radio, while it is undeniable that he lived within a minority community that, by nationalist legislation, was increasingly economically and culturally marginalized. Moves to establish a national language, for instance, at the expense of minority communities were expressed through the aforementioned "Citizen Speak Turkish!" campaign, rules regarding the language of instruction at Alliance schools, and, in Algazi's own case, requirements to romanize the *rashi* (cursive Hebrew) script of his Ladino newspaper.[61] Like all Turkish Jews, Algazi lived as a citizen in a nationalizing state that had not resolved the dilemma of universal citizenship and ethno-religious protections.[62] Further, according to one source, Algazi fled in fear of his life, an understandable reaction in the face of the "measured terror" in the late 1920s and early 1930s, which suppressed political opposition, at times violently, within both the government and society, including journalists, Muslim and non-Muslim like himself.[63] Given such state actions and policies, it is not surprising that, for a high-profile, pro-republican artist like Algazi, official rejection was a betrayal of his support for the Republic and would result in a sufficient decline of his personal and professional life to motivate departure.

Moreover, changing popular vocal styles progressively sidelined Algazi's Ottoman-era stylistics in favor of Europeanized, republican tastes. By the mid-1930s in the commercial world, major record labels appear to have ceased recording minority male vocalists, like Hayim Efendi and Algazi, in part because of their "goy goy" vocal style, which included such alaturka qualities as glottal vibrato, vocal melisma, emotional expressiveness, and high volume.[64] As its technology changed, the recording industry itself had cultivated shifts in musical aesthetics, with the early acoustic recording horn demanding loud vocals or instrumentation, and the later, more sensitive electrical microphone (1926) favoring control of vocal or instrumental dynamics.[65] It is also likely that the promotion of a national language created an environment that curtailed the recording of Algazi's multilingual genres.[66] In the vocal arena, furthermore, a new performance style was emerging, beginning with the concerts of classical singer Münir Nurettin Selçuk (1899–1981), who, after a sojourn in Paris, began in 1930 to perform classical Turkish music in a smoother, more controlled vocal style, while adopting European conventions, such as solo concerts and formal (tuxedo) attire.[67] Moreover, as new technologies, such as radio and film, entered the marketplace, it became more important for artists to be active in a range of commercial ventures in order to obtain recording contracts, which thereby guaranteed sales.[68]

Thus, from its beginnings in rich and varied musical genres, promoted by diverse local agents, the record industry gradually narrowed its productive range, responding to and steering (via its own sales-motivated selectivity) a changing popular music culture.[69] Gazino and radio performances likewise showcased artists representing a changing classical aesthetic. An artist like Algazi, therefore, whose acoustic synagogue performance necessitated vocal volume and emotional expressiveness related to religious texts, was caught between expectations of his religious community and the changing technologies and tastes of the wider society. Retaining a vocal and performative style associated with religious, Ottoman music, ceasing to appear on radio and records, and never performing in gazinos, Algazi lived within a legal, aesthetic, technological, and economic web that reinforced a normative music culture by filtering out less commercially active, minority, and religious singers such as himself. Despite the admiration and support of traditionalist composers in the Republic, by the 1930s in the society at large Algazi was not only a sociopolitical, but also a musical outsider, unsupported by the sources of patronage that had sustained him until then.

By contrast, Algazi's contemporary, Mısırlı İbrahim Efendi, remained in Turkey until his death in 1948, sustaining a successful career in the musical marketplace, as well as in the upper echelons of politics. Given the numerous characteristics held in common by these two Jewish musicians, their contrasting life stories illuminate the pathways by which a minority musician was enabled, or not, to survive, and even thrive, in a period of intensified nationalism. Both Algazi and Mısırlı İbrahim Efendi enjoyed upper-level musical and political contacts, performing in wealthy homes as well as for the president of the Republic. They both recorded prolifically, taught extensively, and were sufficiently politically connected and supportive of the new state to be considered for or to achieve positions in government: whereas Algazi was expecting an appointment to the Board of Ankara Radio, Mısırlı İbrahim Efendi became a member of the Turkish parliament.

The political success of one over the other reveals key differences in each musician's ability to rise in the changing national and musical order. Mısırlı İbrahim Efendi's political relationships and appointments undoubtedly derived from his musical activities, which, in the 1930s, included leading the Türk Gülşen-i Musıki Heyeti in official concerts at the Dolmabahçe Palace and giving a series of concerts in Egypt at the invitation of King Faruq (r. 1936–1953). As a longtime gazino musician, Mısırlı İbrahim Efendi maintained his marketability and popularity in the commercial world of Turkish art music, a popularity that extended into official realms through the ongoing currency of alaturka music in the midst of formal disfavor.[70] He performed with the studio orchestra at Columbia,[71] and his mastery of the cümbüş, a popular instrument in the early Republic, attests to the currency of his instrumental expertise at the time.[72] His instrumental focus allowed him to circumvent new republican vocal tastes, even as contemporary women singers popularized his songs through their own up-to-date recordings.[73] As testimony to his official musical acceptability in this period, he participated in a concert series with Hafız Yaşar, the lead conductor of the president's Turkish music ensemble and a harsh, if unreliable, critic of Algazi's performance for Atatürk in 1932.[74] As a teacher he was known for training Perihan Altındağ Sözeri (1925–2008), a singer who gained renown through her youthful performances on Ankara Radio beginning in 1939. Clearly, in the 1930s Mısırlı İbrahim Efendi actively participated in commercial and official music-making through his extensive experience and growing reputation in the musical marketplace that, in contrast to hazan İsak Algazi, kept pace with changing vocal taste, instruments, and performance practice in Turkish art music of the early Republic.

In the context of intensifying Turkish nationalism, which included the purification and standardization of the national language, accoutrements of Mısırlı İbrahim Efendi's performance career, such as his stage name, also advantaged him over Algazi in the music world. Specifically, the Family Name Law (1934) required the adoption of surnames, in effect suppressing names marked as Jewish, Greek, and Armenian.[75] Acquired in an earlier period reflecting Ottoman patterns of musical nicknaming, Mısırlı İbrahim Efendi's commercial name was already Turkified ("İbrahim," the Muslim counterpart to his birthname, "Avram"), serving him well under the national conditions of the early Republic. In the official and commercial music worlds of the

Mısırlı İbrahim Efendi (*in circle*) in the Türk Gülşen-i Musiki Heyeti in the 1930s. This early republican ensemble was a part of the Gülşen-i Musiki Cemiyeti. Reproduced by permission from Gözlem Gazetecilik Basın ve Yayın, Istanbul.

1930s, formal Turkification of names appears to have been encouraged at the highest political levels to facilitate employment. Atatürk reportedly offered Turkish names to a group of foreign musicians, who performed at his official functions, including an Ashkenazi Jew, so that they could become citizens and effectively pass as Muslim Turks for remunerative reasons.[76] It is also possible that, even if known as Jewish in governmental and commercial circles, Mısırlı İbrahim Efendi's Ottoman-Arab origins ameliorated his ethno-religious provenance in a period when European-identified minorities, such as Jews and Greeks, were viewed as foreigners and when popular understandings of local culture blurred the Turkish with the Arab and Persian, rather than sharply distinguishing each from the other.[77] Although Mısırlı İbrahim Efendi's musical reputation, commercial competitiveness, and political milieu were the primary reasons for his enduring success, something as brief but symbolic as the name by which he was publicly known usefully conformed to the nationalizing ethos of the 1930s and '40s in ways that a Jewish stage name would not. Advantaged musically, politically, and linguistically for upward mobility after the 1920s, Mısırlı İbrahim Efendi thrived under conditions that excluded musicians, like Algazi, who were sufficiently marginalized musically, politically, and economically to leave the country.

In addition to Algazi, other prominent Jewish hazanim and composers left Turkey in the early 1930s for a variety of reasons, including economic, linguistic, and cultural pressures resulting from anti-minority policies and events. For example, Samuel Benaroya fled violence in Edirne in 1934, commonly referred to as the Trakya Olayları (Thrace Incidents), which included the boycott of Jewish businesses and violence against property and individuals. These events occurred uncoincidentally at the same time as the passage of the Settlement Law, which, in the interest of "security," permitted the government to resettle minority populations away from border regions and transportation lines and among Turkish Muslim majorities.[78] As Benaroya recollected decades later:

> It was in twenty-four hours we have to leave the country, to leave the town where we were living. . . . As a matter of fact, in twenty-four hours we start to sell our furniture, our dishes, our things in order to

leave, what do you want us to do? . . . At that time, I went to Istanbul myself. . . . My father was quite old, and I said first I want to secure, God willing, the life of my parents. I rented a room, a place for them. Then I returned to Edirne and I made my possibility to go to Geneva, Switzerland.[79]

Over the next two decades, a growing number of Jews emigrated owing to ongoing anti-minority policies and incidents, among them campaigns against the formal and informal use of Ladino, discrimination in the civil service, forced labor and extraordinary taxation during World War II (the *Varlık Vergisi*, or Capital Tax), and incidents of anti-Greek ethnic violence that overflowed into attacks on Jewish businesses and districts.[80] Some newspapers and journalists published anti-Jewish articles and cartoons, among them pro-German dailies during World War II.[81] These emigrations emptied historically Jewish neighborhoods on the Golden Horn, such as Balat and Hasköy, as rising poverty, educational disadvantages, and the dispossession of the middle class excluded large numbers of Jews from historical avenues of advancement.[82] From an estimated population of 81,400 in 1927, the Turkish Jewish population fell to approximately 46,000 in 1955 through immigration to Europe, North and South America, and increasingly (after 1948) to Israel.[83] Among those going to Israel was Nesim Sevilya: in addition to ostensibly religious reasons, given the timing of his move, it is probable that conditions in Turkey contributed to his departure.

Employing European Emigrés

In the same period of Turkish Jewish communal and musical losses in the early 1930s, the institutionalization of a Europeanizing musical philosophy was moving forward, largely through the recruitment of European artists and theorists. Ottoman patronage of European music and musicians had begun in the early nineteenth century and generated a cultural dispute, framed as alaturka versus alafranga musical styles and education, that continued among republican musicians, intellectuals, and politicians, as they debated what constituted an appropriate national music.[84] By the second decade of the Republic such debates took place in an increasingly nationalist economic and

A Musical Landscape in Flux 71

Nesim Sevilya before his departure to Israel in 1949. Avram Leyon (*right*), the director and owner of the newspaper *Şalom gazetesi*, is, according to the caption, wishing him a good journey (*Şalom gazetesi*, May 12, 1949). Reproduced by permission from *Şalom gazetesi*, Istanbul.

cultural context. Among the early republican policies promoting European-style music and training, the most significant include state funding for schools (the Musıki Muallim Mektebi, a conservatory to train teachers in Western music, was established in 1924), the institution of competitive exams for study at European conservatories (1925), and the closing or proscription of Turkish music programs (at Darülelhan, 1926, and in public schools, 1927).[85] Moreover, as discussed earlier, through the closure of dervish lodges and orders (1925) performers of Ottoman music lost a primary center for musical education and composition.

Music as a measure of cultural revolution in the Republic had begun to appear in Atatürk's speeches in 1928, with the energy of European classical and Anatolian folk music, in contrast to a ponderous Ottoman style, associated with a contemporary Turkish spirit.[86] Moreover, the multiethnic character of Ottoman-Turkish composers and performers appears to have come under implicit criticism,[87] as the notion of a "national synthesis" in music, based on Ziya Gökalp's writings,[88] was promoted as a position between alaturka and alafranga music, that is, Anatolian folk music (alaturka) transmittable through notation and amenable to polyphonic arrangement (alafranga) to forge a music for the future. Supported by their European conservatory education and Euro-Russian precedents, several Turkish composers, collectively referred to as Türk Beşleri (the Turkish Five), used folk melodies, motifs, and historical figures in their symphonic and operatic works.[89] Among the measures intensifying the promotion of such a national music were music classes at People's Houses (1932), a 22-month prohibition of classical Turkish music on state radio (1934), and the development of state performing arts programs by European consultants and teachers (1935).[90]

It was primarily prominent German and Austrian artists, most of whom were Jewish, who filled positions supporting these national arts-building initiatives.[91] Because of the firing of German Jewish civil servants, professors, and lawyers in Germany, as well as the Nazi threat to ideologically unsympathetic artists and intellectuals beginning in 1933,[92] a pool of professionals and academics seeking to leave Germany was available to receiving countries, including a Turkish state pursuing both a national university system based on German educational models and European-style music conservatories.[93] In fact, the German embassy in Ankara, led by Ambassador Friedrich von Keller (1873–1960), presented a vision of German arts that antedated the Nazi regime, promoting German-centric cultural exchange, whether by Jews or non-Jews, that correlated with official Turkish agendas. Thus, whereas the "push" for German emigration to Turkey came from incipient Nazi ethnic and cultural policies, the "pull" included not only a welcoming Turkish government, but also resident German nationalist proponents of home-country high culture in an uneasy relationship with the Nazi regime.[94] Different ideological perspectives in Germany and Turkey regarding modern music for the nation, in the end, benefited the new Republic's cultural initiatives, as supported by an aristocratic German embassy. In official Nazi arts policies, the term "modern" was avoided because of its associations with the pre-Nazi Weimer Republic, and state arts organizations generally supported "German music" (tonal, post-Romantic, local) and not "Jewish music" (atonal, experimental, international).[95] By contrast, among Turkish cultural policy-makers and the German embassy, modern European classical compositions and composers represented the music of the future and the height of elite culture respectively, motivating the employment of the very musicians deemed degenerate in Nazi Germany and Austria.[96]

Starting in the mid-1930s, at least twenty-five German and Austrian performing artists came to Istanbul and Ankara as visiting consultants or long-term employees.[97] In Istanbul, composer Joseph Marx (1882–1964) was hired from the Vienna Music Academy to serve at the Istanbul Belediye Konservatuarı (Istanbul Municipal Conservatory), and later recruited Austrian instrumentalists to Turkey.[98] In Ankara, Paul Hindemith (1895–1963), German violinist, composer, and theorist, whose musical and political reputation among the Nazi regime rose and fell by the mid-1930s, was hired to develop a "Universal and Turkish Polyphonic Music Education Program" for all music institutions in Turkey.[99] Threatened both professionally and personally in Germany (his wife's father was Jewish), Hindemith had decision-making authority in Turkey in his capacity as curricular consultant, becoming a conduit for other German and Austrian émigré artists to work in Ankara.[100] In contrast to some German émigré employees and visiting artists from Russia in the same period, Hindemith objected to presenting music as elite entertainment or avant-garde extravaganza. Rather, his curricular recommendations emphasized the disciplined, long-term music education of the young Turkish *Volk* (folk), who, he believed, had the potential to acculturate to European music if it was rooted in their indigenous folk and military music traditions. In this way, Hindemith's approach resonated with Ziya Gökalp's philosophy of a national music,[101] while uniquely echoing the success story of German Jews assimilating through the arts to German culture beginning in the mid-nineteenth century. Despite competitive tensions with contemporary Russian, and some German and Turkish, musicians in Ankara at the time, the German arts contingent, led by Hindemith, succeeded in moving forward with organizing music education, performance venues, and state arts institutions in Turkey based on German models.

The majority of the German émigré musicians active in these efforts, whether Jewish or non-Jewish, had experienced threats to their musical careers owing to the economic crisis in Germany, increasingly restrictive racial laws, and the Nazification of German music. These musicians generally left Germany after the passage of the Nuremberg Laws (1935).[102] Among the most prominent of these in establishing European-style performance culture in Turkey were actor and director Carl Ebert (1887–1980), who set up opera and theater departments at Ankara State Conservatory (established in 1936); pianist and composer Eduard Zuckmayer (1890–1972), who directed and taught in the conservatory's music department; and conductor Ernst Praetorius (1880–1946), who conducted the Riyaset-i Cumhur Filarmoni Orkestrası (the Presidency's Philharmonic Orchestra) and presented concerts throughout the country.[103] In addition, Hindemith assisted a number of Jewish vocalists and instrumentalists in leaving Germany and Austria, for example, Georg Markowitz (piano), Licco Amar (violin), Ludwig Czaczkes (piano), and Frieda Silbertknopf Böhm (voice)—performers and teachers who trained a generation of classical musicians in Turkey. Most prominently, violinist Licco Amar (1891–1959), who had performed Hindemith's compositions in the Amar-Hindemith Quartet in Berlin (1922–1929) and whose father was Turkish Jewish, taught and performed in Turkey for over two decades, training numerous classical artists, including Turkish violinists Edip Günay (1931–2010), Suna Kan (b. 1936), and Ayla Erduran (b. 1936).[104] Because of the reportedly high salaries, positive professional reception, paucity of alternative destinations, and the outbreak of World War II, with few exceptions German and Austrian émigré artists remained in Turkey for a decade or longer, witnessing, and in some cases participating in, the establishment and training of Turkish state opera, theater, and ballet companies in the 1940s and '50s.[105]

The hiring of political and Jewish escapees from Nazi Germany in the 1930s in Turkey, part of a movement to recruit German and Austrian experts in the sciences, law, industry, and other fields, has been represented variously as an under-recognized national anomaly in Holocaust history; evidence of historical hospitality linked to the fifteenth-century Sephardic emigration from Spain to the Ottoman empire; and the continuation of an ambiguous Turkish legacy that included anti-refugee actions during World War II.[106] From the perspective of Ottoman-Turkish social and musical historiography, what is significant

A Musical Landscape in Flux 75

The Amar-Hindemith Quartet. *From top left clockwise*: Maurits Frank (cello), Walter Caspar (violin), Licco Amar (violin), and Paul Hindemith (viola). With occasional changes in membership, the quartet, which specialized in contemporary European music and premiered Hindemith's own compositions, performed, toured, and recorded between 1921 and 1929. The illustration is by Rudolf W. Heinisch (1896–1956), a German painter and illustrator, who, unlike his friend Paul Hindemith, remained in Nazi Germany, but stopped painting until the end of the Third Reich. Reproduced by permission from Lebrecht Music and Arts/Photographers Direct.

is that historians have studied the episode in isolation rather than in juxtaposition to native Jewish emigration in the same period.[107] In fact, the hiring, and resulting protection, of Austro-German Jewish artists coincided with the loss of employment, and resulting departure, of a significant collection of Turkish Jewish composers and hazanim. Budgetary decisions in the early 1930s, for example employing Hindemith as music curriculum designer and not appointing Algazi to the Board of Ankara Radio, reflect a broader partisan agenda that disfavored not only Turkish Jews but non-Muslims as a whole in the public sector, and promoted European-style music education and cultural institutions over Ottoman musical heritage. Because minority male vocalists were increasingly associated with a style and ethnicity not fitting republican national values, by the early 1930s, when Austro-German Jewish musicians were marginalized by Nazi cultural and racial ideology, the stage was set for an influx of German musical expertise to Turkey, reflecting the government's pro-European, anti-Ottoman cultural platform.

While recognizing that Turkey offered a safe haven to German and German-Jewish artists during the Nazi era and World War II, we must also recognize the country's concurrent loss of Turkish Jewish and other minority artists—two simultaneous movements of peoples, often discussed separately in the literature. Whatever the complex artistic, economic, or ethno-religious motivations in a single émigré's decision, by the early 1930s, different nationalizing agendas in Turkey and Germany created an environment for such movements, aided and abetted by a sympathetic German ambassador aligned with anti-fascist elite cultural values. Musically speaking, the comings and goings of Jewish and other musicians, Austro-German or Turkish, figuratively channeled a republican cultural ideology that valued one over the other. As Europeans, Austro-German Jewish musicians possessed civilizational capital, despite their ethno-religious roots, and were thus viewed as capable of transforming and elevating Turkish musical culture. By contrast, Turkish Jewish vocalists, whatever their progressive politics, represented an Ottoman musical past and non-Muslim ethno-religious presence, viewed as increasingly alien to an evolving national culture. The movements of Jewish musicians occurred within a global context of racialized nationalism in which less racialized, pre-Nazi German aristocratic values took part, representing, on a Turkish ideological level, those who prevailed and those who lost out in a broader debate on national music. After World War II, German musicians continued to find a place in Turkey, especially through visiting conductors in the 1950s and 1960s.[108] It was a full fifty years after the founding of the Republic that, through the political agitation of classical Turkish musicians remaining in Turkey, classical Turkish music education received official funding (1975), opening the way for the establishment of Turkish music conservatories in major cities.[109]

Civic Musical Friendships

As an art music shift took place in Turkey, involving, among others, officially funded (European) or unfunded (Turkish) musicians of Jewish ethnicity in the country, and as growing numbers of Turkish Jews emigrated over time, what was the music scene like for those Jews who chose to remain in Istanbul? Despite increasingly nationalistic and Europeanizing cultural trends, in the 1930s art music life and endeavors did not, of course, disappear from the Jewish and wider community: state reforms and funding priorities were the official face of a more complex music scene. In the Jewish community, prominent instrumentalists, composers, and some vocalists who were not closely associated with the religious realm and remained in Turkey continued to perform and compose. This included Mısırlı İbrahim Efendi, as well as Edirneli Hayim Efendi, who established a coffeehouse, Şark Musıki Kahvehanesi (Eastern Music Coffeehouse) on Bankalar Caddesi in Galata, where prominent Jewish musicians, such as Udi Selim, Menteş Sabah, and Mısırlı İbrahim Efendi performed regularly in the 1930s and '40s.[110] Other instrumentalists performing in the commercial sphere include Udi Moşe Moiz Leon (1908–1983), kanun-player Rafael Kordovero (active in the 1930s), violinist Ama Pepo Taragano, and accordionist Muzaffer Hekimoğlu (b. 1936).[111] Given the difficulty of identifying Jewish commercial musicians, because of Turkified names and negative associations of gazino work, it is probable that the list of Jewish gazino instrumentalists is longer.[112] Of course, in spite of their emigration, artists' records produced in earlier decades (e.g., by Algazi) continued to enter the soundscapes of Jewish and possibly non-Jewish homes, providing a measure of diversity to contemporary commercial production.[113] Such musical products, as with already published treatises, scores, and biographies, continued to circulate among the population beyond the control of national budgets and cultural agendas.[114]

Unlike instrumentalists, however, Jewish religious vocalists remaining in Turkey after 1930 primarily performed music in unofficial, communal spheres. Whereas first-generation republican singers such as Algazi had initially participated fully in changing commercial and official settings, as well as in the synagogue, his students, for example İsak Maçoro and David Behar, inherited the progressively contracting musical sphere for

Jewish musicians of the neighborhood of Hasköy, Istanbul, in the 1920s: singer and percussionist Menteş Sabah (*standing, right*), Kanuni (kanun player) Hasköylü Bohoraçi Levi (*reportedly standing, left*), and Kemani (violinist) Sabetay Sabah (*seated, with violin*). Reproduced by permission from the collection of Mehmet Güntekin.

minority vocalists of the 1930s. As music-making spaces and patronage became less inclusive, younger hazanim practiced their art more and more in inclusive communal spaces free of state and commercial interests, such as the synagogue (in Maftirim sessions and prayer services) and *ev toplantısı*, or home gathering, where performers of classical Turkish music met regularly to converse, meşk, and perform together. Meeting with non-Jewish musicians in these communal settings, as well as apprenticing as young men in both synagogues and conservatories, Jewish religious musicians came into close contact with musicians active in official and commercial spheres, where Jews were generally not employed. Thus, while most fully active in communal realms that reinforced traditionalist musical values, they also developed artistically through friendships with musicians more broadly employed and through immersion in a changing urban musical culture.

Isak Maçoro (1918–2008) and David Behar (b. 1918), students of Algazi who are considered the twentieth-century masters of Maftirim and synagogue music in Turkey, exemplify the musical lives of non-emigrating Jews across the twentieth century. By establishing a line of oral transmission to hazanim such as David Sevi, conductor of the surviving, weekly Maftirim group in Istanbul, they maintained musical links in the present to Ottoman Jewish masters of the past—the very musical pedigree considered so vital to Ottoman musicianship. Contemporaries and classmates, Maçoro was a full-time hazan in Istanbul for forty years until his retirement in 1979, whereas Behar worked professionally as a businessperson and musically as an amateur,[115] playing the kanun, teaching music, and conducting a Maftirim ensemble.[116] By musical education and activity, they were actively involved in the Jewish community, as well as republican learning spaces that officially taught European-style music while maintaining opportunities for meşk. Both learned synagogue music alongside Algazi during prayer services and at Maftirim sessions, with Maçoro assisting Algazi at the İtalyan synagogue as a youth. Both also learned Turkish music from teachers at the Belediye Konservatuarı (Istanbul Municipal Conservatory), the former Darülelhan, which had exclusively taught European music since 1926: Maçoro studied with Alice Rosenthal of Polish Jewish origin, the vocal teacher of Münir Nurettin Selçuk during his sojourn in Paris in the late 1920s; and Behar studied at the conservatory with Eyyubi Ali Rıza Şengel (1880–1953), a prominent composer of Ottoman-Turkish classical music, known for both religious and nonreligious compositions.[117] Such alaturka learning was possible, because, despite its European music curriculum, the school maintained a Türk Musıkisi İcra Heyeti (Turkish Music Performance Ensemble), which Ali Rıza Şengel directed as şef beginning in 1940.[118]

Both Maçoro and Behar thus learned Ottoman-Turkish and European music from a variety of quarters in the mid-century Turkish Republic, Maçoro becoming known for a more popular art music style, and Behar for a more traditional style. Maçoro did interact occasionally with the commercial art music world by invitation: he reportedly sang with Safiye Ayla (1907–1998), and was invited (but declined for religious reasons) to perform with Münir Nurettin Selçuk at the Şan Sineması, after the latter heard him sing at the synagogue.[119] David Behar, by contrast, became well-known among classical musicians as an usul master, as well as an expert in solfège, notation, and the kanun.[120] In this way, by the 1950s Algazi's second-generation republican descendents were participating in synagogue, as well as contemporary civic music-making and learning, to develop distinctively popular or traditionalist approaches common among Turkish classical musicians of the period. Such mixtures of musical education and differing emphases were possible through involvement in oral learning in the synagogue, as well as in changing, officially promoted European-style conservatory learning that retained pockets of meşk opportunity by means of its Turkish music ensembles. Through Maçoro and Behar, then, Jewish religious music kept contemporary with Turkish classical music in the Republic, even as it drew on the legacy and credentialing pedigree of master hazan İsak Algazi.

One primary inclusive, unofficial musical venue that allowed non-commercial, religious musicians like Maçoro and Behar to interact with more widely circulating republican artists was the ev toplantısı, a venue for performers, composers, and aficionados to sustain Ottoman music practices against their growing commercialization in gazinos, records, and film.[121] Concerts and meşk instruction in homes had Ottoman precedents; however, the republican gatherings represented a concerted effort to provide weekly meeting space, patronage, and intellectual exchange to traditionalist musicians in an era of commercialization and official non-endorsement. Hosted by patrons, some of whom were musicians and others not, a typical ev toplantısı of Istanbul centered around fasıl music-making, but also included intellectual discussion, socializing over tea, and religious observance in diverse combinations.[122] It is unclear how mixed attendance was; however, according to Neyzen Abdurrahman Nevzat Tırışkan (b. 1928), who regularly participated in more than one ev toplantısı in Istanbul, non-Muslims attended frequently, but were not trackable as such, because of Turkified names and the nature of amateur music-making at the time, that is, "going here and there," joining different sessions on different days.[123] Tırışkan recalls a meeting in the early 1950s at the home of Cahit Gözkan (1911–1999), an udi and composer whose musical gatherings with master musicians at his homes in Cerrahpaşa and Çiftehavuzlar became well-known in this period.[124] On this particular evening Jewish hazan David Asseo and a collection of rising republican artists of the time attended the gathering, including the Mevlevi musician Kani Karaca (1930–2004), who had recently moved to Istanbul from Adana and later became known internationally as a leading Mevlevi vocalist, instrumentalist, and *hafız*, as well as a performer of nonreligious music on stage and Istanbul state radio.[125] Also in attendance was Alaeddin Yavaşça (b. 1926), a prolific composer and vocal artist on Istanbul Radio at the time. David Asseo, hazan of Knesset Israel synagogue, reportedly studied with Kani Karaca.[126] According to Tırışkan,

> One day I was at Cahit Bey's. . . . Dr. Alaeddin Yavaşça was also there. Kani Karaca came with David. . . . They were all at the house. There Kani Karaca sang something. Conversation had started, and while we were talking about this and that, people requested something from [him]. Kani Karaca began a Hebrew hymn. It came to an end and David put his hand out, saying "When did you learn that?!" [Karaca] said, "When I came [to the synagogue], you were inside giving a meşk lesson. I sat outside. I learned the melody—you repeated it once or twice; the second time I learned the words. I came here and sang it." The hymn lasted about seven or eight minutes. When Kani Karaca sang it . . . everyone was amazed. Alaeddin Yavaşça wanted to meet him; they embraced.[127]

While highlighting Kani Karaca's by now famous, near-instantaneous musical memory, the story also reflects the kinds of friendships and tone of meetings taking place among Turkish classical musicians at the time. On the day of the story, Asseo was teaching Maftirim pieces to boys at the synagogue, where Karaca was to meet him and waited, overhearing and learning a piece himself, until the lesson was over. Later that evening, they went together to the private, weekly home session at Cahit Gözkan's house, where they met other prominent vocalists, such as Dr. Alaeddin Yavaşça, who had apprenticed at home sessions and elsewhere with various composers. Although Tırışkan saw Asseo and Karaca only once at that particular session, in his words, Asseo was a very "likeable, handsome, fine human being" with many close friends, and so likely appeared at other private gatherings. That Asseo effectively introduced newcomer Kani Karaca, who had recently relocated from the provinces, to Yavaşça and others also suggests Asseo's familiarity with such meetings. As a whole, the recollection offers a window onto the relationship of musical friends such as Asseo and Karaca, coming and going together between the primary inclusive classical Turkish music-making spaces of the time, interrelating with other artists such as Yavaşça and, in this case, learning specific pieces across repertoires. In this way, even if Asseo primarily performed at Knesset Israel synagogue, his own musical activity engaged with official, commercial, and non-Jewish religious spheres that intersected, through diverse artists, with communal meeting places.

The example of David Asseo and his musical relationships is one of many reported among Jewish religious singers of this period. According to Yavuz Yekta (b. 1930), neyzen and grandson of Rauf Yekta, Yavuz met in musical circles with hazan İsak Maçoro and other musicians of various backgrounds, explaining that, in this unofficial music sphere of amateurs, "we all knew each other."[128] Along the same lines, Victor Beruhiel, hazan at Ortaköy synagogue, described how his teacher, İsak Maçoro, along with David Behar, Alaeddin Yavaşça, and Kani Karaca were all friends in the 1950s and '60s. In this period Kani Karaca attended Maftirim sessions regularly, and later performed at least two Maftirim compositions on a home recording.[129] According to Beruhiel, such friendships involved religious visitations, in addition to musical and personal discussions:

> Kani Karaca taught a hazan [David Asseo]. Then, at the same time Kani Karaca became friends with Maçoro . . . in the '50s and '60s. Moreover, one evening—a Passover evening—we waited for Alaeddin Yavaşça. . . . We didn't start for fifteen or twenty minutes. [Alaeddin Yavaşça] was also a gynecologist. We waited for him. He was a very close friend of Maçoro's. He was friends with David Behar. We waited for him. In the end he didn't come, but there were many relationships. Later Emin Ongan trained a [hazan] friend.[130] . . . That is, there were relations with Turkish musicians, extremely good relations, close, high quality.[131]

Beruhiel's recollections enrich Tırışkan's testimony about private gatherings by adding Jewish religious occasions and nonmusical discussions to the potential interactions of prominent hazanim and non-Jewish musicians of the time. Fragmented as historical evidence, these third-person stories suggest further meetings at synagogues and homes, and fuller conversations—a broader fabric of relating than limited ethnographic sources can convey. Despite the possible interest of informants in highlighting multiethnic relations in twentieth-century Muslim-majority Turkey (Tırışkan) or their community's links with prominent Turkish vocalists such as Kani Karaca and Alaeddin Yavaşça (Beruhiel), the close friendships implied in their testimonies and confirmed in other sources provided the glue binding a functional, cross-communal classical Turkish music world in the republican civic sphere.

At times, among these musical visitations and interactions, relationships supported specific musical projects. In the mid-1980s, David Behar pursued a way to notate the Maftirim repertoire as currently performed, because of the loss of Kirkor Çulhayan's scores of the 1920s. His close friend composer Yesari Asım Arsoy (1898–1992) introduced him to Fatih Salgar, assistant conductor of the Istanbul Devlet Klasik Türk Müziği Korosu (State Classical Turkish Music Chorus of Istanbul), who worked as a *notacı* (notator) before computerized scoring was introduced. According to Salgar, "[David Behar] gave me the cassette of what they sang in the synagogue. I listened and took down the notation. We worked together at the very end. When I sang it to him, he said whether it was correct or not."[132] Completed in approximately two months, Salgar's scores are those used by David Sevi and David Behar at Maftirim sessions in Şişli synagogue today. Like Chief Rabbi Becerano, whose original scoring project was facilitated by Algazi, Kordova, and Varon, all of whom were introduced to him by Çulhayan, David Behar too was sufficiently embedded in the contemporary classical Turkish music world to network for the skills needed to achieve musical and communal objectives.

Let us return to the question of the fate of late Ottoman music-making and the survival of Maftirim performance into the twenty-first century. To be sure, in an environment of progressive Jewish emigration over the course of the twentieth century, Maftirim gatherings gradually diminished in Istanbul, migrating from neighborhoods vacated by Jews to new areas settled by upwardly mobile members of the community. Current sessions, nonetheless, continue Ottoman and republican Turkish learning and performance practice, and continue to be led by musicians respected as masters. The directorship of the weekly Maftirim group today has passed from İsak Maçoro and David Behar, both pupils of Algazi and other masters in the 1920s, to David Sevi, hazan of Şişli synagogue. Although depleted musically and numerically, current Maftirim performances evidence a chain of transmission cultivated through unofficial channels beginning in the early Republic, reflected not only in David Sevi's pedigree, but also in the memory of Algazi alive across generations in the religious community today.[133] Through a revised periodization of sociocultural history in this period, we can understand the historical underpinnings of the longevity of Maftirim performance. Leading composers, religious singers, and entertainers fully participated in turn-of-the-century commercial and technological opportunities that provided new channels of patronage in an era of reform after the founding of the Turkish Republic in 1923. Jewish migration from the provinces to Istanbul likewise contributed to a musical florescence in the 1920s, when the synagogue and its Maftirim ensembles comprised part of the art music culture of the city.

To be sure, there was also a contrary trend. The growing nationalism of the 1930s—embodying new notions of ethnicity, civilization, and secularism—favored Europeanizing performing arts, which led simultaneously to the employment of European Jews escaping the Third Reich and to the loss of Jewish and other minority vocalists from official and commercial spheres. In the end, however, Jewish religious musicians remaining in Turkey lived their musical lives primarily within a social milieu of amateur musicians of classical Turkish and religious music seeking to sustain Ottoman music forms, in opposition to state cultural agendas and the music marketplace. It is along this civil strand of musical activity that masters Maçoro and Behar orally transmitted the Maftirim repertoire and broader musical knowledge to future hazanim, including the current Maftirim conductor David Sevi. Through friendships with traditionalist musicians and in such community places as the multifunctional synagogue, *ev toplantısı*, and meşk opportunities at conservatories, they taught, performed, composed, and musically networked in ways related to late Ottoman musicians.

Unlike their predecessors, however, religious and traditionalist musicians as a whole faced a growing dichotomization and ranking of Ottoman-Turkish (alaturka) and European (alafranga) music under the Republic, with official, commercial, and civic spheres each advancing distinct, sometimes overlapping, musical interests. While any musician of classical Turkish or religious music in the Republic was affected by cultural reforms, state budgetary priorities, and commercial/technological developments that sidelined Ottoman musical heritage for half a century, Jewish musicians were made doubly vulnerable through their ethno-religious affiliation. In this context of attenuation of both a musical genre and the minority Jewish population in Turkey, we might expect more rapid cultural losses among Turkish Jews. As it is, the weekly Maftirim performance channels Turkish and Jewish musical learning, sheltered across the twentieth century not so much by a concern to preserve a musical heritage as by surviving and changing intercommunal spaces and relationships that evolved from the first decade of the Republic. In this way, one of the dimensions of Ottoman music-making that implicitly motivated nationalizing music reforms—its multiethnic character—was not entirely suppressed, but partially sustained despite musical and minority losses in the Turkish Republic.

Three The Girl in the Tree:
Gender and Sacred Song

As I walk along a bend in the road, the gate of Kasturiya synagogue suddenly appears before me, bordered by a sand-colored stone wall. "That's it!" I exclaim to myself. The rusty iron lattice work, grey stone arch, and red brick sides match in full color the black and white photo I had seen in a guidebook to the historical minority neighborhoods of the Golden Horn. Unsure of ever finding the place on this scorching July afternoon, I had followed the directions of children playing on various street corners, as I climbed further away from the water's edge along dusty, narrow streets. Registering Hebrew letters and a date imprinted on the gate's lintel, I pass by and enter a wide driveway, its steel bar ajar and stenciled in Turkish, "Otopark" (parking lot). I soon find myself drinking tea with a handful of parking lot attendants, idling away the afternoon in the empty lot. They reminisce about their past Armenian and Jewish neighbors in this area, which they call "Avcıbey," and a cab driver who grew up here nods that, yes, the stone wall around the lot was the original garden wall. Within its perimeter once stood a modest synagogue with its nearby gatekeeper's house, and small trees used to grow along one wall.[1] One huge tree, which shelters us now, then stood apart, the oldest and biggest. It extends upward through a hole in the tin roof overhanging the men's makeshift, open-air teahouse, its trunk strung with climbing beans and a dangling detergent bottle. When the men hear Janti Behar's story, they all agree this must have been her tree. Now living in a central district of Istanbul (Şişli), Janti had told me how, as a 10-year-old girl in the 1930s, she had entered the garden of the synagogue in her neighborhood of Kasturiya (its Ladino name), climbed the big tree, and listened, entranced, to the Maftirim suite sung by men inside the building.² I imagine her coming through the massive gate now forming the back wall of a roofed room with a sofa where a young man lies sleeping. As the non-Jewish parking lot workers chat, in my mind's eye I see Janti taking a few steps to the huge tree. From its branches, she would hear the deep voices, melodic ornaments, and diverse rhythms of Hebrew song coming from the synagogue.

"Can you send us some of your photos?" The question returns me to the men sitting comfortably and relaxed in their teahouse. "Absolutely," I respond, as I think, it's their life now. How much did they have to do with the social upheavals that drove Jewish residents to abandon their neighborhood and synagogue for upscale districts or foreign countries? A whole way of life is gone; a new space and livelihood have taken its

Kasturiya synagogue garden gate (2006). The Hebrew date above the gate (5653) indicates it was built in 1893. The synagogue, built within the stone wall and no longer standing, was constructed in 1801. Photo by author.

place. I cannot help but notice that the ground between Janti's gate and tree is where the workers have built their tea and housekeeping nook, dwarfed by the vacant space of the parking lot (busier at night, they tell me). Tea steams on a hotplate; a television, rigged up above a table, buzzes. One man lounges back on his plastic chair, doing a crossword puzzle. Another stares alternately at the television screen and a newspaper flattened on the table. A young man in dark glasses and blue jeans drops by to chat, just as a cab, sparkling yellow, pulls up. The resident from childhood who told me the most about the synagogue, its building and trees, is starting his shift. Posing proudly next to his car, "Will you take my picture before I leave?" he asks.

Kasturiya and its residents remain in the memory of the older generation of the 24-hour parking lot. The quarter was one of seven historical sections of Balat, once a Jewish-majority neighborhood, located on the Golden Horn and near the old center of the city, with its palace, imperial mosques, and marketplaces. It was named after a town in the Balkans from which its first Romaniot (post-Byzantine Greek-speaking) Jewish émigrés came through *sürgün* (forced emigration) to repopulate the city after the Ottoman conquest of 1453. Later, Sephardic Jews expelled from Spain settled in Kasturiya and in other areas of Balat as well as in nearby, ethnically mixed neighborhoods of the Golden Horn.[3] Kasturiya appears not only in the stories of the parking lot workers, but also in scholarship and memoirs about the historical Jewish district and in community-based literature on Istanbul's synagogues.[4] However, as with other minority areas in the city, its history is largely hidden from public view, despite the association of Balat with Ottoman and Turkish Jewry.[5] In fact, located on the outskirts of Balat, its synagogue destroyed, Kasturiya was not suggested to me for a research visit by members of the Jewish community. Rather, I had attended the two active synagogues in central Balat, Yanbol and Ahrida, both frequented today by Jewish residents coming from other parts of the city: the former holds regular Shabbat services, and the latter, chosen for renovation for the quincentennial celebrations in 1992, hosts special holiday celebrations.[6] Already on the periphery of municipal and communal history, Kasturiya and its synagogue came to life for me largely through the childhood memories of Janti Behar and the present-day workers at the parking lot. As I sat with the workers, remembering her interview, the surviving synagogue structures—the garden gate and surrounding wall—together with Janti's tree appeared to me not as ruins but instead as keepers of one girl's musical story. Excluded by religious law from male music-making, Janti confined her religious music activity to the outskirts of the synagogue, yet another periphery within a sectional periphery (Kasturiya) of Balat. With the destruction of a central institution, administered by male congregants, it was understandably assumed that little remained there of communal religious or architectural history. Ironically, it is the peripheral person and her history that have survived the loss of the center.

The life story of Janti, the daughter of a Maftirim conductor in the 1930s, opens a window on the musical lives of Jewish girls and women in the city, contributing new insights to our understanding of gender within Ottoman and Hebrew music-making. Through her acquisition of Ottoman-Turkish art music and a measure of Hebrew song, Janti's musical life story blurs the apparent masculine boundaries around such repertoires as the Maftirim, enriching and challenging a

Parking lot on the site of the demolished Kasturiya synagogue (2006). Photo by author.

predominant perception that identifies Sephardic women with Ladino singing. Furthermore, through her personal choices and navigation of religious, musical, and social norms across her lifetime, her story helps to unravel the interplay of gender, music, and religion among Turkish Jews in the twentieth and early twenty-first centuries.

In the early Turkish Republic, girls like Janti lived and moved in neighborhood spaces—home, synagogue, music cafés, baths—that were animated by musical trends—art music, day and nightlife entertainment, gramophones and radios, popular song publications—held in common with diverse others, even if certain gendered and class expectations held sway. The concept of "soundscape" offers a generative framework for elucidating such daily life in neighborhoods and retrieving participants like Janti, missing from historical accounts based exclusively on textual sources, musical notation, or audio recordings. Articulating an urban soundscape uniquely benefits interdisciplinary historical ethnographies such as this one by enabling sensory, especially auditory, inferences of a past urban landscape.[7] The diverse, changing, and reiterative aural experience of residents emerges not only as indirect musical exposures from such sources as taverns and street vendors, but also as engaged musical listening through, for example, music-making and gramophone-listening at home. We can thus expand our auditory awareness of Turkish neighborhood life beyond visual mappings or musical texts in order to include all those within earshot: for example, a woman at her window catching melodies from an open-air gazino; a girl on a tree branch listening to a sacred suite she cannot join. The concept of soundscape thus provides a tool for appreciating the nature of both passive exposures and active learning at the heart of a musical life neither easily nor exclusively defined by Ladino song.

Janti, a musically adept Jewish girl and woman, found diverse ways to participate in the music of her community, religious and otherwise, embedded as it was in the ambient music of her neighborhood. Are there other women who learned diverse repertoires, musical participants who have been filtered out of cultural histories focused on public performance as the exclusive sign of knowledge and practice? How did they acquire their musical understanding? What is the relationship of their varied knowledge, practice, and expertise to music traditionally associated with women of the community, such as Ladino singing? In raising questions about the participation of women in varieties of music in the community and neighborhood, Janti's story, interwoven with historical sources, affirms efforts to re-theorize gender and Jewish music-making beyond the oppositions of male/female or Hebrew/Ladino by conceiving more continuous, albeit contentious, zones of musical practice. By retrieving music-makers absent from the historical record, moreover, the revised conceptual categories and new ethnographic sources broaden our understanding of how Jewish girls and women moved musically between opportunities and exclusions, among different urban musical cultures, to practice music at a time of communal and national flux.

Questioning Gender in Jewish Music

Until recently, music historians, performers, and listeners have associated women from Sephardic culture areas (including Ottoman territories, and present-day Turkey and the Balkans) with Ladino song, especially the *romansa* ballad linked to medieval Spain. By contrast, Turkish Jewish men have been represented as the exclusive performers of Hebrew liturgical music in the synagogue. To a certain extent, such musical divisions are valid. Jewish religious law, specifically the Talmudic injunction *kol b'ishah ervah* ("a woman's voice is erotic by nature"), prohibited women from singing in the synagogue or elsewhere before male listeners.[8] Historically, Ottoman synagogues separated women from men through balconies or partitions, with men leading services and women expected to sing along, if at all, under their breath. Whereas male children generally attended Talmud Torah religious schools to learn Hebrew scripture and liturgical leadership, girls learned Ladino songs orally from their mothers and grandmothers—repertoires that included pieces for paraliturgical, life-cycle celebrations such as weddings, funerals, and births. Generally, in the divided musical and religious world of Ottoman and Turkish Jewish communities, the public performance of specific musical genres—Hebrew synagogue music and Ladino song—became gendered.[9] There is a rich ethnomusicological literature exploring the woman-dominated domain of historical and contemporary Ladino song, together with their communal-religious functions and the singers who performed them.[10]

Even though the transmission and performance of diverse musical genres generally divided along gendered lines, in music-making practices there were significant areas of overlap between strictly male and female musical realms. Oral transmission between mothers and daughters, and between fathers and sons or male teachers and students, may have been normative, but lines of transmission also crossed. More recent ethnomusicological literature confirms the illusory nature of a rigid gender dichotomy separating men's music (Hebrew, liturgical, high-culture) from women's (Ladino, life-cycle, folk).[11] This division fails to account for several overlapping practices, such as oral transmission and shared compositional tendencies: for example, Ladino songs with Hebrew phrases or poetic aesthetics, liturgical hymns in the vernacular, and Hebrew scripture adapted to Ladino melodies.[12] Evidence of women's song notebooks also challenges an implicit literate/illiterate dimension of the gender dichotomy between men's and women's music.[13] In addition, with the advent of the recording industry, it was Jewish male singers who first began to record the women's domain of Ladino songs of their communities—a development that, despite historically gendered performance practices, indicates that regular exposure to "each other's" repertoires, whether in synagogue or life-cycle celebrations, at home or on the street, allowed both men and women to aurally cross musical lines.[14] Evidence from the Jewish diaspora suggests that Ottoman Jewish women likely knew the Ladino repertoire well and liturgical repertoire partially, with the reverse true of men.[15] Furthermore, past ethnographic scholarship has shown that daughters of hazanim or rabbis were positioned to learn synagogue music more thoroughly than other girls through aural exposure or direct instruction from their fathers at home, or by sitting with them at synagogue services.[16]

Blurring the gendered dichotomy between Hebrew and Ladino song reshapes popular and academic conceptualizations of ethnolinguistically specific Jewish repertoires. However, if we consider the broader urban music environment, the dichotomy itself dissolves in the face of Jewish participation in so-called non-Jewish music—the mixing of musics at the core of this study. Even though Jewish women did not frequent urban locales cultivating Ottoman music in the lives of such musicians as Becerano, Benaroya, Sevilya, and Mısırlı İbrahim Efendi—the palace, Mevlevi lodges, and music schools, among others—the cultural shape of space in Ottoman neighborhoods exposed them to the genre on a regular basis. It is within the environment of the neighborhood that gazinos grew out of Turkish and European-style entertainment venues popularizing court music forms; here, too, the commercial and technological developments of gramophones and records, film and radio progressively spread popularized art music forms into Jewish urban life and homes. Despite the rarity of respectable Jewish women recording, performing, acting, or broadcasting in this period, they nonetheless shared the changing cultural landscape—new forms of musical production and entertainment in which Jewish male vocalists took part—and thus participated as listeners or audience members, and hence were potentially learners if not public performers.[17] Reconfigured by lived urban space, the conventional gendered dichotomy of Hebrew and Ladino song must be transmuted to pair Hebrew religious and Ottoman-Turkish secular genres, which, as performed on gazino stages, records, and radio, included women in their broad sonic net as well as in more direct learning opportunities than women's primary identification with Ladino song would suggest.

Home music-making provided key learning occasions for women in an era when, despite increased schooling for girls, their role as wives, mothers, and homemakers continued to be primary. Besides Ladino songs learned orally from female relatives, women could also learn Turkish art music from relatives, teachers who provided home lessons, and the gramophone. Such home activities took place within broader changes in musical dissemination at the turn of the twentieth century, when, as we have seen, music societies and publications began to increase art music learning in the general population and when records began to fill both leisure and learning roles in families that could afford them.[18] Granted, public performance opportunities of the genre were often limited for adult Jewish women, potentially curtailing refinement of certain musical skills. However, in a period antedating radio and television as fixtures in Turkish homes, women played important roles in home music entertainment, which, depending upon the family, included diverse genres, including popular Turkish forms. In addition to Ladino repertoires, therefore, women were positioned to become proficient in

Turkish art music, learned not only in neighborhood venues, but also via lessons, records, and family music-making at home. Although women may have more commonly become adept at Turkish forms of the genre, as Janti's life story will show, in some cases such musical acculturation and learning formed the foundation for acquiring its Hebrew forms.

In the study of Sephardic women's music-making, if we counterpose the theory and genres of Hebrew religious music with those of Turkish art music, as well as include the home in music-making venues, a revised picture of Jewish women's acquisition of and participation in these interconnected forms emerges. Given the commonplace aural exposure to art music genres, and given the home as an alternative music center within the neighborhood, learning opportunities for girls and women were broader than we have previously assumed. In fact, as other studies have shown, a musical family and individual aptitude, rather than gender, are often key factors in acquiring musical knowledge—in this case, secular Turkish music as the foundation, for some women, of Hebrew religious songs.[19] The training available to Jewish women generated the possibility of acquiring expertise in art music, and at times its Hebrew forms, even if such specialized knowledge remained unperformed on stage or in synagogue, or was a latent potential, in an era of status-changing developments tempered by traditional communal expectations. Primarily taking Balat with adjacent Kasturiya as a case study of Jewish neighborhoods in the late Ottoman and early republican eras, the following pages will explore the musical and communal life of several male and female Jewish residents as a window on the insufficiently recognized involvement of women in both Ottoman-Turkish and Hebrew music-making. By probing the nature of Janti's musical involvement, we can also discover, on a social level, how the multifaceted musical life of one woman embodied and resolved the tensions and contradictions of a changing community and society.

Music-making in Neighborhoods

Despite outsider impressions of Balat as a backward neighborhood of poor Jews, early-twentieth-century residents considered themselves culturally and linguistically rich. Likewise, scholars today recognize that

Balat's modern institutional developments paralleled those of other Istanbul neighborhoods with large Jewish populations.[20] Together with a nearby neighborhood, Hasköy, Balat had been a primary Jewish residence on the Golden Horn since the seventeenth century and historically included other ethno-religious communities—Muslims, Greeks, Armenians, and Gypsies—in diverse and changing demographics.[21] It remained a populous Jewish-majority neighborhood even as eighteenth-century disasters (such as fires), economic opportunities, and communal-institutional developments pushed well-to-do Jews to Galata and Pera, districts that became central to the community's sociocultural life by the late nineteenth century through the establishment of influential businesses, publishing houses, and later the chief rabbinate offices. Among the Europeanizing developments that Balat shared with other Istanbul neighborhoods were two Alliance Israélite Universelle schools, established for boys (1875) and girls (1882), which promoted European educational and political values, with classroom instruction in French.[22] An Alliance vocational school for girls also operated between 1884 and 1905.[23] Moreover, the neighborhood was known for its many rabbinical scholars, whose religious legal judgments reflected the generally progressive leanings of Ottoman Jewish hahamim and chief rabbis appointed in the post-Tanzimat reform era.[24] As we shall see, in addition to musical changes across the late Ottoman and early republican periods, such educational and religious developments affected the lives of girls and women, with ambiguous consequences for musical careers.

Because of its multiethnic composition and social economy, Balat had a soundscape both distinctive to its particular population and related to other multiethnic neighborhoods in late Ottoman cities. Before turning to musical venues related to the genres under discussion, we can gain a general impression of neighborhood sounds through personal reminiscences and architectural evidence—sounds elucidating the neighborhood as lived, acoustic space in which not only boys and men, but also girls and women moved and heard in specific ways. Divided into seven sections, including Kasturiya and its largely Gypsy-inhabited area, Karabaş,[25] Balat contained numerous synagogues with congregants of Balkan origin, Greek Orthodox and Armenian churches, and mosques, most notably the Molla Aşkı Mosque, where the Ottoman composer and teacher of numerous hazanim, İsmail Hakkı Bey, served as lead muezzin in the late nineteenth century.[26] Depending upon where they lived, Balat residents would have heard such multireligious sounds as church bells and *ezan* (call to prayer), and would have witnessed religious processions related to holidays or funerals as well.[27] Inhabitants of Balat and Hasköy describe the calls of street vendors and boatmen, in addition to music from open-air cafés, cinemas, and spectacles in summer months.[28] In the interwar period, "there were greengrocers who sold their fruit and vegetables, and fishermen their fish, singing songs about them," according to resident Salamon Bicerano. "The songs of vendors mingled with the music coming from the tavern. . . . The synagogues were once so full that the sound of praying was heard from the streets."[29] Noise also pervaded certain areas, sometimes drowning out music: "Due to the creaks, squeaks, rattling, welding and pounding sounds coming from warehouses, one [could not] hear the calls of fishermen, lemon-sellers or shopkeepers until one [entered] the market."[30]

As in other ethnically mixed Ottoman neighborhoods, the marketplace and indistinct ethnic boundaries in Balat brought multiple languages into street life, even as Ladino, spoken by the Jewish majority, predominated. Former Balat residents confirm a measure of Greek usage in Jewish homes, because of the adjacent district of Fener (a Greek-majority area), family traditions of sending Jewish children to Greek schools, and the pervasive presence of Greeks throughout the neighborhood.[31] "Greeks and Jews lived close together," according to one resident. "Therefore, the children learned each other's language."[32] As in Salonika, where memoirist Leon Sciaky listened to the languages and songs of the ethnic groups near his changing residences, areas of Balat with Jews and Gypsies (Karabaş), for example, or Jews and Armenians (Kasturiya) contained slightly different mixes of languages.[33] Amid such linguistic diversity, Jewish testimonials from the first half of the twentieth century confirm "how people enjoyed speaking their Ladino openly, and loudly, without concern of being overheard by strangers, from window to window, on the streets, and with the roaming street vendors."[34] Ladino melodies were heard regularly from the *şamaz* (Heb. *shamash*, beadle), who roused people on Shabbat evening and morning for candle lighting and prayers, as well as on religious holidays.[35] Jewish women took the lead in singing for life-cycle events both within and outside the home, including one of the major celebrations, the wedding, with its extensive Ladino repertoire.[36] In the local baths, such as Balat's Tahta Minare Hamamı, frequented by Jews, women and their children socialized with friends, eating and singing together, and in some cases playing musical instruments.[37] Jewish families of Golden Horn neighborhoods recall the common music-making of summer leisure time, such as picnic excursions and singing with neighbors from windows or doors opened in the heat.[38]

The multifaceted soundscape of Balat—dominated by Ladino-speaking Jews, diversified by the presence of Greek, Armenian, Gypsy, and Turkish-speaking residents, resounding predictably and unpredictably with its distinctive street life, noise, songs, and silences, and offering a shifting aural experience based on an individual's mobility and location—provided the aural backdrop for places cultivating Ottoman-Turkish music. Whereas street life exposed residents indirectly to Turkish musical structure—from street vendors' tunes to calls to prayer to songs from open-air gazinos—active learning emerged from personal and urban histories of neighborhood venues showcasing Turkish art music, which extended exposure and entertainment from an apparent male-only purview to interested women and girls of the community. To be sure, the same changes in patronage affecting Jewish male performers from the late empire into the Turkish Republic—that is, increasingly commercialized musical performance, instruction, and production—also enriched the musical lives of Jewish females, even if remunerative public performance was not generally a goal. In fact, famous for its historical multiplicity of male public spaces—taverns, coffeehouses, and wine merchants—nineteenth-century Balat boasted well-established drinking and entertainment enterprises that laid the ground for late Ottoman and early republican gazinos presenting art music programs to mixed audiences.[39]

The development of Balat's socializing establishments and gazinos appears roughly to parallel that in Ottoman urban centers as a whole.[40] Balat abounded with venues like the *meyhane* (tavern) and *kahve* or *kahvehane* (café), which antedated and later coexisted with gazinos, including the celebrated Çuhacıoğlu meyhane from the first quarter of the nineteenth century and at least twenty-one places of ethnically diverse ownership (at least seven by Jews) in the 1880s.[41] A space offering tea and card-playing, the kahvehane in some cases doubled as a meyhane: according to Eli Şaul, in early republican Balat the Kamburun kahvehanesi and Baba Kemal kahvehanesi each turned into a meyhane at night.⁴² Echoing historical trends among earlier Ottoman coffeehouses, the famed Café of Perendeoğlu in Karabaş, owned by a successful Jewish businessman, served as a base for a volunteer firefighting unit of Balat, cultivating the perception of coffeehouses as community protectors, despite rabbinical disapproval.⁴³ A çalgılı kahvesi, Perendeoğlu's business evidences the popularity of fasıl venues in the neighborhood at the turn of the twentieth century: presumably fearing competition, the owner blocked the establishment of a musical café in his area by Laz boatmen.⁴⁴ Another widely celebrated meyhane, Bahçeli à Balat, in particular presages a later gazino culture, offering as it did alaturka entertainment associated with the early çalgılı kahvesi, while serving alcoholic beverages later associated with the gazino.⁴⁵

Jewish residents not only attended entertainment venues such as these in Balat, but also patronized establishments in nearby neighborhoods on the Golden Horn, especially the adjacent districts of Eyüp and Fener. Established by the late nineteenth century, the Pierre Loti Gazinosu (in Eyüp) and the Fener İskele Gazinosu (in Fener) illustrate the growth of gazinos from their earlier entertainment spaces, becoming favored gathering places for Balat Jews on non-workdays. According to Jewish informants born in the early decades of the twentieth century, one of the favorite pastimes later in the day on Shabbat was to go to a gazino to hear Turkish art music.⁴⁶ The musical café in Eyüp was reportedly the traditional place for marriage proposals to be sealed, with both members of the couple present.⁴⁷ Residing in Balat between 1920 and 1937, Eli Şaul (b. 1916) confirms the beauty of the Pierre Loti Gazinosu enjoyed by Jewish residents: "[It] was on the backside of Eyüp and you could see the whole Golden Horn from there. I couldn't get enough of the view. On clear days it was possible to see as far as Unkapanı and across the Galata bridge."⁴⁸ The district of Fener, easily accessible from Balat by road or stairway,⁴⁹ was even more popular in his youth, according to Şaul.

> On hot evenings in the summer, the people of Balat—Turks, Jews, Greeks, Armenians—everyone would pour into Fener. It was a ten-

View of the Golden Horn from the Pierre Loti Café (2006). Photo by author.

minute walk from Balat to Fener. During the summer there were two ince saz [takımı, or art music ensemble] gazinos open in the evening and at night in Fener. In particular, there was one fantastic gazino located adjacent to the Fener ferry dock, right over the water. It was spotless. Meze [appetizers] and beer were inexpensive. And best of all, there was an ince saz takımı performing the historic Turkish music that our family loved. At night this gazino was full. The ince saz takımı would begin with a peşrev, then a beste, a few şarkıs in the middle, and, at the very end, a saz semaisi.[50]

One of the most famous turn-of-the-century gazinos in Istanbul, the Fener İskele Gazinosu, sported a large waterside building with a spacious garden behind and a front section stretching out over the water of the Golden Horn; well-known singers and instrumentalists of Istanbul performed there.[51] Such gazinos were newer venues for socializing in ways (drinking, enjoying music, eating non-kosher food) that Ottoman rabbis had disapproved of since the eighteenth century.[52] To be sure, their intensified attention to such activities by the late nineteenth century suggests that such behaviors were sufficiently pervasive and threatening to their conception of social order to warrant a firmer hand.[53] Nonetheless, the ethnographic evidence from Balat exposes the real-life gap between rabbinical texts and actual social behaviors through evidence of liberal local religious rulings, nonobservant Jewish residents, and business activities not conforming to religious law.[54] In fact, testifying to their participation in the local entertainment culture, Balat Jews incorporated "gazino" into their spoken and sung language: one Kasturiya informant called Purim festivities "gazino," making an analogy between religious and nonreligious partying, while a popular Ladino song includes the line, "En el gazino del Fener ay un saksi de rozas" (in the Fener gazino there is a flowerpot of roses).[55]

Rabbinical texts delineated distinctive gendered spaces and roles, but the historical record suggests gradual and increasing female participation in gazino culture. Venues similar to the Fener Gazino of the early twentieth century, such as the Çubuklu Gazino, provided afternoon hours exclusively for women and evening hours for men, a pattern maintained across the century that, it is reasonable to assume, was shared by such a major venue as the Fener Gazino.[56] Moreover, at least by the 1930s, at times women went to gazinos in couples, thus chaperoned during mixed evening performances.[57] In this period of social flux it is probable that the patronage of gazinos by Jewish women correlated with lower levels of familial religious observance, the proliferation of public fasıl performances over time, the availability of companions, and, in the case of deluxe gazinos, personal wealth.

Fasıl music, in addition to being enjoyed in afternoons and evenings in the gazinos, was also popular in the home, as we can see from Eli Şaul's reminiscences of his father, an ordinary doctor, and siblings in his household:

> Everyone in my whole family were alaturka lovers. In his youth my father played the kanun. My brother Robert also took kanun lessons for three years as a young man. As for me, from middle school on, I took ud lessons from the famous Avni Bey.[58] My father and sister had very beautiful voices. At home we pretty much had an ince saz ensemble. Because of this, we often went to the Fener Gazino. All of us knew Turkish music.[59]

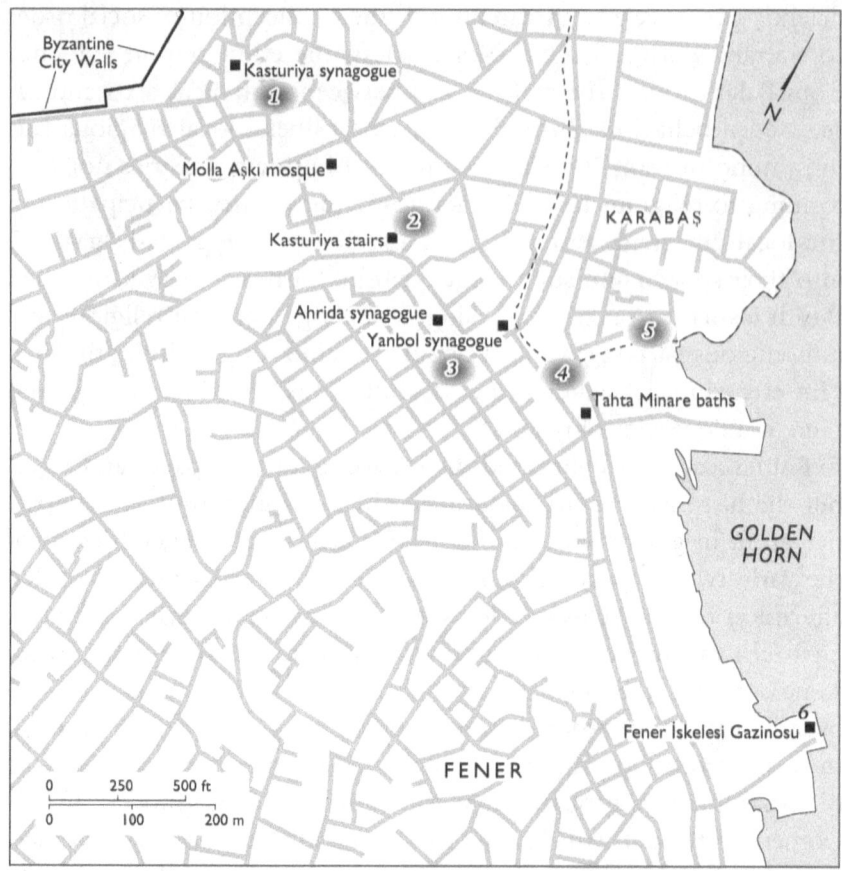

The district of Balat, 1910s–1930s. Music and socializing venues were located near Kasturiya synagogue (Yusuf Toros kahvehanesi 1) as well as lower areas accessible by the Kasturiya stairs (las eskaleras de la Kasturiya): an open-air gazino 2; Baba Kemal kahvehanesi 3; Kamburun kahvehanesi 4; Café of Perendeoğlu 5; Fener İskelesi Gazinosu 6. Although the exact opening and closing dates of the venues are not known, Reşat Ekrem Koçu lists thirty kahvehanes and twenty meyhanes in Balat by 1948 (İstanbul Ansiklopedisi, Istanbul, 1960, p. 1964).

The growth of privately owned musical societies and music shops offering services such as lessons and notation, particularly after the Second Constitutional Period (1908), contributed to the spread of art music learning among Istanbul residents.[60] By introducing practices divergent from historical master-pupil apprenticeships, particularly through the payment for services and notational documentation, these businesses extended the reach of music instruction beyond individual apprenticeships. In a biography of Adel Samanon (b. 1905), whose father was an official Ottoman legal advisor, we read about musical life and learning at home, led by a music teacher. Growing up in Hasköy, across from Balat, Adel remembers "red fez wearing, mustached, and at times bearded gentlemen," including Chief Rabbi Hayim Nahum,[61] visiting her father, troubling her by speaking a language she didn't understand (probably Turkish), and enjoying coffee and sweets prepared by her mother and the servants.

> Later the guests would gather around the brass brazier and sing a fasıl under the direction of music teacher Leon Efendi. . . . Whenever she heard Dede Efendi pieces [years later] on the radio, Adel would remember the part-enchanting, part-agitating scene she used to watch from the doorway. It was as if it brought back the men whose language she didn't understand well, as they gathered around the stove, keeping the rhythm by beating their knees with their hands. And of course, in their midst would be her beloved father with his sad features and velvety voice.[62]

Clearly, from Adel's descriptions, Leon Efendi was directing, at least in part, historical Ottoman musical pieces and practices: Dede Efendi (1778–1846) was a major Ottoman composer,[63] and beating the usul on knees is a key mnemonic element in Ottoman oral learning methods. On occasion, women in the family participated in such home music learning:

> Sometimes during the evenings, Leon Efendi would come to give music lessons only to members of the family. At those times, Adel's father [Jak] would always call his wife to his side: "Come here, Eliza Hanım." The young woman's eyes would be shining bright; like all members of the family she adored singing. Her husband's showing even a little interest in her made her very happy. After Jak's death, her mother wanted Adel to play these songs on the piano. As she listened once

more to the Nihavent and Rast melodies of fasıl ensembles of the past echoing through the family home, tears streamed down her cheeks.[64]

Later, in 1911, the family moved to Kadıköy on the Bosphorus, following a migratory pattern in which affluent Jews settled in such waterside neighborhoods after the nineteenth-century construction of the sultans' palaces (Dolmabahçe and Yıldız) on the Bosphorus.[65] Adel remembers, together with the fine "alafranga" furnishings from Syria, a new piano and both European and Turkish-style music-making: "For music lessons there was a Zimmerman piano. Colorful candles were placed in brass candlesticks rising on each side; in the candlelight Spanish romances, Turkish art music, and Vienna waltzes were played."[66]

Although Eli Şaul and Adel Samanon grew up in very different households—one in the modest home of a neighborhood doctor, the other in a well-to-do family of an Ottoman civil servant—both individuals participated in the music-making of their families. Amid the musical and other cultural developments of the period, Şaul's family clearly came down on the side of Turkish-style aesthetics, while the Samanon family favored Sephardic songs, Turkish art music, and European classical styles, common among French-identified Ottoman Jewish professionals of the capital.[67] Despite differences in musical taste, both Eli and Adel testify to the way Istanbul Jewish families made fasıl music at home in the early twentieth century—music-making that included female relatives. With the gradual changes in leisure activities among Jews, it is possible that Eli's sister or Adel and her mother frequented entertainment venues in the company of men or during gazino matinees. Even if they did not, these musically inclined women lived in music-cultivating families that played and sang together, and at least in Adel's case, took Turkish music lessons at home. Together with the increase in private music learning in the early twentieth century, the absence of radio and television at the time, according to numerous Jewish memoirists and informants, motivated much self-generated entertainment at home among family, friends, and neighbors.[68] It is significant that, whether or not women attended gazinos regularly in the early twentieth century, we nonetheless know that, in the home, female relatives participated actively, and often enthusiastically, in oral learning and family performance of Turkish art music.

Kasturiya: One Girl's Story

Home music-making is one facet of the multidimensional musical childhood of Janti Behar, whose family life included religious and commercial music-making, Ladino folk singing, urban musical entertainment, and individual performance opportunities and curtailments reflecting the ambiguous play of gender in Jewish musical and religious life in the early Republic. Janti Behar grew up in the 1930s in Kasturiya, one of two upper villages of Balat, which, in contrast to the poorer areas closer to the Golden Horn, had a reputation among Jews for being healthier, more comfortable, and well-to-do; several families of wealthy entrepreneurs and manufacturers lived there.[69] This upper district had its share of musical venues: by the late nineteenth century there were reportedly at least five meyhanes in Kasturiya, with two owned by Jews, in addition to an open-air gazino established in the 1920s and frequented by Jewish locals on Sundays.[70] The meyhane of the Greek Podromos (dates unknown) was a regular destination for Jews, and at the beginning of the twentieth century, former residents recall, men frequented the coffeehouse of Yusuf Toros situated near the synagogue.[71] Janti Behar's highly musical family included a father, Yomtov Sulam, who was a Maftirim şef (conductor) at Kasturiya synagogue, brothers who played instruments for enjoyment and for pay, and a mother who sang regularly:

> One brother played accordion, the other played violin. They were professional, not amateur. My brother went to gazinos and performed. My father sang songs at home. I also sang. [Judeo] Spanish folk music, but very old songs. Every day, all day there was music at home. We didn't have a radio, because we already had music at home. My brothers were at home and friends would come. They would play music. My father would sing songs with his beautiful voice. My mother would sing. I would sing. What would we have done with a radio?[72]

According to Janti, Hebrew singing and learning typically took place in the synagogue, whereas Ladino folk music was sung at home:

> Our kind were [Judeo] Spanish-speaking. The songs I sang were from a hundred and fifty or two hundred years ago. I learned them all from my father and mother. My brothers didn't learn much, as they

> weren't interested. . . . My father had students from there, from the synagogue. Every Saturday after prayers they had a *se'uda* [the third Shabbat meal]; they ate and then gathered. He would teach these [Maftirim songs] to the students; they would prepare for the holidays. My father had a very, very beautiful voice; my brothers did, too.[73]

In his role as a Maftirim conductor in the 1930s, Janti's father imparted extensive musical knowledge to his daughter and sons at home.[74] An amateur classical musician in the Ottoman sense—highly artistic and musically educated, without being paid for his music activities—he began to acquire his musical training through his natural vocal talent and religious observance, which prompted him to be chosen for synagogue and Maftirim performance at an early age.[75] Desiring to learn more about Turkish art music for his Maftirim activities, Janti's father took kanun lessons, as well as learned from friends who were well versed in the genre. Clearly, he taught his children a religious repertoire, as he and his family presented a series of synagogue concerts in 1936.[76] Janti remembers learning and performing as a girl for a specific religious holiday, as well:

> For holidays there were beautiful [Maftirim] pieces. I sang with my brothers. For example, on the second night of Passover there is a piece called "Pithu li." I was ten years old. Because my father was a Maftirim professor, he taught us this piece at home [Janti sings "Pithu li"]. Now there is a section here that I sang all by myself. . . . I sang at the teva [hazan's platform], the only girl.[77]

Although "Pithu li" is not, in fact, a part of the Maftirim repertoire as Janti implies here,[78] and although we do not know the extent of religious music she learned from her father, Janti's testimony nonetheless confirms her inclusion in Hebrew music learning at home, as well as her performance in the main body of the synagogue, despite the normative exclusion of girls and women from the teva.[79]

> I was young, so it was okay. Whenever you have a menstrual period [it is prohibited, but] I was ten years old and didn't have periods. [Normally] they don't accept you at the teva. They asked my mother, because it [normally] wasn't allowed; it would be a great sin. So, my mother [first] said no, she is still a baby. Again [later] they didn't accept me. I had grown up.[80]

Gender and Sacred Song 107

Flexibility in the observance of religious laws among reform-minded Balat rabbis or the potential for vocal talent to trump religious legal considerations may have made room for Janti's performance in the synagogue on Passover.[81] In an example of liberal observance, according to early twentieth-century informants, a rabbi in Kasturiya did not believe in ritual cleansing of women (*mikveh*) before marriage, forbidding his daughter to participate in a "harmful superstition" with little hygienic value.[82] Potentially supported by rabbinical latitude in her neighborhood and certainly supported by music at home, Janti was enabled to learn Ladino, Hebrew, and Turkish singing—to performance standards of the time—from musically knowledgeable family members who conducted or performed publicly (father and brothers) or sang in the home (mother).

Excluded as a girl from the weekly Maftirim ensemble and discouraged from attending paraliturgical events as a child, Janti found her own way of hearing, learning, and enjoying this Hebrew religious music in the public sphere:

> I wasn't a boy, so I couldn't [join]. At that time things were more backward. After eating, at three o'clock up to Arvit [evening prayer service], everyone was in the synagogue . . . Monsieur Moiz Daron played the kanun . . . My father worked as conductor. There were six men: one played kanun, the others [sang]. They would sit at the teva. Those wanting to listen sat in the synagogue. Of course [women came]. . . .
>
> Everyone had a God-given natural gift, a beautiful voice. There was Alhadeff [for example]; what God-given voices. . . . It was very crowded. Everyone came to the synagogue [to listen]. There wasn't anyone who didn't come.
>
> It was so, so beautiful. I loved it so much that I went to the synagogue. There was a garden at the synagogue, very beautiful and big. I used to climb up the tree. I was a child, ten years old. I climbed up to listen to these [singers]. It sounded just like a fasıl ensemble, a Turkish fasıl ensemble.[83]

Representing yet another indirect way of hearing art music forms (such as from a café or open-air gazino), within the larger soundscape of the neighborhood, Janti's tree-climbing likewise conveys the intense desire, pleasure, and motivation of a musically inclined girl to listen to

Janti Behar's tree on the grounds of Kasturiya synagogue (2006). Photo by author.

the music she loved—particularly, it appears, during the same year she performed for Passover. It is notable that her actions took place in the exclusive domain of childhood, like her performance in the synagogue: just as climbing a tree was a part of child's play, so too was singing at the teva permissible to her only before young adulthood. As a woman, Janti would leave behind both circumventing and unsettling the normative exclusion of girls or women from the all-male Maftirim ensemble. Her childhood story, however, contains further ambiguous meanings in an era of religious and educational reform, intertwined with communal stability. Even as her musical interest and skill may have been blossoming, Janti nonetheless describes a lack of comprehensive learning of Hebrew song. The holiday song "Pithu li" appears to be the main Hebrew verse she could sing "cleanly" because her father

Gender and Sacred Song 109

taught her at home, while all the others, including Maftirim music, she heard, but did not learn completely because "I listened clandestinely. They wouldn't take me into the Maftirim."[84] Janti's incomplete knowledge of Hebrew-language music confirms the limits on learning within gendered performance and religious norms.[85] For Janti, overhearing Hebrew song led to a certain level of knowledge, whereas instruction honed one's skills, and practice, specifically for performing in the synagogue for Passover, made perfect.

Other musical occasions and encounters allowed Janti to listen to Maftirim singing and to learn Turkish art music pieces, the latter becoming the music she loved and sang. Her descriptions of nighttime Maftirim concerts convey the overlapping of synagogue and entertainment culture at the time. At the Kasturiya synagogue, on certain Saturday evenings, the Maftirim ensemble performed to benefit one or another family in the community who needed help. On these occasions, according to Janti, the synagogue was packed with women in the balcony and men below, coming to experience the beautiful *müzik ziyafeti* (musical feast) and give a *bağış* (donation) for the family in need.[86] Like the previously noted integration of "gazino" in sung and spoken Ladino, Janti's use of the phrase "musical feast" for these benefit concerts reflects her contemporaneous immersion in gazino music, since the phrase was conventionally applied to gazino programs, implying the link between eating and entertainment at such establishments.[87] Her comparison implies that the Maftirim singers actively engaged in contemporaneous musical aesthetics of fasıl music, which in 1930s gazinos was dominated by older, complex Ottoman-Turkish compositions.[88] Janti certainly lived and learned in the midst of such venues and musicians, with meyhanes and at least one gazino in Kasturiya, as well as one brother who worked as a gazino instrumentalist. Significantly, at the age of fourteen, according to her testimony, she would go to Fener Gazino with her parents.[89] In addition, Janti learned Turkish art songs from a Jewish girlfriend with whom she worked:

> I was fourteen or fifteen years old. My friend and I used to sew gloves together at a shop. . . . She lived above a meyhane. . . . This girl Emily and her siblings had very beautiful voices. Whenever any part of the

fasıl ensemble was missing [from the meyhane], these friends would fill in there and earn money. . . . There were instrumentalists there. It was fasıl music, not [Turkish folk] music. . . . My friend would go down and earn money there. While we were at the shop, I also loved to sing. So, she taught me a song [Janti sings "Farığ Olmam"].[90]

While her father restricted his singing to Hebrew religious music, Janti loved and sang alaturka or fasıl heyeti (fasıl ensemble) compositions; her daughter Viki claims that her mother knows hundreds of classical Turkish songs.[91] Thus, despite (or because of) her exclusion from synagogue music, Janti learned and sang from the popular fasıl repertoire surrounding her—the Turkish art songs performed at gazinos and on records and radio in the early Turkish Republic.[92]

Unlike her friend Emily, however, public or commercial performance was not an option for Janti:

My brother's wife was secretary for Blumenthal Records. One day she took my brother aside—I was twelve years old—and said her voice is very beautiful. Let's bring her here to the shop and make a record. She will make a big profit, a lot of money. My brother said okay, maybe. But my father and mother—ooh! All hell broke loose. "Are you making my daughter into a [gazino] singer?" Among Jews there wasn't such a thing for girls. They didn't give me permission.[93]

It is testimony to Janti's talent at a relatively young age that her brother and sister-in-law suggested making a record with the Blumenthal Brothers, by then the local agent for Columbia Records.[94] However, the differing stories of Janti and Emily—one disallowed, the other allowed to sing publicly and commercially—reflect perceived differences in class among Ottoman, and later republican, Jewry. While sharing peripheral musical status with Janti as a substitute singer, Emily was permitted as a girl to earn money singing in a meyhane, whereas Janti continued to learn and sing Turkish art songs without ever singing or recording publicly. As articulated by Janti's daughter, Jews in Kasturiya were split between the "aristocratic" and the "low-profile," with Emily's family—headed by an apparently alcoholic father who permitted "inappropriate" work and performance by girls—in the latter category.[95] Thus, Janti's generalization that public performance wasn't possible for girls in fact refers to her own Jewish class and family, which evidently observed more closely gendered roles and spaces in the neighborhood than Emily's did. Later, Janti moved with her family to Beyoğlu—part of a demographic trend that, in conjunction with out-migration under the Republic, would leave Balat and Hasköy nearly empty of Jews after the 1950s. As an adult, marrying in 1946 and giving birth to her first child, she actualized three aspects of a woman's lifecycle within one year—marriage, birth of a son, and his circumcision. Her son's *pidyon* (redemption ceremony for the firstborn), as Janti described it, became a special honor for her good fortune as a wife, mother, and woman within her community, celebrating her publicly for these maternal successes, if not for her artistic talent.[96]

Janti's musical history portrays a Turkish Jewish woman engaging in art music in the early Republic—she was passively (though extensively) exposed to Maftirim music and publicly performed Hebrew verse once, while gaining considerable knowledge of popular Turkish art music of which her religious musical tradition was a part. Her story illuminates how an artistically inclined girl, growing up in a musical household and among neighborhood gazinos, was enabled to become proficient in multiple genres of music. In the context of general and local rabbinical latitude, and with a father as a Maftirim conductor, Janti performed Hebrew-language verse in chorus and solo at the teva for Passover. However, as her tree story shows, the doors to participation in more complex religious music were closed to her, as was commercially recording popular Turkish art music. In the life stories of Eli Şaul and Adel Samanon we also encounter sisters and mothers, or daughters and wives, who were avid Turkish music performers within their families, exposed to Turkish art music forms not only through neighborhood gazinos, but also through teachers and/or knowledgeable parents and siblings active in the family sphere of learning and performance. The home, a "woman's place," was often a key musical space in this period. Even if typically peripheral to Hebrew religious singing, women became musically engaged in a different communal center where family-generated entertainment in diverse genres flourished before the proliferation of television and radio.[97]

Although Janti emphasizes exclusively live music in her home and Adel describes real-life teachers, in some families the advent of the gramophone certainly provided alternate forms of oral learning, without necessarily preempting family music-making. Through the audio collection and textual transcriptions of another Emily (Emily Sene), who lived in Edirne and Istanbul between 1911 and 1925 before immigrating to the Americas, we learn about a selection of records popular among Turkish Jews in the interwar period. Among her "old country" materials are a few Ladino romances, but many recordings of her contemporary Edirneli Hayim Efendi singing Ladino folk and popular songs, as well as liturgical compositions (at least one Hebrew Maftirim song) and Turkish songs.[98] It is significant that, allowing for diverse preferences among Istanbul families, including more classically inclined tastes for such recording artists as Algazi or Karakaş, Sene's recordings confirm the popularity of mixed genres and vocalists in the entertainment and record industry of the time, connecting the home and women to the street, in a sense, rather than primarily to romansas of a historical Ladino repertoire.[99] Although not a musician or singer herself, Emily Sene, her audio collection, and unpublished notebooks are nonetheless suggestive of the home-life exposure to popular urban genres through the record and gramophone industry, booming as it was in Istanbul and other urban centers in the first decades of the twentieth century.

Within their neighborhoods and homes, then, whether through live or recorded music or both, women could develop diverse musical knowledge, including Ottoman and Turkish art music, with artistic interest, ability, taste, and income likely determining different levels of Turkish-style music-making in individual families and among individual women. Even if proficiency and performance in Turkish, rather than Hebrew, forms would have been more common among Jewish girls and women, there is evidence that proficiency in Hebrew song was possible for some women. Samuel Benaroya, a credible informant as a Maftirim master, reported that, at the turn of the twentieth century, a Jewish woman in Edirne knew the entire Maftirim repertoire by heart, singing compositions from her balcony, another peripheral space, to listeners below on the street.[100] In mid-century Izmir, a musically talented girl joined the all-boy Maftirim rehearsals, reportedly not singing with them in the synagogue mainly because of a physical disability.[101] Moreover, because the Maftirim repertoire contained adaptations of well-known Ottoman and Turkish compositions of the day, as well as pieces by contemporary Jewish composers such as

Gender and Sacred Song   113

Nesim Sevilya and İsak Varon, a musically inclined woman listener would most certainly recognize the melody—and in some cases the Hebrew—of a range of Maftirim compositions.[102] Add to this the practice of girls sitting with fathers during services as effective "participant-observers,"[103] and we can conjecture that, depending upon a woman's musicality, urban circulations, home life, and religious observance, the ability not only to recognize but also to reproduce Hebrew compositions would potentially increase, even if remaining a primarily latent or publicly unperformed knowledge.

Together with these musical potentialities, Janti Behar's social life can be understood within the probably more common experience of other women of her generation—caught between institutional changes in female education, workforce, and religious values, on the one hand, and the conceptual lag in gender expectations among the community at large, on the other.[104] Rewarded for the birth of a son, but not awarded a record contract; singing at the teva as a girl, but sitting in the balcony as a woman, Janti had noteworthy musical opportunities as a child, but as an adult lived out ongoing familial, class, and communal values that foreclosed the possibility of public or religious singing without abating her personal acquisition of Turkish art songs throughout her life. Paradoxically, Janti's musical experiences reflect both a tradition-based narrowing of performance opportunities and an increasing attraction to and acculturation in Turkish, rather than Hebrew, musical forms, thus both reinforcing communal norms for women and encouraging their participation in the wider society. Her story suggests the personal choices and compromises of a highly musical woman in an era of reform and restraint across the nineteenth and twentieth centuries—both silencing (in religious and commercial spheres) and singing (in home and city life), enforced or chosen, to engender acceptance by family and community.

Hidden Legacies

In present-day Istanbul, members of the Jewish community are concerned that the Maftirim repertoire, as well as classical Turkish aesthetics in religious services in general, will fade away with the next generation. A number of activities and projects address this concern. For example, the two Maftirim groups practicing in the city welcome younger men who are interested in carrying on the tradition. The Ottoman-Turkish Sephardic Culture Research Center has completed an extensive publication of archival recordings, notation, and historical scholarship on the Maftirim repertoire.[105] As well, special musical instruction is being provided to a select group of adolescent young men, with the goal of training the next generation of hazanim.[106]

Janti's story suggests that it may also be the older generation of Jewish women, acculturated to gazino fasıl music popular in their day as well as to master Maftirim musicians of the 1930s and 1940s, who possess the musical foundation for learning a religious repertoire linked to Turkish art music. In the absence of unlikely institutional changes in women's place in liturgical performance, of course, we will never know to what extent such changes might have cultivated cultural growth (by potentially doubling the number of performers through the inclusion of girls and women) or might prevent imminent losses

Janti Behar, Istanbul (2006). Photo by author.

(by taking advantage of latent female knowledge). However, the significance of such foundational knowledge becomes apparent under attenuating cultural circumstances. In fact, across the twentieth century, as the number of community members shrank, Jewish women remaining in Istanbul arguably increased both their knowledge of Turkish art music and Jewish religious genres through the expansion of Turkish and sometimes Hebrew linguistic fluency, public participation in gazino and concert performances, and musical exposure through the expanding film industry and radio.[107]

According to a number of senior hazanim, it is this very immersion in the genre of Turkish art music, whether on television, radio, or records, that provides the crucial ear-training necessary for accurate learning of Maftirim and synagogue music—cultural conditions that, for many reasons (including loss of gazinos and changing musical tastes) no longer exist for youth in Turkey today.[108] In view of the significant obstacles to learning, at least one hazan has decided not to teach younger men who have no familiarity with makams or usuls, among other elements in Turkish music theory.[109] By contrast, Jewish women in their middle years and beyond did grow up surrounded by Turkish art and Hebrew synagogue music, and some of them acquired extensive knowledge. In fact, a few blocks from the Şişli synagogue, where a Maftirim group meets on Shabbat, stands the apartment building of Janti Behar who, now in her eighties, still recalls listening to her father's group from her girlhood tree and is still able to sing from her voluminous art music repertoire, if not in the voice that nearly won a record contract. Whatever her education or performance status as a woman, Janti remains a vital source of musical knowledge from a past era of popular and religious music-making of her childhood neighborhood, Kasturiya in Balat.

Four Staging Harmony,
Guarding Community

The Etz Ahayim synagogue sits at the turn of the main street in Ortaköy, pressed between shops and nightclubs of this bustling, waterside neighborhood. A few steps beyond stands a Greek Orthodox church, Ayios Fokas Rum Ortodoks Kilesisi Vakfı, while behind, near the restaurants catering to strolling tourists, is a compact, ornate mosque, Büyük Mecidiye Cami. A few blocks inland, away from the Bosphorus, are two active Armenian churches. Like other villages along the Bosphorus, including both Kuruçeşme and Arnavutköy to the north and Kuzguncuk across the water, Ortaköy historically was inhabited by communities of mixed religion and ethnicity, with affluent Istanbulites, including Jews, expanding the population in the nineteenth century, as Ottoman palaces moved from the Golden Horn to the Bosphorus.[1] The diverse surviving religious structures of the neighborhood reflect historical demographics, while vacated residences, such as the row of eighteen Jewish houses on Bulgurcu Sokak,[2] attest to the migration within the city and abroad that has nearly emptied the neighborhood of its past minority communities. Today Jewish congregants who attend the Ortaköy synagogue generally come in from outlying neighborhoods of the city.

I first visited the synagogue in 2005 during the Jewish High Holy Days, for the Selihot vigil preceding Rosh Hashanah, the Jewish new year.[3] For clearance I had completed my paperwork at the chief rabbi's offices, arrived at the synagogue at 4:00 AM, identified myself to a guard in a booth next to the front door, and pressed the intercom button under a surveillance camera. Inside a secured vestibule a man took my passport and questioned me, then opened the heavy steel door into the synagogue's courtyard. Before I ascended the steps to the women's balcony, I saw a panel on the wall explaining an eighteen-month closure of the synagogue for security renovations after the November 2003 bombing outside Neve Şalom and Şişli synagogues. Later, I would find similar security precautions at all the active synagogues of the city, while at Ortaköy, befriending the guards on my regular research visits, I came and went, in the end, as easily as a congregant.

Later, on the first evening of Rosh Hashanah, I sat with a handful of women in the balcony. Below us the hazan led the Arvit (evening) prayer service, facing the men and singing with them, then turning toward the ark and singing alone. There was a sudden pause. The ezan (call to prayer) resonated from the Ortaköy mosque behind. The long melismatic tones, ascending on "Allah," impressionistically echoed the vocal style of the hazan just heard in the synagogue. The congregants remained silent throughout the ezan. I wondered if it was to respect the muezzin, to avoid acoustic competition, to distinguish between religious traditions, or a mixture of all three. In any case, I was acutely aware of being an unusual, non-Jewish visitor in a highly secured house of worship, a place where it was increasingly rare for community outsiders to experience these aural musical connections between different religious institutions.

After the early Selihot service preceding Yom Kippur, I hopped into a cab in which the driver was fasting for Ramazan and listening to Qu'ranic chant on the radio. As he sped me away from the synagogue, I informed him of the upcoming Jewish fast on Yom Kippur. He raised his eyebrows in surprise: "They fast, too?" he asked. Listening to the intoning of Arabic on the radio, recalling the intoning of Hebrew at the vigil, I reflected again on urban walls, whether steel or sociocultural, erasing the record of historical cultural confluences of communities, erasing the public knowledge of alternate holy days.

On a cool winter Saturday afternoon I joined the weekly Maftirim session in the balcony of Şişli synagogue, located several miles from the synagogue in Ortaköy. The makam of the day was Nihavend. The second song sounded familiar. It was the same melody we recently sang in a non-Jewish classical music *koro* (chorus) I had recently joined: "Tole Eretz al Belima" here, and in the koro, "Seni Hükm-i Ezel Aşub-ı Devran Etmek İstermiş" by İsmail Hakkı Bey. Delighted by the familiar melody, I felt my two separate worlds coming together in my imagination and in the synagogue: the light-hearted rehearsals of a nonreligious community chorus for a public Nihavend art music concert and the weightier sacred Hebrew suite sung weekly in the enclosure of Şişli's balcony.

Attracting my attention and redirecting my research focus, these personal impressions motivated inquiry into what, taken together, they pointed toward in the urban landscape of synagogue music today. The current security measures at Istanbul synagogues have their roots in previous attacks before 2003, one in September 1986, which killed twenty-two worshippers at Neve Şalom synagogue, and another in March 1992, which claimed no casualties.[4] Unlike the 1986 killings, the most recent attacks in 2003 involved car bombs outside Neve Şalom and Şişli synagogues, killing both Jewish congregants and non-Jewish residents, with Turkish nationals held responsible for the crime. Police protection and Jewish community security has risen at synagogues and other institutions following these attacks, with increased steel reinforcement structures, such as those at the Ortaköy synagogue, and with the removal of signage at the Jewish museum, newspaper, and other organizations. Attendance at services has reportedly dropped, particularly among families with children,[5] while the conviction of Turkish citizens in the 2003 attacks has increased a sense of alienation from the broader society among some community members.[6]

In the context of increased synagogue security and Jewish communal isolation in Istanbul, what has become of the practice of Hebrew religious music? To what extent have cross-religious relationships between musicians of classical Turkish and synagogue music, witnessed at least through the mid-1980s, transformed themselves or effectively ended, as sociopolitical and urban conditions have changed? In addition to the protection of Istanbul synagogues, by the 1990s the aging of musical masters and composers, and the waning of an active Turkish art music scene through the closure of gazinos, had already diminished remaining relationships between Jewish and non-Jewish classical musicians. Concomitantly, amid ongoing religious music-making (Shabbat and holiday services, life-cycle celebrations), by the mid-1990s there remained a single practicing Maftirim group, led by hazan David Sevi. While Sevi's group has made music solely within the synagogue, at the end of the decade a second Maftirim ensemble formed that has performed for both the community and the public: for religious holidays in synagogues, and in Istanbul concert halls, for diverse Jewish and cross-religious cultural events.

By tracing the development of these two Maftirim groups—their genesis, composition, raison d'être, and activity—we can more fully understand the state of Jewish religious music-making in Istanbul today as well as the broader social, cultural, and political currents of which it is a part. As we shall see, not only has Jewish participation in the classical Turkish music world waned or been walled off, but the practice of paraliturgical Hebrew religious music, visible in the example of the Maftirim, has become more or less bifurcated musically and socially. That is, each group represents a distinctive historical trajectory: one focuses exclusively on cultivating and transmitting musical and religious culture within a community, the other acts as a bridge between the community and the broader society, thus participating "on the outside" in what theoreticians of culture might call commodified and politicized productions.[7]

Concerts reconstruct in particular ways the inclusive "Ottoman music world" that has been a focus of this study, offering the largely non-emigrating, security-conscious Jewish community a public forum for their relatively positive Ottoman past and thus representations of social tolerance as ideals for present and future national integration. Reduced to musical and historical, religious and national iconography, the concerts likewise support contemporary Islamist party politics through reclaiming an Ottoman imperial past as an alternative to secular republican historiography. Increasingly, then, Turkish synagogue music divides itself between in the community and on the stage, where historiographical motives, the Jewish and Islamist, meet to reconstruct a shared music world. As a result, such divided Jewish religious music-making appears to hide religious communal culture and highlight it as cultural product in a changing sociopolitical, urban world. The following discussion, however, will avoid the problematic dichotomization of "authentic" and "artificial" religious performance as well as, contrariwise, the uncritical view that both phenomena exemplify changing cultural forms awash in a pool of options, unmoored from social and music history.[8] Rather, the in-synagogue group aims to continue the musical knowledge and religious practices of an older generation credentialed through Ottoman-Turkish master-pupil chains. The public performance group, composed of a mixture of generations with a leader less credentialed in the Ottoman sense, sings Maftirim music inside and outside the synagogue, participating in the repertoire's musical changes over time while publicly performing a religious facet of Turkish Jews today through mutually beneficial (to the politics of the Jewish community and a national party) stagings of a shared Ottoman past.

The broad trajectories of these two groups can be contextualized within the changing and politicized urban landscape of Istanbul over the past three decades. For Turkish Jewry, greater synagogue security has taken place within a longer history of province-to-capital migration and emigration to other countries, together with upwardly mobile, intraurban moves of remaining Jews within Istanbul.[9] These demographic trends have effectively vacated outlying provincial Jewish communities, particularly in Thrace, as well as historically Jewish districts in Istanbul, such as Balat and Galata, concentrating Jewish residents closer to the commercial center of the city and its suburbs.[10] The city has swelled enormously through rural-to-urban migration since the 1950s, and has become a global city since the 1980s.[11] Moreover, in the context of secularist-Islamist cultural and political debates of the 1990s, the revival of Istanbul as an Islamic city has gained ground.[12] It is within this changing and contested urban environment that the twin tendencies of Maftirim practice take place today, one more self-cultivating and communally enriching, the other intentionally self-representational within the broader social and political landscape. Whereas the cultivation of historical religious genres now occurs primarily intracommunally, behind secured doors, its public face, in part, performs a harmonious historical culture in prominent concert venues of Istanbul, where contemporary Turkish Jewish and Islamist self-portrayals intersect. Such communal divisions, as reflected in divergent patterns of Maftirim performance, are aspects of social adaptation and negotiation in the Turkish Jewish community as a distinctive minority. As such, a transnational comparison with European Jewish cultural productions is useful in highlighting further distinctions within Jewish social history: in contrast to cultural revivals by non-Jews in Europe, Maftirim concerts in Turkey exemplify the official face of a community seeking a place in the nation.

Behind Steel: Living Practice

> Here, with all its mistakes, is a chorus that represents the whole of the Maftirim. . . . Sixty or seventy compositions have survived today, and every Saturday we sing in different makams, but [over time] try to sing them all. We don't just do four, five or six songs. [We] represent the entire repertoire. Yes, we are trying to preserve the Maftirim repertoire. For us it is not important to perform on stage. [This is] only in the synagogue.
>
> David Sevi, personal interview, January 5, 2006

David Sevi, who grew up listening to a "strong" (*güçlü*) Maftirim group with good singers (*iyi okuyanlar*) at Neve Şalom synagogue in the 1960s, now leads the remaining, in-house gathering at Şişli synagogue in Istanbul.[13] Considered one of the few remaining masters of the genre, Sevi took over leadership of the group after its longtime conductor, David Behar, emigrated to Israel in the mid-1990s. The singularity of the group meeting in one synagogue in the city correlates with internal migration patterns of Istanbul Jewry in the past five decades: until the late 1950s, Maftirim groups met in synagogues of Balat and Galata, but gradually diminished and migrated themselves, as Jews emigrated from Turkey and remaining middle- and upper-middle class residents moved away from Galata into the neighborhoods of Şişli, Nişantışı, and Kurtuluş.[14] In contrast to the historical practice of meeting before prayer services on Shabbat, the current group, like the Neve Şalom gathering of previous years, meets in the afternoon before Minha, the third service of the Sabbath ritual cycle. The more convenient hour has attracted audiences, at a time when attendance, once in the hundreds, had dropped to less than ten.[15] Such adaptations to current smaller numbers of observant community members are reflected in other gestures to draw in singers and listeners, including the extensive provision of food and beverages for the participants.

The character and tone of the Maftirim session, as well as Sevi's philosophy behind the current group, convey its embeddedness in religious liturgy and learning, embodying functions of both spiritual edification and musical transmission.[16] Meeting in an upstairs room behind the women's balcony in Şişli synagogue, male attendees are often dressed formally (suits and sometimes ties) for Shabbat, rising upon the rabbi's entrance, while simultaneously enjoying a relaxed, socializing atmosphere during a singing session accompanied by food and drink. Although the sequence of the session may vary according to leadership and liturgical calendar, in general a sacred fasıl of four to six Maftirim songs in the same makam is framed at the beginning by reciting the kiddush, and an introductory vocal taksim, and at the end by a homily on the Torah reading for the week (usually by the attending rabbi) and the kaddish, the prayer for the dead, recited voluntarily by some members.[17] In this way, the session combines the musical, intellectual, and devotional through religious singing, theological teaching, discussing, even debating, and praying. After the Maftirim session, most of the men descend from the balcony into the main section of the synagogue for the last prayer services of Shabbat (Minha and Arvit).

As in the Maftirim sessions of his childhood, according to Sevi, the current group seeks to learn the entire extant repertoire, although the social pressures for high-quality performance, and the requisite knowledge, no longer prevail. In the past, singers at Neve Şalom met for a separate rehearsal immediately before singing Maftirim songs for the congregation, which numbered in the hundreds: "It was necessary to make absolutely no errors, or at least have a minimum of errors. . . . There were very strong Maftirim singers . . . [so] we had very serious rehearsals."[18] Today, the intention to learn is clear, but the absence of an informed audience or public performance objectives allows for frequent mistakes, particularly among the younger, less-experienced members. Typically drawing close to thirty-five participants by the final rabbinical homily, the group includes a range of experience, from five or six older knowledgeable singers, occasional crossovers from the newer performing Maftirim ensemble, and a majority of silent listeners and beginning learners:

> What we sing here every Saturday . . . represents the entire Maftirim [repertoire]. . . . When we sing there are many mistakes. There are places we forget . . . we start all over again. It isn't important. It's just between us. We are trying to sing. We are doing this for God. We are doing this work simply for emotional fulfillment. For this reason we don't want something where it's important whether it's right or wrong.[19]

Again, based on its present-day aims for religious community, the session does not require the stringent standards of the past—a flexibility that, like the comfortable hour and fare, serves to include more potential learners of a repertoire with few remaining masters.

Despite the challenges, David Sevi has chosen to devote his musical expertise solely to his role as hazan and Maftirim conductor within the synagogue. In 1996 he participated in the "İstanbul'un Ayrıcalığı" concert (March 2, 1996) at Cemal Reşit Rey concert hall, in which several stronger Maftirim vocalists performed under his leadership in a multireligious celebration of Jewish, Christian, and Muslim music of the Ottoman empire and Turkey. Later a CD of the concert, *İstanbul Müziğin Renkleri*, was produced, sponsored by the Istanbul Büyükşehir Belediyesi (Greater Istanbul Municipality) and the historical society Türkiye Ekonomik ve Toplumsal Tarih Vakfı (Foundation for Economic and Social History of Turkey), one of a number of sponsorships by the new Islamist city administration to foreground Istanbul during the Habitat II international meetings.[20] However, concerns about his own professional life and preservation of the music led Sevi to discontinue public productions in 1999 and leave the formation of a performing Maftirim group to another Istanbul hazan, Aaron Kohen. For someone earning his living as a professional hazan, the time-consuming challenge of teaching amateur singers not acculturated to classical Turkish music proved too onerous.[21] Moreover, his concerns about maintaining the historical performance practice of the Maftirim repertoire became paramount:

> Particularly on the subject of traditions, I'm a rather conservative person. And from the past, from our ancestors, our fathers, our grandfathers, the Maftirim is an enormous legacy. There is nothing like it in the world. The source is here. People come from all over the world to learn about it. . . . Someone had to [continue] it. . . . This was my one concern, the loss of the Maftirim. Despite my lack of knowledge, I dared to keep it going. I taught and learned at the same time. By doing this I became more knowledgeable. As they say, the teacher by teaching learns. . . . I never think that I'm the last generation, because you can never know.[22]

Just as he attempts to situate and sustain historical Maftirim singing within the present Jewish community, Sevi chooses to practice his liturgical art as a whole in terms of spiritual communication within his religious setting alone. Using a vivid metaphor, he explains his role as a prayer leader:

> A hazan is a bridge between God and the people who have come. Through his music he must awaken people's spirits. If the music he makes is not beautiful, if it doesn't give anything to people's emotions, if it doesn't awaken their spirits, people will sleep. Then the hazan breaks the prayer, he makes no bridge. . . . Just like nonreligious music, whether allegro, moderato, whatever, if our music inspires different feelings, it's the same thing, whatever name you put on it.[23]

Asserting that there is no difference between great secular art music and great *hazanut* (cantorial music) and that inspiring human emotion makes them fundamentally the same, Sevi nonetheless eschews modes of performance—whether Maftirim or otherwise—that remove his singing from its religious setting and his role as prayer leader. When explaining his avoidance of recording studios and musical notation, for example, he described their tendency to break his concentration on communicating through his religious singing.[24] Clearly, through his metaphor of a bridge, Sevi seeks musical and spiritual continuity with his congregants toward union with God, rather than taking synagogue music out of context for listeners, learners, and researchers outside the Jewish community and religious experience. From his work as professional hazan to his leadership of the Maftirim sessions at Şişli, Sevi concentrates his expertise on deepening communal culture within daily, lived liturgical experience, which, owing in part to synagogue attacks and security, has become increasingly isolated from the surrounding society. In contrast to broader circulations before the mid-1980s, as exemplified by David Behar, İsak Maçoro, and David Asseo, Sevi's choices reflect individual preferences within a new urban landscape and declining forms of Turkish Jewish heritage. Whatever the potential musical or social losses, such choices currently exclude participation in public cultural productions, which involve the second Maftirim group in politically interested performances reflective of both Jewish communal and broader cultural politics in Turkey today.

Staging an Ottoman Music World

> First of all I thank God who has brought this beautiful project to life. . . .
> For us it is a great honor to set our hearts on this tolerance, on this partnership and unity. I congratulate everyone from the bottom of my heart.
> Menahem Eskenazi, SHOW Channel, October 30, 2004

Menahem Eskenazi, another practicing hazan and since 2002—taking over from Aaron Kohen—the conductor of the current performing Maftirim group, thus commented on the concert series *Birlikte Yaşamak* (Living Together) during a television interview/performance.[25] He joined artistic director Taşkın Savaş and Armenian conductor Nişan Çalgıcıyan in discussing the longtime, municipally sponsored concert series that celebrates the coexistence of Judeo-Christian-Islamic religious communities in the Ottoman empire and the Turkish Republic. According to Savaş, the concerts traditionally take place following the commemoration of the conquest of Istanbul by Mehmet I (May 29) to showcase the dhimmi communities officially recognized by the Ottoman imperial administration.[26] From the series' inception in 1995, singers of Jewish religious music have participated, beginning with a group led by Cako Taragano and later showcasing the current Maftirim group. The Armenian chorus performs under the direction of Nişan Çalgıcıyan, and the Tasavvuf Sufi group of Taşkın Savaş, Yakarış Müzik Topluluğu, takes center-stage along with the concert's artistic director.

The *Birlikte Yaşamak* concerts are only one of numerous public, multireligious performances in which Menahem Eskenazi's Maftirim group has participated. In 2005–2006 alone these public performances included the "Rumi and Tolerance" concert directed by filmmaker Fehmi Gerçeker and using similar community choruses at Cemal Reşit Rey concert hall in October 2005; a concert at the "Hatay Medeniyetler Buluşması" (Hatay Civilizations conference) in Antakya in September 2005; and a second *Birlikte Yaşamak* organized independently of Taşkın Savaş, taking place during the 2006 International Istanbul Islands Culture and Art Festival on Büyükada.[27] In addition to participating in such musical celebrations of religious plurality, the Maftirim group also performed during the European Day of Jewish Culture, the Istanbul program of an international Jewish festival, which focused on Turkish Jewish musicians, artists, dramatists, and photographers, performing or

Program for the "Rumi and Tolerance" concert, October 2, 2005, at Cemal Reşit Rey concert hall in Istanbul. The Sinagog Maftirim Korosu performed with Greek (Fener Rum Patrikhanesi Korosu), Armenian (Vartanants Teganni Heyeti), and Muslim (Üsküdar Hafızları) groups. Collection of the author.

exhibiting in historic Jewish sites in Galata.[28] Finally, during the year the group performed for six Jewish holidays in synagogues in Istanbul, rotating among different congregations throughout the liturgical calendar. According to the group's logistical coordinator, Bensi Elmas, the ensemble has also sung at life-cycle celebrations (circumcisions and name-giving ceremonies), as well as official visits related to the chief rabbinate.[29]

On the one hand, Menahem Eskenazi's group, Sinagog Maftirim Korosu, shares several elements in common with David Sevi's weekly gathering.[30] Despite its public performing profile, the group similarly participates within the religious community, presenting Maftirim compositions historically related to specific religious holidays, such as Sukkot, Hanukkah, Purim, and Shavuot. Although differently trained in some respects and less credentialed in historical terms, the group's leadership has been held by hazanim who have grown up acculturated to in-synagogue religious music, as well as to the classical Turkish music of their day on radio, television, and film. Additionally, the activities of the group reflect philosophically related, though differently actualized, preservationist concerns. While the singers do not meet every Shabbat amid prayer services, as in historical practice, the holiday Maftirim singing perpetuates a historic subset of the repertoire. Individual choices on the part of leaders or members likewise reflect an urgency to preserve: the first conductor, Aaron Kohen, notated a series of Maftirim compositions and produced a CD in 2001, *Maftirim: Judeo-Sufi Connection*,[31] while coordinator Elmas is a younger member, self-admittedly unacculturated to classical Turkish music, who views himself responsible, as the "last generation," for not letting the tradition pass away.

The genesis, rehearsals, and performances of the Sinagog Maftirim Korosu, on the other hand, diverge from the Şişli gathering in distinctive ways, forging its function as a bridge between the community and the Turkish public through multireligious concerts projecting a conciliatory historiography in support of official representations and tolerance within the nation today. As such, the group's public performances are a religious and musical example of a variety of current representations of Turkish Jewry to mixed public audiences in Turkey. During 2005–2006, Sephardic music concerts in Istanbul included performances by Rosa Zaragoza, Hadass Pal-Yarden, and Sefarad. Each of these concerts showcased primarily Ladino song, in contrast to the Hebrew, religious genre of the *Birlikte Yaşamak* series; however, the performers presented a spectrum of Turkish Jewish cultural integration on stage, from a past Iberian utopia of Abrahamic faith (Zaragoza), to a historical-ethnomusicological focus (Pal-Yarden), to Sephardic youth as an integral part of Middle Eastern culture through both Ladino and Turkish songs, and bellydancing interludes on stage (Sefarad).

It is through their participation in public performances that the Sinagog Maftirim Korosu articulates a distinctive bridging and ameliorating role for the Turkish Jewish community today. As we have seen, in 2005–2006 four out of five of its public events represented multireligious celebrations, particularly related to the historical and contemporary coexistence of Judaism, Christianity, and Islam in Turkey and the Ottoman empire. For over fifteen years the *Birlikte Yaşamak* annual concert series has presented social coexistence through the lens of the historical interconnectedness of religious music within a Turkish national context.[32] The thirteenth annual concert, on June 11, 2006, took place at the Atatürk Kültür Merkezi (Atatürk Cultural Center), located in the central Istanbul neighborhood of Taksim. At that concert, two large Turkish flags hung on either side of the stage. The three conductors of community choruses appeared together, raised up from below on a moveable platform. Massive applause greeted them. After the master of ceremonies introduced the program, the concert began with a call to prayer, then each choir—Jewish, Armenian, and Sufi—sang a religious piece to the accompaniment of a Turkish instrumental ensemble. Several sets of round-robin multireligious pieces followed, punctuated by whirling dervishes turning onstage, as multicolored pastel lights glowed on their white garments. At the end of the first half of the evening's program, the choirs sang "Alleluia" in unison, a piece by artistic director and conductor of the Sufi group, Taşkın Savaş.

The annual *Birlikte Yaşamak* concert thus showcased Muslim, Jewish, and Armenian religious compositions as part of a larger, unified Ottoman vocal and instrumental tradition. The round-robin sets of hymns in Turkish, Hebrew, and Armenian allowed listeners to impressionistically grasp an underlying musical commonality, as the whirling dervishes provided a visual locus of spiritual unity—the Mevlevi order—appearing to unite the three religions, or at least to form a benevolent basis for historical coexistence and religious tolerance. The initial call to prayer likewise established the majority religion within which the minority religious communities historically and currently resided, while the enormous, banner-like Turkish flags draped on the stage confirmed governmental sponsorship of the religiously toned event.

Significantly, the concert followed on the heels of "Conquest Day" on May 29 in commemoration of the anniversary of the taking of Constantinople by Mehmet I, thus reinforcing, with the holiday, national pride associated with establishment of the Ottoman capital in the city. Celebrated as a quincentennial in 1953, the first "Conquest Day" of the Republic—held over the course of ten days from May 29 to June 7—was a state-sponsored event with a clear religious dimension: although not formally linked to today's Conquest Day, the annual *Birlikte Yaşamak* concerts generally fall within a similar ten-day period.[33] The quincentennial in 1953 represented the outcome of dissension in the public sphere, which continues today, regarding the place of religion in public and political life. Reflecting agitation against the single-party regimes and platforms of Atatürk and İnönü, the expansion of political parties and provincial newspapers after 1945 promoted debates about state-led secularism in addition to a public reworking of the place of the Ottoman past in Turkish national history.[34] Through historical novels, films, newspaper articles, and textbook revisions, the empire was increasingly represented not as oppositional to but as containing the democratic and nationalist seeds for the Turkish nation-state.[35] Cultural contestations beginning in the mid-1940s, then, were precedents to current ideological debates in Turkey, reflected in such recent phenomena as Conquest Day.[36]

Remaining low-profile and unofficial for decades, the celebration of the Muslim conquest of Constantinople reemerged in the 1990s amid the electoral successes of Islamist parties. Beginning at the municipal level, with Recep Tayyip Erdoğan's mayoral victory in Istanbul in 1994, the Islamist Refah Partisi (RP, or Welfare Party) has tangled with dominant secularist cultural narratives through debates about secularism, Islam, and alternative historical markers in Turkish national historiography. After a series of political victories and censures at the national level, the Islamist Adalet ve Kalkınma Partisi (AKP, or Justice and Development Party) under Erdoğan's leadership today continues such interventions into secularist interpretations of Turkish history and social life. What is important here in the extensive and growing literature evaluating the political character of the party, is the dimension of cultural production, specifically moves to reclaim Ottoman heritage and Istanbul as an Islamic city, in contradistinction to Ankara and the founding of a secular republic.[37] In fact, in the 1950s the Democratic Party and Prime Minister Adnan Menderes moved forward on the construction of a major mosque in Ankara, a gesture that, although connected to the capital city of the Republic and not of the empire, was a precedent for reclaiming Islam as a part of national architecture and history.[38]

As examples of such productions, both Conquest Day and the *Birlikte Yaşamak* concerts represent an Islamist municipal and national administration's investment in public programs grounding Turkish national history in an imperial and religious past.[39] Both events prominently display Turkish flags—flying on the old city walls or framing the choirs onstage—clear choices to make imperial Ottoman history Turkish through panegyric historical reconstructions that could as easily warrant historically accurate Ottoman banners.[40] Moreover, Conquest Day commemorates, and nationalizes, founder and founding event in distinctively religious terms, as a prophesized Islamic conquest rather than the Turkish military victory of school textbooks.[41] In the same vein, the concert foregrounds religion through a Turkish Islam encompassing dhimmi choruses under its wing: the Mevlevi *sema* projects a positive, inclusive, and tolerant Islamic tradition in Turkey and the Middle East, yesterday and today. The touristic lighting of the dervishes and the whirling fragments withdrawn from their ceremonial context reduce the Mevlevi *sema* to visual punctuation marks—icons denoting unity, benevolence, and enlightenment in relationship to the ethno-religious diversity of the choirs. As such, the motif represents a growing trend to insert the whirling dervish as a fragmented and folkloric image in a variety of contexts (for example, shopping malls, weddings, and private parties), divorced from religious settings and practices.[42] Through this and other elements in the staging of the concert, the productions utilize commercial design in the interest of entertainment. The sociopolitical aims of the performance, moreover, are conveyed in the free-to-the-public ticketless exchange as well as in the front-row attendance of municipal officials.

Although the concert presents apparent markers of peaceful cohabitation—the Mevlevi *sema* as benevolent symbol and collectively sung *ilahi*s (religious songs) as musically linked to non-Muslim religious music—the program itself reflects a tension, in common with Conquest Day and related Islamist political events, between representations of dominance and triumph, on the one hand, and on the other, conciliation promoting ethno-religious pluralism. In the political arena, triumphant Ottoman commemorations, as well as proposals to architecturally Islamicize the city, have coincided with overtures to non-Muslim religious minorities,[43] thus combining valorization of majority culture as Turkish and Islamic, together with the appearance of ethno-religious inclusiveness. The *Birlikte Yaşamak* concerts, in their inception, conception, and production, convey a similar contradictory dynamic. First organized in the Istanbul municipality by a cultural agency instituted in 1994 by the newly elected (Islamist) Welfare Party, the first concerts reflected tensions in the early years of the series. Organizers refused a request by the leader of the first participating Jewish group to end the program with a Hebrew song, reasoning that "The country is Turkey. The majority are Muslim. If I were in Israel I would not sing the last song. A Jew should sing the last song. . . . But here . . . I will sing the first and last song." Further, religious history reinforced this line of argument: "If your prophet had been the last prophet I would have allowed this, that is, if Moses had come last into the world, go ahead. [But] here it goes according to the sequence of prophets, the people of Moses, Jesus, and Mohamed."[44] Accordingly, Islam's prophetic chronology and Turkey's Muslim majority justified the musical order of the program.

Together with the performance of national and religious hierarchy, however, the apparent message of the concerts is to "show Turkish culture . . . how interconnected we are with Armenians . . . how interconnected we are with Jews . . . how much each of us, how much Turks did in the area of aesthetics and music. . . . In cities everyone lived together and played Turkish classical music."[45] In this way, the programmatic concept of *Birlikte Yaşamak* encompasses seemingly egalitarian relations based on historical court music culture, which are nonetheless embedded in power relations based on nation-state Muslim majoritarianism linked to particular forms of Islam. Given these contending dynamics, the artistic concept as a whole excludes the possibility of a final Hebrew song. Lest this arrangement appear natural and unsurprising in Muslim-majority Turkey, in another concert celebrating the music of dhimmi communities, "Beraberliğin Ahengi" (Harmony of Togetherness, February 2004), Jewish music took center stage in a performance commemorating past ethno-religious diversity in the neighborhood of Kuzguncuk to launch a book by the same name, written by architect Cengiz Bektaş.[46] At this concert the order of the musical program correlated roughly with historical population numbers of Kuzguncuk.[47]

The debates surrounding the first *Birlikte Yaşamak* concerts in the early 1990s signal the uneasy tensions in producing such a program, which in the end were resolved by maintaining the majority's pride of place, and finding a new Jewish conductor and choir agreeable to the performance arrangement.[48] The resolution of the conflict among concert personnel implies the inherent conditionality of the program's design, that is, minority religious inclusiveness on condition of Muslim majority predominance. As in the electoral arena, where, for example, proposals for a mosque in the commercial center of town coincided with reaching out to minority communities in the district, the apparent contradiction between dominance and diversity resolves itself as a particular form of religious nationalism maintaining political power through not appearing narrowly Muslim.[49]

From the perspective of the Jewish group currently performing in the *Birlikte Yaşamak* concerts, their participation reflects both individual and official motivations. For example, conductor Eskenazi interprets a spiritual basis for the musical performance of unity, while other members highlight the potential to promote intercultural education and to influence the decision on Turkey's accession to the European Union.[50] In the official realm, the performance correlates with public representations of communal social history sanctioned by Turkish Jewish institutions today. The Quincentennial Foundation, established in 1989 by Jewish and Muslim community and business leaders, promoted an overarching narrative of Ottoman-Turkish-Jewish peaceful coexistence shaping the five-hundredth-year anniversary celebrations in 1992, as well as later productions, such as Naim Güleryüz's *Türk Yahudileri Tarihi 20 Yüzyılın Başina Kadar* (Turkish Jewish History until the Early Twentieth Century) in 1993, and the opening of the *500. Yıl Vakfı Türk Musevileri Müzesi* (The Quincentennial Foundation Museum of Turkish Jews) in 2001.[51] In the same period, the *Birlikte Yaşamak* concert series aligned itself with favorable Turkish Jewish historical narratives for both the Ottoman and republican eras by performing historical musical linkages and adaptations to an Islamic majority culture, with contemporary continuities implied through an active, participating community chorus. Related events, such as the

Rumi Project and Hatay Civilizations conference, have involved the Maftirim group in similar historical portrayals of the Jewish community. Performances on less positive themes have not received support from communal officials, for example the filming of a movie about the Capital Tax, a trend highlighting an official avoidance of casting shadows on the Turkish Jewish past, and resulting in favorable public perceptions of the historical position of Jews in Turkey, in contrast to that of other non-Muslim minorities.[52] This reticence on the part of community institutions has its roots in the 1970s, when the state began to cultivate a relationship with and representation of Turkish Jews as a model minority: the invasion of Cyprus by Turkey and the first assassination of a Turkish consul by Armenian nationalists publicized Greek and Armenian grievances and motivated an official response to foster a multicultural national narrative of tolerance.[53] Such narratives and the cultural productions representing them support diverse governmental public relations campaigns at home and abroad, including in the area of European Union accession talks.

Sinagog Maftirim Korosu in concert at the Büyükada Turing Kültür Evi in the Third Annual Princes Islands International Festival, July 16, 2006. Called *Birlikte Yaşam* (Life Together), the concert is distinct from the annual Birlikte Yaşamak (Living Together) concerts after Conquest Day, but includes similar programmatic content. Photo by author.

Funded by the Greater Istanbul Municipality and communally supported by the chief rabbinate, the *Birlikte Yaşamak* concerts and related performances thus stage an Ottoman music world in which contemporary Islamist and Jewish versions of Turkish history intersect. The nationalization of an Islamic-Ottoman heritage, through music, locates the nation's foundations in a pre-republican golden age, retrograding Turkish national history back from 1923 to 1453 and raising up alternative founders and national heroes to Mustafa Kemal Atatürk, specifically Mehmet the Conqueror.[54] The benevolence of "Turkish Islam" and an Ottoman administration of millets infuse this historical portrait with multiethnic coexistence, completing a usable past for a range of Islamist party interests in the present.[55] Arguably, such contemporary cultural productions are the logical outcome of two five-hundred-year celebrations of historical origins, the Conquest Day of 1953, which recently resurfaced to challenge secularist republican national history, and, in 1992, the commemoration of the Sephardic expulsion from Spain, which narrated a favorable history of Jews in Ottoman and Turkish lands, in contrast to contemporary Armenian and Greek claims. Although official and individual motivations may diverge in complex ways, both historiographies meet onstage to fold an Ottoman music world into officially sanctioned Islamist or Jewish presentations of Turkish history. Both historical narratives strategically elide the republican period for distinctive reasons: one to trace national roots to a presumably pre-secular imperial and religious past, the other to emphasize Jewish culture in the Ottoman period over twentieth-century adversities to represent and motivate integration in the present.

If we return to the nonpublic performances of Maftirim music at Şişli synagogue, how can we understand these two groups, the broader community and Turkish society, in relation to each other? Whereas one appears embedded in an active liturgical life largely hidden from public view, the other performs both inside and outside of the synagogue, making contact with non-Jewish audiences and enabling Islamic-Ottoman heritage productions. The apparent tension between a hidden living community and a harmonious public face, as reflected in these two groups, correlates with other recent ethnographic scholarship on Turkish Jewry focusing alternatively on citizenship and nonmusical productions. For example, research on Turkish Jewish views on citizenship has posited a consistent tension between "invisibility" and "loyalty," that is, a belief that cultural survival depended on repressing Jewish cultural or religious difference, while maintaining a self-representation of nonthreatening loyalty to the Turkish nation.[56] Likewise, a semiotic study of Turkish Jewish cultural negotiation probed the seeming contradictions between community discourses of threat, fear, and security needs following the 1986 Neve Şalom attack, and official declarations of five centuries of Turkish tolerance of Jews. The celebration of a publicly absent tolerance is prescriptive rather than descriptive, "[casting] not a backward glance but instead a wishful eye toward the future and a secure legacy for Turkish Jewry."[57]

Similarly, the two Maftirim groups play out two sides of the same coin by seeking to sustain historically informed versions of Maftirim practice in a secured community, while officially publicizing a peaceably embedded minority in Ottoman-Turkish-Islamic musical culture. In this way, real-life interaction between Jewish and non-Jewish master musicians is effectively foreclosed, while real-life risks to community are seemingly avoided through positive socio-musical stagings. As only one of numerous groups performing diverse Turkish Jewish music in Istanbul, the performing Maftirim group nonetheless shares in a current pattern of positive publicity for Jewish culture and history in Turkey. It remains to be seen whether the group's particular adaptation to artistic concepts such as the *Birlikte Yaşamak* concert series has the potential to go beyond obscuring historical adversities and to promote new knowledge, awareness, curiosity, or social relationships. That is, to what extent does the group's performance *represent* historical coexistence and to what extent might it *generate* genuine social inclusion as expressed in the motivations of individual members seeking humanistic unity and multicultural education? Further, if sociocultural conditions in Turkey increasingly tolerate reckoning with difficult knowledge, particularly around twentieth-century minority histories,[58] will groups like the Maftirim chorus transform their roles in a changing public Jewish historiography or, alternatively, will the conditions and interests of secured, centralized communal institutions themselves militate against such changes?[59] Whatever the future holds, as it stands now, the two groups—through their distinctive and overlapping spaces, activities, and aims—reflect deeper sociocultural tensions in the Turkish

Jewish community, securing and hiding active liturgical life, while simultaneously adapting to a staged Ottoman music world framed as Islamist national history.

A Transnational Perspective

As an example of staging imperial Jewish music and society, the *Birlikte Yaşamak* concerts can be situated among wider trends to reconstruct and commodify historical communities in general and Jewish communities in particular. Outside Turkey, the subject of Jewish culture and its contemporary reconstruction has drawn attention from a variety of scholars, with a particular focus on post-Inquisition Spain and post-Holocaust Europe. Especially after the end of the Soviet Union, a European Jewish cultural revival grew from investigations into Jewish and minority cultural histories, and second- and third-generation quests for family heritage.[60] In Spain, the medieval Sephardic legacy has been reconstructed through Jewish museums, renovated Jewish quarters, and Sephardic music festivals.[61] In central Europe, Jewish culture has experienced a revival through artifacts (museums and renovations), musical performances, scholarly conferences, and Holocaust memorials.[62] Since 1990, interaction between the tourist industry and tourists themselves has led to an upsurge in Jewish tourist itineraries regionwide.[63] If we contextualize Turkish Jewish cultural activity within broader Jewish heritage phenomena, how does it compare transnationally and what additional insights at the national level might we gain? Specifically, in the area of Maftirim and synagogue music, to what extent does its performance in the community or on the stage share elements with Jewish cultural revival in areas of low or no Jewish population today in Spain and central Europe? How might the Turkish case reflect imperial or national contexts particular to Turkish or other non-European Jewish culture regions?

Turkish Jewish cultural productions in general, and religious music in particular, participate in worldwide transnational trends today. At the same time, a comparative perspective can assist us in understanding what is unique about the Turkish national case. On the one hand, the global interest in Turkish Jewry parallels the rise in Jewish tourism and historical commemoration in Europe, expanding since the quincentennial celebrations in 1992 in Turkey, Spain, and elsewhere.[64] The Quincentennial Foundation spawned commemorative celebrations and a Jewish museum, increasing tourism to historic Jewish sites in Istanbul initially through tours sponsored by the foundation, as well as scholarly research and publications related to Turkish and Ottoman history.[65] Sociocultural divisions in Turkey and Europe alike have often sealed off communal life from cultural production. In Italy, for example, Jews may celebrate a yearly religious holiday in the synagogue next door to a popular entertainer reconstructing Yiddish musical theater for a largely non-Jewish audience—and never the twain will meet.[66] In Spain, touristic, entertainment motives so overshadow Sephardic festivals that the resulting imagined Jewish communities are fraught with historical and religious incongruities.[67] In a similar vein, this chapter has posited a distinction, however blurred and overlapping, between one Maftirim gathering as cultivating in-synagogue religious life and the other participating in commodified and politically involved *Birlikte Yaşamak* concerts. Indeed, my own in-synagogue experiences have measured the distance between the public at large and observant Jews engaged in real-life, if little known, musical commonalities with fellow Turks. In such a social environment, ethno-religious stereotypes may persist, understandings of violent histories remain superficial, and substantive cross-communal relations rarely develop. In fact, the *Birlikte Yaşamak* and Rumi Project concerts testify to these possibilities through the isolation of choirs and the absence of interreligious communication backstage. A concert organizer, furthermore, voiced conventional anti-Semitic views, despite the humanistic ideals of the *Birlikte Yaşamak* series. In his words, Jews, unlike Armenians and Greeks, generally transferred their way of making money ("cheap, easy, quick") to their way of composing music (adapting non-Jewish compositions to Hebrew texts).[68]

On the other hand, in Turkey there are no spaces equivalent to European Jewish landscapes, vacated in the course of an Inquisition or Holocaust, to fill with "things Jewish."[69] In Europe much historical reconstruction takes place in cities with few or no remaining prewar Jews, and sometimes in towns or villages uninhabited by Jews since the fifteenth century.[70] Moreover, minimally there is public awareness, even if not extensive knowledge, of the historical destruction of Spanish and European Jewish communities in the region, and the revival of past Jewish populations includes significant commemoration through memorials to the dead. By contrast, in republican Turkey, it was not mass marginalization and murder, but primarily dispossession through economic and cultural nationalism that pushed Jewish communities—progressively rather than precipitously—to emigrate.[71] Owing in part to official Turkish and Jewish historiographical cooperation, these departures under duress remain largely in individual and family memory, and to a lesser extent in independent scholarship.[72] In fact, some justify public silence on the Capital Tax during World War II by noting differential suffering, that is, compared to European Jewry under Nazism, Turkish Jews were relatively protected.[73] Thus, as a sharply reduced population outside a geography of killing fields, the culturally active, relatively stable and non-emigrating Istanbul community relies not on a relatively underinformed citizenry, but on its own members to represent "Jewish culture" to the public. Unlike the phenomenon of Jewish revivalism in Europe—primarily by non-Jews fulfilling individual purposes, national agendas, and the demands of the tourism market[74]—in Turkey Jewish musicians, artists, writers, scholars, and curators produce work for audiences largely unfamiliar with their community.

Through a comparison with trends in European Jewish cultural productions, then, we can appreciate the dimension of historical *self-representation* in Turkish Jewish public art. To be sure, as an example of diverse public presentations, the Sinagog Maftirim Korosu's participation in multireligious concerts—and not, for example, in more confrontational or politicized multiethnic art—reflects official selectivity involved in publicizing the community to Turkish society. But, however official, nationalist, or Islamist in design, reconstruction of things Ottoman, such as an Ottoman music world, provides a public platform for linking Jews to other Ottoman and Turkish religious communities and thereby reclaiming aspects of Turkish Jewish history that, in contrast to the history of Jews in Christian Europe, exclude the excesses of the Inquisition and the Holocaust. Although the *Birlikte Yaşamak* concerts include elements of extravaganza and iconography (the Mevlevi lightshow, moving stages, whirling fragments), the Maftirim performance itself stands apart from the touristic "pseudomitologia" of, for example, some festivals of Sephardic culture in Spain.[75] Whatever their differences with the non-public Maftirim gathering, the group is nonetheless continuous with a range of current in-community practices through holiday performances and a leadership musically and religiously educated in-residence. In its role as bridge, then, between Turkish Jews and their Muslim majority fellow citizens, the Sinagog Maftirim Korosu presents musical selections of living contemporary religious life on stage, blurring the lines between real-life and staged culture and the strict bifurcation between hidden and harmonious, public and private faces of the community. Among diverse musical and other public presentations by Turkish Jews today, its performances represent a minority within a minority (observant Jews) at a time when highly secured Turkish synagogues have ceased their multifunctional roles of the past. Adapting to a hierarchical Ottoman Islamic staging of Turkish national history—through music—the group indeed exemplifies the official, public face of Jews remaining in Turkey today. In contrast to many European Jewish revivals missing local Jews, however, Turkish Jews themselves are motivated to participate on stage as a resident minority pursuing avenues—and one could say compromises—to be, and become, part of the Turkish nation today.

Five Into the Future:
Texts, Technologies, and Tradition

One spring day I step into the sitting room of a dental office near Şişli mosque, its walls painted bold royal blue and its window splashed with the broad leaves of plants. A television chatters the evening news; a black sofa and chairs encircle the space. A spread of fruit, cookies, and soft drinks on the coffee table attracts my attention, as I sit waiting for members of the Sinagog Maftirim Korosu, the publicly performing Maftirim group, to arrive for rehearsal. Meeting regularly in the professional offices of a member, the singers—all men—arrive in pairs or singly. They laugh and converse, eat and drink, then begin to rehearse a piece for an upcoming performance.

Today the rehearsal is out of the ordinary. Conductor Menahem Eskenazi usually leads the group solo in the sitting room: he hands sheet music (notation and lyrics) to all the men, even though most don't read musical notes and acquire songs orally in the course of the evening. Today, however, we make our way to a small back office and gather around a cassette player. We listen to an instrumental version of the vocal piece "Yekav-Yeşurun," the Maftirim composition to be performed for the upcoming religious holiday of Lag B'Omer.[1] The recording was arranged by guitarist Izi Eli on the computer with the use of electronic Turkish instruments.[2] Returning to the sitting room, Menahem Eskenazi leads the group in a first run-through of the song, joined by a visiting senior musician, Rıfat Dana, who comments throughout the rehearsal on the group's performance. He demonstrates an ornamental turn or two absent from the notated scores, corrects intonation on notes needing to be flatter, and points out to the singers where the composition modulates from one makam to another (Acemaşiran to Saba) and where the usul changes (from Sengin

Semai to Yürük Semai). A regular attendee at in-synagogue Maftirim gatherings in the 1950s in his childhood neighborhood of Balat, Dana had also been invited to contribute to David Sevi's Maftirim sessions at Şişli synagogue during the reading of Perkey Avot, between Passover and Shavuot.[3] In both settings Dana shares his understandings of classical Turkish style and theory, cultivated through his own past oral learning and missing from paper documents.

A single rehearsal utilizing 5-staff notation, outsider commentary, and computerized cassette recordings provides a window on contemporary methods of musical learning among Turkish Jews. The range of approaches exemplifies shifts in technologies of musical transmission across the twentieth century within a historically orally transmitted art form. That Eskenazi distributed scores fits with the widespread trend toward the scoring of classical Turkish music that began in the twentieth century. But since most of the singers in his group cannot read notes, the rehearsal also illustrates the persistence of ear learning and performance in republican Turkey.[4] Other supplementary methods in this rehearsal likewise reinforce oral learning. Dana's corrective comments on ornamentation and intonation indicate the limits of notation, at least for less acculturated singers, in capturing the full complexity of the piece as remembered by Dana. Like fellow musicians in Turkey, Dana approaches printed notes on the page as a skeleton of the piece, to be fleshed out by knowledge held in ear and memory. The cassette recording—an obvious technological departure from meşk methods through documentation and electronification—nonetheless resembled other cassettes used by the group that were drawn directly from vocal renditions recorded in the 1980s by those considered the last remaining masters, İsak Maçoro, David Behar, and David Sevi: it supports learning by ear within the community through local use of tapes during rehearsal, rather than mass production and distribution for a listening public. Compact disc recordings of these same masters, moreover, form the basis of a more recent documentary project (2009), an initiative by the Ottoman-Turkish Sephardic Culture Research Center (Osmanlı-Türk Sefarad Kültürü Araştırma Merkezi) in Istanbul, providing archival recordings, lyrics, and scores of the extant Maftirim repertoire, and raising similar issues related to orality, textuality, and practical usage.

Diverse documentation of "traditional" oral forms raises important questions shared by global cultures today regarding living transmission and the representation of heritage, the constitution of musical masters, cultural authenticity, and artistic change over time.[5] In particular, the latest comprehensive Maftirim project, a culmination of the varied oral-textual-recorded documentation of the repertoire over time, reflects impulses to preserve heritage by a minority population with aging or deceased masters, and is thus invested with the power, as a primary historical and instructional source, to represent the music to congregational learners and international scholars into the future. It is for this reason that tracing the changing transmission and documentation of the Maftirim into the twenty-first century provides a fitting conclusion to a social history of this sacred song. Broad shifts from the oral to the textually or aurally documented, especially in numerically declining groups, have often alerted scholars of oral art forms to the demise of musical and poetic practices. Indeed, a shift from people to paper, as it were—the textualization and recording of a music that had been a historically live, communal, and intercommunal practice—may cause musical and sociocultural losses linked to the disappearance of the oral dimension. Through apprenticeship relations, for example, students learned, imagined, and recollected the music in specific ways, honing ear and memory to actualize compositions during performance. Like oral art forms in general, a composition-in-performance represents rich variability—a range of performative possibilities, whether through individual musical alterations, a version learned from a particular master, or change over time through oral transmission. For the Maftirim, documentation through texts and recordings potentially forestalls such variability, creating a seemingly fixed or frozen repertoire as the Turkish Jewish legacy to future generations of musicians, scholars, and synagogue singers.

The actual use of documents like the recordings and scores at the Sinagog Maftirim Korosu rehearsal described above, however, complicates our understanding of musical learning and our assumptions about a straightforward developmental shift in transmission patterns. Indeed, recent scholarship on orality and textuality commonly assumes blending, rather than sharp divisions, of the oral and textual in social and literary history. The Maftirim repertoire is a case in point. Its oral transmission historically included certain kinds of texts: embedded as it was in Ottoman instructional and performative practices, the repertoire appeared in manuscripts of non-notated song-text collections with mnemonic devices for oral methods of teaching, learning, and performing.[6] In the first decade of the Republic, several projects documented the repertoire in both historically grounded and unprecedented ways in Istanbul: the song-text collection *Shire Yisrael be-Erets ha-kedem* was uniquely comprehensive and published for distribution, and at the same time resembled in format past manuscripted songbooks and published works in other Ottoman cities.[7] The Maftirim notation project sponsored by Chief Rabbi Hayim Becerano, which provided the first notated scores of the repertoire, remained unpublished. It was only after a gap of fifty years, into the 1980s, that we witnessed a flurry of preservationist efforts: the recording of masters of the genre; notations by David Behar and Fatih Salgar; a commercial CD of one Maftirim group; and the recently produced Maftirim project based on 1980s recordings.

Because of the advantages of musical documentation to music historians and younger-generation learners, there can be a tendency to value uncritically any effort to record (aurally or textually) an orally transmitted repertoire, such as the Maftirim, and a tendency to remove such recording efforts—because they are valuable to us today—from the historical context shaping them. In tracing the history of documenting Maftirim compositions, particularly from the late Ottoman through the republican eras, we will interpret new and unprecedented initiatives in the 1920s to document the music as continuous with Jewish cultural concerns of the period as well as with broader Turkish classical music trends in which Jews participated at the time: that is, ongoing oral learning together with wider dissemination of musical publications and adoption of European notational methods, which, however, were variably used in practice.[8] Only after the 1980s do we witness increasing efforts to document the music for cultural preservation objectives, culminating in the current Maftirim project of the Istanbul research center. Given significant waves of emigration, especially after 1948, and a small remaining population, we might expect the documentation of music to have happened earlier or not at all. Like other regionally and ethnically diverse non-emigrating minorities, however, Turkish Jews often consolidated themselves in fewer close communities and their institutions, a trend that, in the decades from the 1920s through the 1980s, incubated historical music-making in a variety of ways.⁹ The neighborhood synagogue remained a site of orally transmitted classical music learning, not only through liturgical services, but also through Maftirim sessions as meşk opportunities and concert-like entertainment. Like local gazinos and coffeehouses, synagogues offered opportunities to learn and enjoy classical Turkish music learning and performance, albeit in a religious register, during an era of official exclusion from conservatory curricula.

Moreover, unique characteristics of urban synagogue culture arguably cultivated and maintained oral learning in particularly intensive ways, in comparison with the surrounding classical Turkish music world. Jews remaining in Turkey continued to live in relatively close neighborhoods until a few decades ago, supporting synagogues with a dense liturgical calendar, despite secularizing trends and unevenness of religious observance. Not only would such social proximity and regularity of services promote oral liturgies, youthful attendance, and musical education, but also Jewish congregants themselves, whether more or less observant, contributed to classical music transmission through their extensive knowledge of Turkish art music and involvement in liturgical and paraliturgical performance. Thus, despite unique threats to Hebrew musical culture owing to progressive Jewish emigration from Turkey, the consolidation of remaining residents within diminished urban centers in fact led to ongoing oral transmission of the Maftirim and synagogue music, and a paucity of preservationist initiatives until relatively recently. The publication by the Istanbul research center in 2009 reflects a surviving critical mass of material, as well as fears of cultural loss today. How can we understand the dynamic role of synagogue, neighborhood, and audience in the oral-textual history of the Maftirim—the in-community processes linked to civic musical friendships of masters? How significant is the broad shift in orality and textuality to the performance, transmission, and representation of the music in the future? By publishing single compositions that existed in multiple forms in the past, the most recent project may risk significant musical losses in common with initiatives globally to preserve oral art forms. Even so, does the contemporary publication have a larger story to tell about texts, technologies, and a "tradition" that has always been embedded in an oral Ottoman and Turkish music world?

The Persistence of Oral Transmission

"Your Thighs Would Get Red"

> As far as the Maftirim goes, most of the time we didn't know notation, so . . . "Dum tek-a, dum tek" is how we learned. It was in the Turkish classical music method we learned—always master-apprentice relationships.
>
> Yusuf Altıntaş, personal interview, January 31, 2006

According to Yusuf Altıntaş, who attended Maftirim sessions as a youth in Galata in the late 1950s, there were no scores for learning the repertoire:

> When I was young I took Maftirim lessons with [David] Behar. It was at Neve Şalom and Knesset Israel [synagogues]. . . . We learned the usuls. It was necessary to sit down and do it on our legs. . . . For the first lesson it was "dum tek-a, dum tek" to keep the tempo, then we did the songs. . . . Behar would say the usuls—this is düyek, this is aksak . . . this is aksak semai. . . . There were no notes. Yes, it was just like meşk [beats usul] . . . your thighs would get red.[10]

The teacher of Yusuf's lesson, David Behar, to be sure, was considered an usul master among classical musicians in Istanbul.[11] Here he is teaching in a traditionalist meşk fashion by beating the usul, a primary mnemonic and core element of oral learning, which correlated in intimate ways with melody and lyrics.[12] Masters typically modeled the usul first, then sang the entire piece and reviewed it section by section, correcting or repeating areas that students did with difficulty or mistakes. In his teaching Behar represented, as we have learned, the ongoing interaction between Jewish and non-Jewish traditionalist musicians in meşk venues in the civic republican realm, in this instance, teaching separate groups of boys like Yusuf Altıntaş.[13]

While the usul offered one mnemonic device during meşk, the song-text collection (*güfte mecmuası*) offered another, and was generally used in oral learning. Singers at David Behar's Maftirim session probably read from the song-text collection *Shire Yisrael be-Erets ha-kedem* (henceforth *Shire Yisrael*), published in Istanbul circa 1921, which, according to Samuel Benaroya, was also used in Edirne before his departure in 1934. The work remains in the libraries of older-generation hazanim and congregants in Istanbul today, and forms the

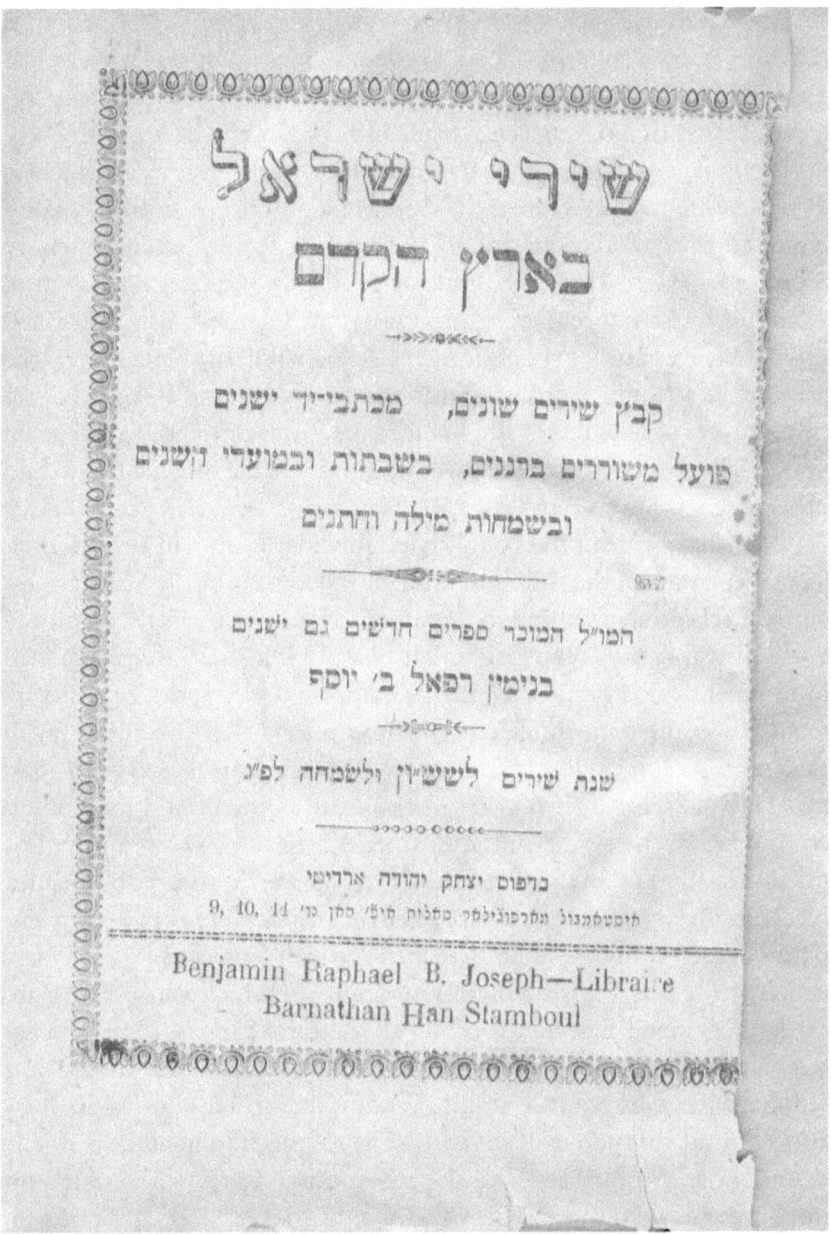

Title page of the song-text collection *Shire Yisrael be-Erets ha-kedem*, published in Istanbul circa 1921. Reproduced by permission from the estate of Hazan Samuel Benaroya, belonging to Judith Amiel and on loan to the Sephardic Studies Initiative, University of Washington.

basis for learning in David Sevi's in-synagogue group.¹⁴ In practice, the *Shire Yisrael* collection would have provided Maftirim learners like Yusuf Altıntaş the equivalent of manuscripted Ottoman song-text collections, that is, lyrics, makam, usul, and composer's name, with compositions arranged according to makam. However, the songbook also introduced new characteristics: whereas manuscripted books were intended for personal, instructional use and not for documenting entire repertoires, *Shire Yisrael*, printed by Benjamin Raphael B. Joseph in Istanbul, was comprehensive, incorporating for their historical value songs that were probably no longer performed.¹⁵ In the words of the preface, "the singing group Maftirim and the erudite İsak A. Navon (1859–1952) [toiled] to salvage many songs from tattered, worm-eaten manuscripts, some of them three hundred years old, which would otherwise have been lost."¹⁶

The songbook can thus be situated in wider Ottoman Jewish intellectual currents of the time and understood as a part of Jewish enlightenment scholarship aiming to document Jewish history and culture in a scientific fashion—scholarship that boasts a long, if underrecognized until recently, history.¹⁷ Its preface, composed of a series of endorsements by prominent intellectuals of the period (Chief Rabbi Hayim Becerano; Soloman Rosanes, 1862–1938; Abraham Danon 1857–1925; and Hayim Nahman Bialik, 1873–1934), extols the book's methodical comprehensiveness and cultural value in a time of social and political upheaval. The endorsing scholars congratulate the publisher for recording Jewish musical culture after the displacements in early twentieth-century conflicts, in particular the Balkan Wars and World War I, which witnessed Jewish emigration from former Ottoman cities, including occupied Edirne, the center of Maftirim singers, to urban centers within shrinking imperial borders and abroad. Rabbi and scholar Soloman Rosanes points out in his endorsement that musical mastery and cultural unity had declined owing to the fragmentation of the empire after World War I and the incorporation of Jewish communities into other nations.¹⁸ The Ukrainian-born poet and writer Hayim Nahman Bialik, moreover, enlarges the mission of the book by referring to the paraliturgical Maftirim songs as "folk music" capable of renewing Hebrew culture as a whole, conveying notions of Jewish heritage based in German Romanticism, and Hebraist and Zionist trends of the period to cultivate linguistic and artistic national culture. In his words, "if Hebrew song is destined to be revived, there is no doubt that it will draw its strength from the vast well of Eastern music," and not presumably European or Ashkenazi Jewish music.

Through its preface, then, the song compilation conveys the intellectual documentary mission of contemporaneous Ottoman and Eastern European Jewish scholars and rabbis to rescue and revive Jewish culture, its music feared in peril because of wars and fragmentation of the empire as well as secularization among Jews in general.[19] In practice, *Shire Yisrael* was used like Ottoman-era manuscript song-text collections—in an era of high Maftirim activity in Istanbul, bolstered by the very migrations motivating *Shire Yisrael*'s publication. In fact, the book joined a wider trend since the early twentieth century of publishing and disseminating music in songbook and notated form for a Turkish public continuing to learn orally from music societies, private lessons, gazinos, and records.[20] Yusuf Altıntaş's memories, moreover, evidence the ongoing utility of non-notated, lyrics-only learning aids into the late 1950s.

The Maftirim notation project, completed in the same decade (1926) by Kirkor Çulhayan under the auspices of Chief Rabbi Hayim Becerano's office and motivated by preservationist and modernizing objectives, was, as discussed earlier, never published. Referring to the importance of the scores as an addendum to the song collection, the endorsers discuss the fragility of orally transmitted music and, in Bialik's view, "the primitive style of notation currently included at the bottom of each page, which only hints at the melody." His Eurocentric perspective echoes similar views of late Ottoman and republican musicians, afraid that past compositions might be lost in an era of changing learning philosophies and concerned with representing the music in a legitimate, modern manner. In fact, Çulhayan completed the Maftirim scores in the mid-1920s, at a time when republican music schools such as the Belediye Konservatuarı (formerly Darülelhan) and Darüttalim-i Musıki undertook extensive notation projects, with musicologist Rauf Yekta Bey (1871–1935) heading the musical-scoring projects of Darülelhan's Türk Musıkisi Tasnif ve Tesbit Heyeti (Turkish Music Classification and Notation Committee), established in 1926.[21] Likewise, Çulhayan's scores, intended for publication but remaining in manuscript form, can be understood as a similar effort to modernize and document

150 Into the Future

oral forms of Hebrew religious music.²² Apparently, the manuscripts left the country with emigrating hazanim İsak Algazi and Moşe Kordova, who, to the best of our knowledge, divided the materials between them in their respective cities of Montevideo and Tel Aviv.²³ Representing a documentary loss to the Istanbul Jews, the scores nonetheless lacked practical utility for congregations that in the end maintained non-notational transmission during subsequent decades.

Even though it is uncertain what written or printed texts Yusuf Altıntaş used as a youth attending Maftirim lessons and sessions in the 1950s, it is clear which documentary impulses in the shifting musical sands of the 1920s prevailed into his childhood decades later. The published songbook and manuscript scoring initiatives, unprecedented in Jewish religious music-making, in part reflected interests among Ottoman Jewish scholars and their European counterparts in empirically grounded documentation of cultural history and in part paralleled trends in Turkish musical society toward practical music publications

Maftirim group under the leadership of David Behar (*seated, with back to the camera*), circa 1985. The group, performing in the Ahrida synagogue in Istanbul, includes David Sevi (*in profile, left of Behar*). Reproduced by permission from Gözlem Gazetecilik Basın ve Yayın, Istanbul.

and modern documentation of Ottoman oral forms. Their respective use and nonuse, however, confirm the persistence of oral transmission in both classical Turkish and Hebrew religious music: the active and intensive scoring of compositions in the early Republic did not eclipse oral learning, but rather resulted in the partial use of notation, whether for modern appearances or for mnemonic suggestion.[24] Synagogues as sites of Maftirim sessions correlated with widespread, contemporaneous public venues for meşk learning in Istanbul, such as music societies, home salons, or informal radio sessions, active in the first fifty years of the Republic.[25] As such, mnemonic aids such as usul-beating, printed lyrics, and vocal repetition were the learning tools that furthered acquisition of the Maftirim repertoire. Moreover, since Maftirim performances were also attended by non-Jews, for example, Kani Karaca and others,[26] and since there were interreligious interactions between musicians in the civic realm, the synagogue was not an isolated enclave of traditionalist practices limited to a religious minority, but rather a meşk venue like others in the city supporting relatively open performances.

"A Beautiful Bouquet of Flowers Comes Out"

The meşking of Maftirim music represents only a part of the ongoing aural-oral dimension of synagogue liturgy. Though not unusual in religious worship across cultures and historical periods, the oral dimension of republican-era Turkish Jewish liturgies is significant because it reflects continuities with Ottoman patterns of transmission and improvisation through its reliance on memory skills, developed with the help of mnemonic aids during meşking. Hazanim who participated in paraliturgical Maftirim gatherings performed prayer services using the same musical skills. Specifically, in addition to Torah cantillation and the performance of precomposed songs and congregational singing during services, hazanim engaged in *serbest okuma*, or "free singing," which made up the bulk of their solo singing and demanded the aural-oral skills of a fine ear and memory.[27] They drew upon a wide pool of both religious and non-religious classical music in order to improvise and adapt during serbest okuma. As hazan Victor Beruhiel explains, his teacher İsak Maçoro was one of his musical sources: "Memory is important. In the moment, you create things out of your head and present them to the people. These melodies are connected to all the rehearsing you have done. Even now Maçoro's melodies come to me. I hear his voice in my ears."[28] Hazanim also drew on classical music performed outside the synagogue:

> Whenever Turkish classical music was on the radio or television, we try not to miss it. Why? So our ears would become full of this music. Whenever we sing at the teva, at least one of these melodies comes to you.[29]

> [Free singing] could come from *sanat müziği* [art music]. I heard [things] from hazanim. These [kinds of songs] were in melodies I heard since I was a child. These impressed themselves on my ear and I blend them with my own feelings and sing them out.[30]

By its content, serbest okuma reveals historical connections between synagogue music and classical Turkish compositions, and by its manner of creation, parallels the skills and processes necessary to improvise in all classical music. For example, in order to perform taksims, an improvisatory form to introduce or modulate to new makams, one also needs a storehouse of remembered and retrievable melodic material.[31] Historically, this form was performed vocally in the synagogue for musical reasons identical to those in nonreligious contexts:

> The same way there was a taksim that instrumentalists did in the introduction—an introductory taksim or a modulating taksim to another makam—these same taksims were improvisations done vocally. It's as if it came from inside, but within a definite framework of rules, within a definite makam—expressing feelings of that moment.[32]

Again, memory and a wide absorption of classical music by ear were skills vital for performing taksims in the synagogue. According to David Sevi, he repeats the first prayer of the service as taksim to aurally establish the makam of the day, drawing upon an internalized core of classical song, absorbed over time:

> [Memory] is absolutely important. However much you know, however many pieces you know . . . because every piece has its own special melody and emotions, each very different. If you make a bouquet from these, a very different synthesis comes out. It's very important for improvising. . . . However many pieces you listen to and know and learn, you take a line from here, a line from there, a line from another place, and a beautiful bouquet of flowers comes out.[33]

Unlike precomposed songs and cantillation of the Torah portion for the week, vocal taksims and serbest okuma are performance-generated compositions:

> When I begin to sing, there is just the beginning makam in my head. That day I have an idea of the makam. Say, today we'll do Hicaz makam. That's all I think of, but what will come out, I have no idea. We'll do Hicaz, but what will go with Hicaz, what music, what influences, I don't know. . . . I don't prepare for this. I just begin and later things come to me. . . . [The music] comes from everywhere, from all the melodies and music in my memory, [acquired] over the years.[34]

For such improvisatory forms what was required of hazanim was extensive classical music skill and repertoire knowledge—facility with using makam and memory for both religious and nonreligious pieces in creative permutation. In fact, in Ottoman meşk musical memory was considered even more important than other endowments, such as a fine voice, for acceptance as an apprentice to a master, because it supported retaining single pieces, passing on entire repertoires, and recollecting heard songs for improvisatory forms.[35] While pre-composed Maftirim compositions required a skilled ear and memory for acquisition, the composition-in-performance of serbest okuma and vocal taksims demanded the ability to recollect from a large reservoir of memorized pieces. Since improvisatory forms constituted significant parts of the prayer service, the aural-oral prerequisites for their performance arguably promoted, until relatively recently, the cultivation of memory and oral arts in the synagogue. Their creation also rested upon immersion in nonreligious music, the classical Turkish genres heard on radio, television, and gazino stages. This popular dimension, of course, was shared by congregations that, through their interest and knowledge, also influenced performance and transmission patterns in the synagogue.

"They Clap, They Say 'Bravo!'"

In order to understand continuities in musical transmission between 1920 and 1980, it is important, as well, to visualize the urban environment of Istanbul's synagogues and their congregations—environments that intensified the dimension of oral learning among Turkish

Jews, and possibly other ethno-religious communities, in comparison with Turkish music education in the general society. As a religious minority, Turkish Jews historically lived in neighborhoods that regularized and intensified exposure to their congregations' musical forms through such cultivating elements as an active daily and annual liturgical calendar. A number of the current hazanim in Istanbul, now in their middle years, grew up in such districts, after which, under conditions of accelerated emigration, they moved to outlying communities initially reconstituted around new synagogues. As Victor Beruhiel remembers:

> Every day, every morning, every evening we would go to the synagogue. When we were students, before we went to school we'd go to synagogue for prayers. Then we'd go to school. When school was out, we'd go running to the synagogue again. The synagogue was only about 50 meters away.[36]

Menahem Eskenazi reports much the same experience:

> In the past we lived in a nearby neighborhood. We lived in Galata. Our house was close. The synagogue was close. We would get out of school and finish our lessons. In the early evening we'd hear hazanim in the synagogue. . . . In this way we learned over time. In the past more hazanim joined morning and evening prayers, so learning by ear was easier. . . . We listened morning and evening. On Saturdays we listened to them.[37]

For Beruhiel, who grew up in Küledibi in the 1950s, such communal, religious, and musical intensity came from sharing a common language and religious law within close multiethnic living quarters:

> In the past we lived in one place . . . not way out in Sarıyer or Beykos or Avcılar.[38] When you opened your window you'd see Moşe across the way . . . you'd see Christo or Yaşar Efendi or Mehmet Efendi. You can't see them anymore.
>
> For Purim, near Apollon synagogue Jews would sell candy, but all in Spanish.[39] Fish-sellers—all in Spanish. Green grocers—all in Spanish. For example, "give me a kilo of this or a kilo of that." The pharmacist, too: "give me something for a rash" [in Judeo-Spanish].
> On Shabbat we couldn't go to Beyoğlu . . . [(because] cinemas and theaters were there. [If we did] we'd be punished: "You can't go to

two [religious] classes." We would cry! It was a big deal, because we had no other entertainment.[40]

Beruhiel's lack of entertainment combined with maternal pride to encourage religious and musical education:

> When the women got together, they'd say, "Do you know, today my son sang Shaharit [morning service]." Oh, really? "Today my son sang Musaf." Another would say, "Today my son read the Torah portion." Or "Today my son sang Song of Songs." This kind of talk happened among our mothers. So, it created competition among us. What did we have to do? We had to learn. We knew our mothers would talk.[41]

Not unlike the interest (and perceived pressure) of neighborhood mothers, the support for the local synagogue came from Jews' attendance at services and reportedly large and enthusiastic audiences for Maftirim performances. Most hazanim and others growing up in Istanbul in the 1950s and '60s remember the social intimacy of these sessions, bringing together large audiences of men, women, and children, and echoing listeners' enthusiasm for classical Turkish music in general. In the early 1960s, according to David Sevi, five or six hundred people came to the session at Neve Şalom synagogue: "The whole synagogue was filled. . . . It's as if I have a photo in my mind of this."[42] "[Neve Şalom] wasn't crowded," commented Victor Beruhiel, "it was super-crowded."[43] And in 1950s Balat, Yanbol synagogue was "full, top to bottom," according to childhood resident Rıfat Dana, as were the sessions at Selaniko synagogue later, the site of the last Maftirim gathering in Balat at the end of the decade.[44]

The weekly audience at synagogue and Maftirim gatherings was significant in the ongoing performance and transmission of Hebrew religious music. Whatever the size, an audience, in effect, can co-create a performance through its musical taste, knowledge, and interaction with performers, thus affecting the quality and frequency of transmission.[45] The Maftirim repertoire in particular attracted devout and less devout listeners, blending as it did the religious and nonreligious, the historical and the contemporary, through its pieces by Ottoman-Jewish composers (e.g., Tanburi İsak and Avtaliyon) and republican Jewish composers (e.g., İsak Varon and Hayim Becerano); adaptations of popular non-Jewish compositions (e.g., by Yusuf Paşa and İsmail

Hakkı Bey); and works on both religious and twentieth-century topical social concerns.[46] According to attendees and performers in their middle years, the gatherings encompassed entertainment and worship, providing a weekly venue to hear a classical fasıl with religious content. In the eyes of one hazan, "[crowds came because] everyone listened to the radio, where they broadcast live music. People weren't longing for American or European things."[47] For one current Maftirim vocalist, the pieces included a meaningful religious dimension through the Hebrew texts, while simultaneously satisfying his love of classical Turkish music.[48] Alternatively, for Yusuf Altıntaş, his lifelong interest in the nonreligious classical repertoire developed from the Maftirim sessions he attended as a boy.[49] Such rich mixtures in the sacred fasıl and its interplay between the religious and nonreligious drew an audience acculturated to the classical Turkish music of the day. Through their informed receptivity and participation, congregations became essential to musical performance and transmission within the synagogue.

Currently expressed in terms of losses, the cultivating qualities of synagogue audiences included a musical taste for classical Turkish music, extensive knowledge of makam usage, and constructive interaction, both negative and positive, with religious singers. As Victor Beruhiel regretfully relates, "The old taste has gone. . . . [In the past] everyone knew the language, the makam, which makam would be sung on which day—everybody knew and they looked for it. [They'd notice] if something doesn't sound right. But now you could sing Isfahan or Kürdilihicazkar makam [and it doesn't matter]."[50] Such familiarity with makams was pervasive among music aficionados. Jewish listeners in the synagogue were able to identify, sing, or request a range of makams.[51] During a visit to a synagogue in 2006 I met several members over the age of fifty who sang and labeled makams with ease during our conversation. Likewise, in the past, says Victor Beruhiel, "on Shabbat evenings everyone waited to sing with the makam. Now people don't want to. When you do something like this, you need a good crowd of [informed] people."[52] Moreover, listeners knew the music well enough to critique performers: "In our time all hazanim had to know everything, because the people wanted it. If a note sounded wrong, a melody sounded wrong, the voice sounded wrong—the people paid attention to these things."[53]

Whether inviting correction or anticipating appreciation, hazan Beruhiel remembers showing off his musical skill in the past because of the audience:

> When more knowledgeable people come, you try to be better. . . . That type of reaction, that type of chemistry, no longer exists. The people are very important. You do something, they like it. They clap. They say "Bravo!" [Now] they don't say "bravo" anymore. They don't clap. If you learn something or not, it's all the same. The old taste isn't there anymore.[54]

Thus, through the 1970s Jewish congregants themselves helped to regulate and enrich synagogue performance, providing a kind of quality control through their own musical knowledge and expectations. In turn, hazanim were more likely to extend their expertise to please listeners and fulfill their high standards. The audience-performer relationship had empirical impact on the quality and complexity of performance, and therefore transmission of the same to youth, as evidenced by one experienced hazan's more recent simplification of his own skills based on new listeners seeking greater musical uniformity and shorter services:

> When you sing a makam you don't settle on one makam, but pass from one to another, for example, from Hüzzam you go to Nikris makam, from there you go to Rast; from Rast you go to Hicazkar; from there to Kürdilihicazkar; from there to Saba. But unfortunately, the youth don't like this now. They like it all in one makam.
>
> [Choices] are connected with the hazan's discretion. If it's his discretion, if the people behind him are on the same wavelength, the hazan can do various things. But if the people behind him are putting pressure on him, thinking, "Come on, Victor, quick, let's get going," as a hazan we say okay, we simplify things, we do fewer makam modulations. The old synagogue discipline is not with us anymore, unfortunately.[55]

Thus, congregants and their musical taste, knowledge, and willingness to spend time in the synagogue—the so-called old synagogue discipline—directly correlated with the complexity, length, and quality of this hazan's performance. Aside from the performer's experience and skill, it was the presence or absence of audience ap-

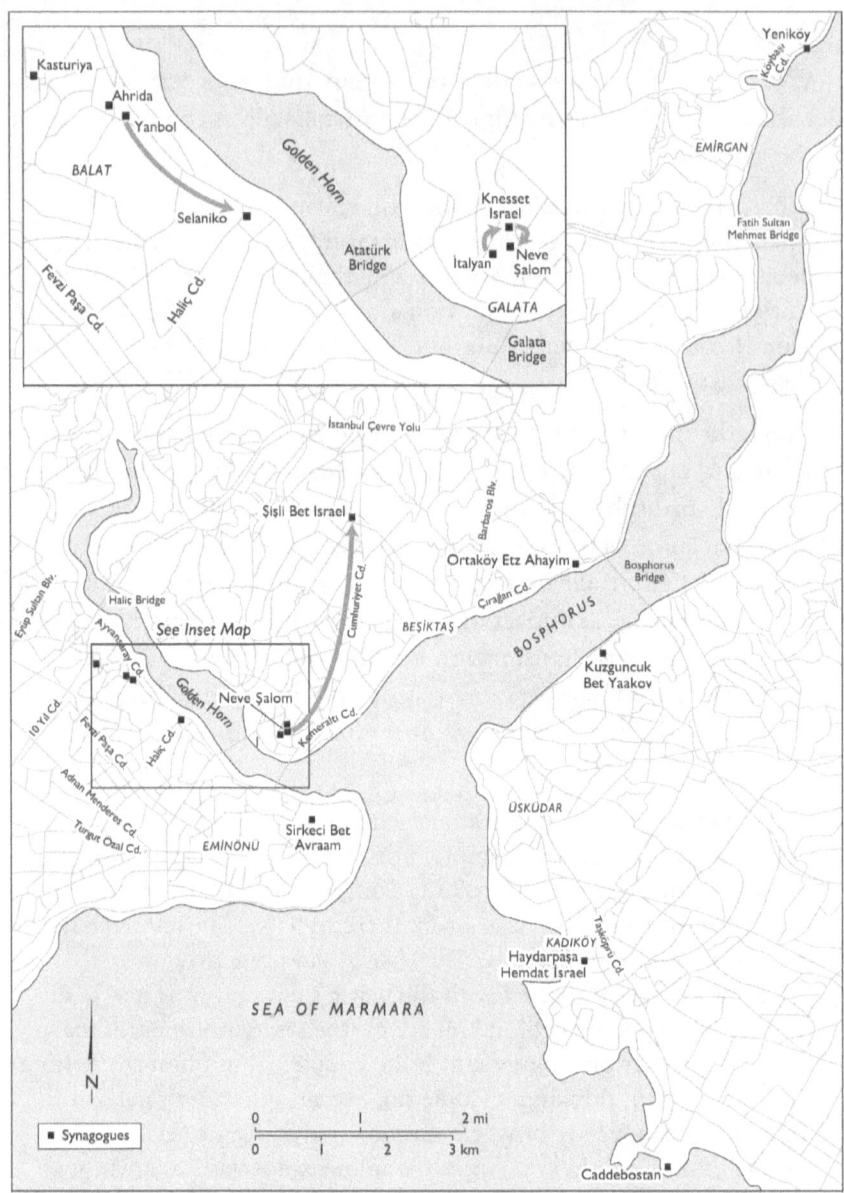

Maftirim gatherings in twentieth-century Istanbul. On both sides of the Golden Horn synagogues hosted Maftirim groups. In Balat, Maftirim gatherings moved from abandoned to active synagogues: Ahrida and Kasturiya (up to 1937), Yanbol (through the 1940s), and Selaniko (1950s). In Galata, groups moved from smaller to larger spaces to accommodate audiences in the first half of the twentieth century: İtalyan (up to 1922), Knesset Israel (1920s–1940s), and Neve Şalom (1950s). The current Maftirim group at Şişli Bet Israel (1960s to present) reflects intraurban movements of Turkish Jews away from historical central districts, especially in the second half of the century.

preciation that determined whether he transmitted a soundscape of multiple makams and their modulating patterns or a single makam during his prayer service—and greater or lesser musical material to potential learners.

One of the reasons for the ongoing significance of community to musical transmission is that, even as large-scale emigration of Turkish Jews, especially after World War II, and changing residency patterns in Istanbul emptied older neighborhoods of Jewish residents, in the new communal clusters in outlying districts religious life initially circulated around newer synagogues. On the one hand, emigration caused a reduction in the size of communities, and thus also a reduction in religious and musical activity, while on the other hand, it promoted the coalescence of the remaining Jews around new urban centers.[56] For example, the synagogues in Şişli and Caddebostan, renovated or built in the early 1960s, began to serve residents who were moving, or had moved, from older districts, where synagogues closed from the 1960s through the 1980s, beginning with Balat and Hasköy (Maalem and Selaniko synagogues closed in the 1960s), then Galata (Zülfaris and Knesset Israel closed in 1978 and 1982 respectively).[57] In part because of long-term factors cultivating Hebrew religious music—the intertwining of neighborhood, synagogue, and art music—initially religious observance and Maftirim performance reconstituted themselves at these newer synagogues. To the best of our knowledge, Maftirim sessions diminished and migrated with the movement of Jewish residents: in the 1950s there were regular performances in Balat (at the Yanbol, then Selaniko synagogues) and Galata (Neve Şalom and to a lesser extent, Knesset Israel), after which, by 1961, singers and listeners met at Şişli synagogue.[58] Such reconstitution provided a measure of musical continuity and transmission, until subsequent changes in residency and religious observance: "There aren't hazanim that [young people] can listen to. Because they don't live in nearby neighborhoods, they can't come [to synagogue]. It's necessary to come continuously and absorb the melodies into your ears. But they can't listen. They can't always come even on Saturdays."[59] Currently, young Jews often live far from the synagogue, in contrast to many middle-aged hazanim, who grew up in older neighborhoods where the synagogue was an integral part of the neighborhood. These

The ruins of Selaniko synagogue in Balat, located on Mürsel Paşa Caddesi (2006). A Maftirim group reportedly met here in the 1950s, and holidays and weddings were celebrated in the synagogue until 1969. Photo by author.

demographic trends together with a decrease in the number of classical masters and changes in musical taste motivated preservationist activities of new texts and recordings after 1980.[60]

Mourning Musical Losses

Concomitant with the unraveling of densely populated Jewish neighborhoods and the observance of daily, local services, changes in the popularity of classical Turkish music and gazino entertainment in the general society have meant a significant decrease in the necessary musical foundation for effective ear learning, even among young, observant congregants attending synagogue. Most hazanim in their middle years included in their childhood descriptions a social life offering leisure and enrichment through listening to live radio performances of classical Turkish music as well as to records and Maftirim sessions themselves.[61] Moreover, because of the onerous task of teaching young people, perceived as enjoying different pleasures today (the internet, multichannel television, and cars), some professional hazanim choose not to teach youth, even if they are motivated and interested, further reducing opportunities for master-pupil apprenticeship:

> I can't teach young people. . . . I ask them, "Do you listen to Turkish classical music." "No." "Do you know any songs." "No, I don't. . . ." "What do you listen to?" "Pop," they say. If you teach Turkish music, but they don't have the voice and ear, it's not possible to get the outcome you desire. . . . After teaching one or two songs, it ends.[62]

The synagogue shares such changes in taste and audience with other classical music venues in the city, testifying to its ongoing integration with Turkish musical culture. In particular, both synagogue and gazino performers offer similar melancholy reports about the "taste" (*zevk*) and quality of their audiences, bemoaning declines in listeners' knowledge, expectations, and performer-audience chemistry. Whereas informed congregations had interacted productively with hazanim to enliven, enrich, improve, and extend performances in the synagogue, today some performers complain that this kind of "old taste" or "discipline" has been lost. Musical responses to new expectations have included simplifying and speeding up prayer services through reducing makam usage or avoiding new material. Likewise, gazino musicians have mourned the "dramatic qualitative decline in taste" of audiences in the 1990s, adjusting to new listeners in ways not unlike hazanim, such as including more folk genres and rhythms in their programs for the younger generation.[63] Although their adjustments may differ in detail, musicians in both contexts have expressed a sense of alienation from audiences lacking expertise in classical music.

Despite disdain for or resignation to changing musical tastes and listeners, both synagogue and gazino musicians have attempted to bolster audiences in different ways for different reasons. In an era of declining religious observance, synagogues have sought to increase attendance at services by, for instance, using music as an enticement: "One must not use makams that make people stay away from the synagogue. There are only 1,000 people wanting to come and pray, with five, six, or seven active synagogues. If a makam is too sentimental, people might leave and not come back."[64] Moreover, through his music the hazan must guide attendees, once in the synagogue, toward the divine and not into difficult emotions: "The hazan doesn't want to break the relationship with God. Hymns are like a bridge to God. If the makam is too sentimental or melancholy, people will leave in a sad mood."[65] Some hazanim respond to requests by members for specific makams on Shabbat, thus satisfying the desires of (probably) older-generation congregants, and intentionally or unintentionally encouraging their return.[66] Gazinos in the 1990s shared a similar concern about enlarging audiences, in their case for commercial interests, with musicians making spontaneous musical changes in performance to alleviate perceived audience indifference and to retain loyal customers, for example through improvising, changing to a faster rhythm, or altering the makam.[67] In these musical strategies, then, classical musicians in both the synagogue and the gazino have generally adapted their expertise to a restricted pool of choices for the purpose of retaining, pleasing, and energizing new audiences for either religious or commercial ends. Depending on the musician, such choices can embody an uneasy tension between a sense of musical decline and a willingness to hold listeners' attention by compromising expertise. In the case of Jewish hazanim, some have focused on irrevocable decline, as in the expression above of the waning taste and enthusiasm of audiences, whereas others, choosing, for example, makams inspiring worship, are responding to the pragmatic needs of a new era.

New Technologies: Photographing Proteus?

A series of factors sustained oral transmission of liturgical music in synagogues until approximately 1980, despite a progressive and significant emigration of Jews from Turkey. Those considered master musicians continued to interact with their counterparts in the republican civic realm, remaining current with classical music developments and transmitting expertise to youth in the synagogue. Maftirim sessions and lessons represented opportunities for meşk-style learning, while improvisatory aspects of Jewish liturgical services in particular called for the cultivation of ear-learning and memory arts necessitating meşk methods and oral transmission. Socially, relatively close neighborhoods and daily prayer services promoted religious and musical learning among youth, even as Jewish lovers of nonreligious classical music productively engaged with, or co-created, religious performance through their own musical expertise and expectations. With the increasing intraurban dispersion of Jewish residents in Istanbul, changing musical taste and knowledge, and the emigration (David Behar) or death (İsak Maçoro) of those considered masters, by the end of the twentieth century oral learning appeared insufficient for transmitting the Maftirim repertoire, and in response diverse documentary projects were undertaken. Until then, Maftirim singers and Jewish hazanim had participated in broader trends in Turkish classical music, continuing to learn via Ottoman-era methods in an era promoting European music and practice. Communal opportunities expanded, moreover, through the social cohesion, religious observance, and secular musical interests of a numerically declining religious minority.

Starting in the 1980s several notational and recording initiatives documented the extant Maftirim repertoire in diverse ways. The retirement of Maftirim masters and step-by-step reduction of orally transmittable pieces were among the perceived musical losses motivating such initiatives.[68] Projects included scores by Fatih Salgar with David Behar in the mid-1980s, recordings of three masters (Isak Maçoro, David Behar, and David Sevi) in 1987, and a CD by the Sinagog Maftirim Korosu under the direction of Aaron Kohen in 2001.[69] Most recently, the Ottoman-Turkish Sephardic Culture Research Center produced a major multimedia Maftirim publication in 2009. Interestingly, despite their documentary media, the scoring and recording projects of the 1980s can be understood as preservationist initiatives to intensify the longtime oral learning already taking place at the time or anticipated in the future. An examination of the real-life use of the new media as well as the people using them, like those in the Sinagog Maftirim Korosu rehearsal, challenges assumptions about textualization and loss of orality. The single recordings, not released commercially, were reportedly made for teaching purposes and, as aural media, would provide opportunities for ear-learning from those considered masters of the repertoire.[70] To be sure, the scores by Fatih Salgar translated live performance into a textual and visual medium (notation) but, through the nature of their transcription and use, they were integrated into aural-oral rehearsal practices rather than introducing significantly divergent methods. By remaining written (but not published or photocopied) and utilized as a mnemonic guide for the conductor only, the scores did not widely disseminate single versions of variable orally transmitted compositions—a tendency in print media—but rather were used as skeletal guides by teachers maintaining oral learning and variation.[71] The teachers themselves, moreover, as older-generation musicians acculturated in meşk methods, would be unlikely to fully integrate new media into their teaching.[72] Such instructional continuities maintained a communal function of oral transmission, that is, learning within earshot only, as musical leaders did not proceed with wider dissemination of scores through replication.[73] The later commercial CD production of the performing Maftirim group in 2001 does disseminate particular arrangements, interpretations, and vocal sound to a wider audience in a global marketplace, and, as the only popular CD currently available, may standardize listener reception of the repertoire. In general, however, before the current research project, new media for the Maftirim repertoire may appear to diverge from past transmission patterns, but in fact were intended or utilized to promote oral learning from earlier decades for present and future learners in a diminishing local community.[74]

The Maftirim project of the Ottoman-Turkish Sephardic Culture Research Center is a striking turning point in the documentation of the music. As a multimedia initiative (recordings, lyrics, and notation) with translations into multiple languages, published, sold, and distributed, the project carries with it the broadest mediatization, linguistic diversity, and dissemination of all the cultural preservation efforts thus far. Clearly, the project communicates the music beyond the hearing of Turkish Jewry alone to a diverse, potentially international audience. The overall mission of the sponsoring research center is to collect, archive, and document Sephardic Turkish cultural forms to promote the survival of traditions and the Ladino language, as well as the understanding of diverse urban centers where Sephardim historically resided. Focused on the arts, religion, the press, and culinary arts, the center has chosen to document the Maftirim repertoire, in part because past ethnographic researchers have concentrated almost exclusively on Ladino folk music to the exclusion of Hebrew religious music and its Ottoman-Turkish theoretical system. In collaboration with the Hebrew University of Jerusalem, the center has produced compact discs of the 1987 archival recordings (Maçoro, Behar, and Sevi), printed notation, Hebrew lyrics with translations into Turkish, Ladino, and English, as well as a historical introduction by ethnomusicologist Edwin Seroussi.[75]

Justifiably heralded as the most comprehensive research-based archival project on the Maftirim repertoire to date, the project contains rich material for investigating the implications of diverse mediatization and the distribution of a centuries-old orally transmitted practice. How will the publication shape the legacy of Maftirim music for future generations of scholars, students, and local residents? Will its textual and recorded documentation reduce complexity and variability through the loss of the oral dimension? What impact will the project have on how we hear, understand, learn, and think historically about Maftirim music—its social history and urban landscape—in the future?

In any music-related archival or documentary project, questions of audience, musical content, type of media, and distribution come into play, influencing the project's academic use, listener reception, and practical application.[76] On the one hand, the publication represents rich academic source material for a repertoire with few remaining masters and a history of attrition of compositions. Project choices, such as university sponsorship, translation of lyrics and academic text into Turkish, Ladino, and English, and notated transcriptions of all pieces expand the potential audience beyond previous initiatives for in-house use among Turkish Jews to non-Jews in Turkey, international scholars, interested musicians, and diaspora communities. Like any documentation of oral forms, on the other hand, the music as recorded has the potential of becoming "*the* song" to an academic, musically literate audience: "Proteus [is] photographed," according to a classic of oral theory, arresting the multiple past versions performed by vocalists for their audiences.[77] Moreover, readers and listeners of scholarly, research-based productions may grant authority to the work in a way that influences perception, or reconstruction, of what constitutes tradition.[78]

In republican Turkey, the concept of "*the* (classical) song" has gained ground primarily through the gradual acceleration of notating Ottoman and classical Turkish compositions. In the 1920s both the Belediye Konservatuarı and Darüttalim-i Musıki undertook extensive notation projects, as outlined earlier, with the former seeking to establish "authentic originals" closer to European notions of classical composition, and the latter maintaining an Ottoman sense of versions-within-limits, that is, compositions actualized in performance and legitimized through reference to the masters who transmitted them. For example, an Ottoman performer might have said, "Ben bu eseri üstadlarımdan böyle meşketmiştim, değiştirilmesine de razı değilim" ("I learned this piece in this way from my masters; I'm not willing to change it").[79] Whereas in an instructional world of master-pupil chains, such versioning was not considered a problem, later, the increasing notation of Ottoman-Turkish pieces cultivated an assumption that originals existed or could be reconstructed.[80] Even though some early republican composers themselves published versions of their own pieces (for example, Refik Fersan, 1893–1965) and musicians continue to modify pieces in performance, what was historically considered "the enemy of the theory of music" (notation) has itself become the enemy of orally transmitted versions, with well-respected musicians and theorists (for example, Rauf Yekta and Suphi Ezgi) authenticating certain scores as "original" to the exclusion of other possibilities.[81] Thus, currently a tension exists between divergent notions of fidelity to classical composition, one seeking authoritative, single sources to notate, the other echoing past notions of versioning through altering notes.[82]

Similarly, the Maftirim repertoire, filled as it is with Ottoman Jewish compositions and adaptations of non-Jewish pieces, was historically actualized in performance. Transmitted from master to pupil, the repertoire certainly perpetuated versions of compositions, even in the twentieth century, when more than one Maftirim gathering, led by different conductors, was held in Istanbul. Despite oral patterns of performance and instruction, however, 5-staff notation is highly esteemed by numerous Jewish informants, including hazanim who learned orally and cannot read notation.[83] This trend is unsurprising in a twentieth-century world of Turkish music education, in which European instructional methodologies have been valorized and musical literacy conceptually conflated with other, modern forms of literacy, prioritized through the Ministry of Education since the early years of the Republic. The coexistence of historical oral transmission with notational tendencies among Turkish Jews follows a trend in classical music-making in Turkey: a clash between actual oral practices and documentary ideals, between fidelity to variants and fidelity to absolutes. What is interesting about the current Maftirim project, however, is that recordings accompany printed scores that a musician notated by listening to the recordings themselves. The descriptive character of the scores, correlating with specific recorded performances, may enable the understanding that one is studying or learning a specific master's vocal interpretation. If viewed prescriptively as standard compositions, the pieces as performed would be misperceived as authentic originals.[84]

In addition to documentation through notation, "*the* song" may also be represented as such through its aural recording. Single recorded sources survive, and are treasured, partly because of the ephemeral nature of oral transmission and performance, as well as legal injunctions against recording Maftirim songs in the synagogue on Shabbat.[85] Recordings, nonetheless, result from a process of selecting from a pool of innumerable singers, in the end potentially representing particular performers as "masters" or "stars," and their performances as "authentic." Moreover, the production of compact discs duplicates and disseminates to a global audience single versions of compositions that were performed and transmitted locally in multiple forms in the past. This contrasts with the use of the archival cassette recordings in the 1980s, which, like the manuscripted notation of Salgar and Behar, continued to support actualization-in-performance because they were not mass-produced, but rather used in the context of individual oral learning, teaching, and performing. The current CDs, however, showcasing those considered masters of their genre can offer opportunities to learn through a kind of *sanal*, or "virtual" meşk.[86] Ear learning and memorizing of Maftirim pieces are possible through repetitive listening to the CDs of Maçoro, Behar, and Sevi, or through their use with a teacher or conductor.[87] Conceptualized as a selection of past masters and versions drawn from a largely lost pool of historically orally transmitted pieces, the Maftirim repertoire would then be understood in terms of Ottoman notions of music composition, transmission, and performance. The documentation of the music would give scholars and learners the opportunity to analyze or acquire compositional versions performed and authenticated by specific masters in historical master-pupil chains.

Publication and distribution patterns of Maftirim songs in the twenty-first century hold the potential for masking and de-historicizing the Ottoman social and artistic context of the music. In the end, the transmission and historical representation of the repertoire will depend on its reception by readers and listeners. Viewed as "one of one," Maftirim composers, compositions, and performers will be conceived of as singular and authentic for their audience, whether academic researchers or musical learners, in a manner departing from Ottoman notions of performative variability and master-based versions. As "one of many," however, the pieces as performed would not be reduced to "*the* songs" through the project's diverse mediatization and publication, nor would oral learning necessarily end. Rather, the multimedia document would represent a next step in older transmission patterns in practice until recently among Turkish Jews and in line with the complex musicological, social, and urban practices of an Ottoman legacy.

Epilogue

"It's the first time I ever heard my father cry," remembers Judith Amiel, the daughter of Samuel Benaroya. It was the fall of 1952, and the Benaroya family had recently moved to Seattle from Geneva, Switzerland, where her father had settled after leaving Turkey under duress in the mid-1930s. In Seattle he had accepted the position of hazan at Sephardic Bikur Holim synagogue through the mediation of David de Sola Pool, rabbi of the Spanish Portuguese congregation in New York, as well as Senator Warren Magnusen, who circumvented the immigration quotas at the time for Turkish citizens, allowing the family to immigrate. On the evening of Yom Kippur, Benaroya had led services in the synagogue and was preparing to leave for home. To his surprise, the *gabay* (lay leader) approached him and held out some keys. "Tomorrow," he declared, "if you sing as long as you did tonight, you'll have to lock up the place yourself." Returning to his house, Benaroya silently entered his study and closed the door, leaving his wife and daughter to overhear the private aftermath of his first major liturgical performance in the United States.[1]

It may not be surprising that Benaroya's virtuosic vocal style and lengthy delivery, cultivated in late Ottoman synagogues and music spaces, exceeded the expectations of some Turkish Jews who had resided in Seattle for several decades. Since their first arrival at the turn of the twentieth century from Marmara, Tekirdağ, and Rhodes, the immigrant congregations had been led by Ottoman-born rabbis and hazanim, who, nevertheless, interacted with both a first generation and second generation growing up in a new social, musical, and political environment. Benaroya had sent a record from Geneva of two popular liturgical songs for Yom Kippur—"Avinu Malkeinu" and "L'Ma-ancha Elokai"—and, despite dissent by a community leader on the holiday itself, the first-generation congregants reportedly raised their hands in unison to hire Benaroya immediately on the basis of the two songs alone. He is remembered, moreover, as having the power to make congregants weep with his singing, especially on Yom Kippur. He made it a priority to pass on his liturgical expertise to his grandsons and youth in the synagogue, including those who became longtime hazanim in Seattle, such as Isaac Azose and Frank Varon, and, indirectly, those exposed to the singing of his students who relocated to other parts of the United States. At the same time, sociocultural conditions had an impact on, for example, exposure to language, repertoire, and vocal style among a second generation from which religious singers arose.[2] In addition, Benaroya adapted his services to the evolving preferences of his local congregation, relegating certain music-making of his youth in Edirne, such as Maftirim singing, to his home and to interested scholars decades later.[3] Like Ottoman-born émigré religious singers before him—İsak Algazi, who settled in Montevideo, Uruguay, in 1935, and Salonikan singers who immigrated to Tel Aviv before the Holocaust—Benaroya found himself in new social circumstances where he alone bore the memory and mastery of Hebrew Ottoman music.[4]

The present study has investigated the intimately interwoven and changing nature of sociopolitical and musical structures in the late Ottoman empire and Turkish Republic of Benaroya's youth. It has pursued the linked histories of the Turkish Jewish community within an emerging nation, and the sacred Maftirim suite within the urban landscape of Istanbul, to elucidate multireligious Ottoman music-making transitioning and transforming across the twentieth and twenty-first centuries. On the broadest level, the book has written against a cultural narrative of decline that typically parallels the numerical decline of minorities such as Turkish Jewry crossing the empire-nation divide. It has approached music-making in terms of its material and social conditions rather than particular compositions, utilizing ethnographic methodologies and untapped primary and secondary textual sources within the framework of urban space to foreground a musical cross-pollination more complex and sustained than previously believed. The study has made three central arguments. First, late Ottoman Jewish musicians of both secular and religious music and of differing social status circulated variously within the places and practices of Ottoman music-making to facilitate cultural flows integral to the Maftirim repertoire. Their careers at the very center of Ottoman and Turkish musical life revise national music historiography by retrieving Hebrew-only composers, lesser-known religious practitioners, and the synagogue itself from previously assumed social isolation to reintegrate them into a larger social history. Second, the performance of Maftirim songs today stems not only from an interest in Sephardic heritage, but also from the fertility of the Ottoman and Hebrew art music culture that thrived in the first decade of the Turkish Republic. A non-national historical periodization accommodating minority lives, new technologies, and popular culture at the turn of the twentieth century unmasks the unmistakable, albeit fragile, continuities of musical interaction and master-pupil chains until relatively recently, despite the state's European-leaning cultural agenda and anti-minority legislation. Finally, diverse documentation of the Maftirim from the early years of the Republic onward suggests a broad shift from orality to textuality across the century. Oral methods of learning and performing, nonetheless, have proved long-lasting among Turkish Jews. Correlating with ongoing meşk practices at large, in-community oral use of new technologies, co-creation by informed audiences, and the proximity of synagogues in neighborhoods with a shrinking population, oral transmission has intertwined with the visual (texts) and aural (recordings) not to be eclipsed but rather to potentially sustain the historical variability of master-based versions within even the most recent Maftirim productions.

The Jewish composers, entertainers, and religious singers populating this study moved around the late empire and the new nation in ways that imply a wide circulation and exchange of music among urban centers and are linked in some measure with Benaroya's own emigration from Turkey. Hayim Moşe Becerano crisscrossed the Balkans to escape violence and secure employment, going from Zagora to Rusçuk to Bucharest to Edirne, before settling as chief rabbi in Istanbul toward the end of his life. Nesim Sevilya left Istanbul to serve as hazan in Sofia for ten years; Mısırlı İbrahim Efendi moved from his birthplace in Aleppo to Istanbul, touring other areas, such as Egypt, during the early Republic. Ordinary itinerant hazanim, moreover, commonly served modest, outlying communities, while preeminent Jewish musicians left the provinces for the palace to perform. Under pressures of late Ottoman wars, Jewish musicians fled wartime conditions or lost Ottoman territories, including Maftirim singers from Edirne, who bolstered the musical culture of their new homes in the first decade of the Republic. As a city of flight in the late empire, Istanbul has provided the primary terrain for teasing out the quotidian lives of Jewish musicians interacting with their non-Jewish counterparts. These earlier wider musical trajectories, however, testify to historical Jewish involvement in both central and provincial intraurban spaces to meet, perform, learn, and worship, reflecting common Ottoman patronage patterns, aesthetic understandings, and master-pupil relationships, and maintaining—contingent upon a musician's religious rank, personal intermediaries, and commercial or liturgical performance—the synagogue as an urban venue for regularly hearing and learning a sacred fasıl.

After the establishment of the Turkish Republic, Jews like Benaroya progressively left the country in waves stirred up by anti-minority events and policies. Learning of the hazan's plans to emigrate, İsak Maçoro expressed dismay at the departure of such a valued religious singer from an already diminishing Jewish population.[5] It was left to Jewish musicians like Maçoro and Behar to transmit the Maftirim repertoire and their theoretical musical knowledge to a younger generation of Turkish Jews. The roots of their transmission can be found in the burgeoning music scene of Istanbul in the first decade of the Republic—its gazinos, recording studios, and synagogues increasing in number to accommodate musical refugees, notably their teacher Algazi. Under decades-long official patronage of German-Jewish musicians and European curricular development, Turkish Jewish musicians circulated with their musical counterparts among unofficial spaces and patrons, such as home gatherings, practicing court music forms in the synagogue and society at large until the first Turkish music programs were established in conservatories in the mid-1970s.

By then, Benaroya had settled, however uneasily, in his North American city, where he taught Sephardic youth liturgical song by beating the usul, singing verse by verse, and bringing together a whole piece without the use of notation.[6] He had wished he could pass on his musical knowledge, meant for male performers, to his daughter Judith, who showed an ear and enthusiasm for the music, even if untrained, as is clear in her reproductions of melodies, recognition of theoretical elements, and emotional response to poorly rendered songs. "It's not their fault," she would say after her father's death. "They didn't learn it right. To me it's unrecognizable, so it hurts."[7] Others, like her sons and other male members of the congregation, learned liturgical music, if not Maftirim songs, through assiduous instruction from her father before he retired in 1980. In a similar case of gender and religious Jewish music in twentieth-century Istanbul, by reorienting our attention to neighborhood and home we have been able to recapture peripheral and non-performing artists like Janti Behar, exposed not only to

Samuel Benaroya and his daughter, Judith, in Geneva, Switzerland (circa 1948). Reproduced courtesy of Judith Amiel.

Ladino song, but also to soundscapes of Turkish art music that for some girls and women facilitated learning its Hebrew forms. Older-generation women like Janti and Judith represent a hidden legacy of exposure and learning from master fathers and home music-making within divergent social circumstances. Their latent knowledge gains currency in new contexts of preservation-minded communities with few or no surviving master musicians.

In 1998 the CD *Ottoman Hebrew Sacred Songs* was produced by ethnomusicologist Edwin Seroussi, based on recordings of Samuel Benaroya singing Maftirim songs in Seattle in the late 1980s and early 1990s. In 2009 the Maftirim project of the Ottoman-Turkish Sephardic Culture Research Center was published, showcasing remastered archival recordings of David Behar, İsak Maçoro, and David Sevi singing Maftirim songs in Istanbul in the 1980s. Both productions reflect the interest of scholars and community members in capturing and documenting musical heritage feared to be lost through the passing away of musical masters. In both Seattle and Istanbul oral transmission of liturgical music has been relatively long lived, with new technologies such as cassette recordings passed hand to hand for local oral learning rather than commercial distribution. The sale of the CDs through internet sites today, however, extends Maftirim music to those outside the immediate community. In Istanbul this expansive phenomenon coexists with the complexities of living as a small Jewish minority in Turkey: the live and historically informed in-synagogue Maftirim gathering is, in fact, relatively inaccessible to non-Jews, whereas stage productions of Ottoman heritage provide a venue for conciliatory Jewish self-representation in harmony with Islamist political platforms. Beyond Istanbul, the new technologies of the most recent Maftirim productions have the potential to carry music from descent communities and their specific national circumstances to transnational affinity communities composed of aficionados held together by personal interest alone.[8]

Who will listen to the voices of Samuel Benaroya and İsak Maçoro, David Behar and David Sevi in the coming years? How will they understand these songs, rendered in particular ways through chains of masters to students—compositions by Jews or adaptations of non-Jewish pieces performed by innumerable others? Even such a skilled practitioner as Benaroya misinterpreted an Ottoman piece performed by Necdet Yaşar as an adaptation of an original Hebrew Maftirim composition, and not the other way around. His musical circulations as a hazan in Edirne and his distance from Istanbul as an émigré in Seattle shaped the contours of his Ottoman and Turkish music worlds. There are many open questions about the future reception of such migrating musics as the Maftirim. This study has called us to remember the stories embedded in the historical urban landscape of the sacred song as it traversed imperial and national orders. Between the musical lines of contemporary productions, whether notated or aural, we may then find clues about the complex, changing, and conflicted intercommunal history of the music, its makers, and their social spheres. We may then listen to a Maftirim master sing and hear not *the* authentic song, but one of many—and understand why.

Reference Matter

Notes

Introduction

1. Approximate population figures are based on Justin McCarthy, "Jewish Population in the Late Ottoman Period," in *The Jews of the Ottoman Empire*, ed. Avigdor Levy (Princeton, NJ: Darwin Press; Washington, DC: Institute of Turkish Studies, c. 1994), 387, and Kemal H. Karpat, *Ottoman Population, 1830–1914: Demographic and Social Characteristics* (Madison: University of Wisconsin Press, 1985), 408. Figures for late Ottoman Jewry in 1911–1912 refer to the Jewish population living in what is now the Turkish Republic. Şule Toktaş cites a population of 20,000–25,000 in 2003, down from an estimated census figure of 81,400 in 1927. Şule Toktaş, "Turkey's Jews and Their Immigration to Israel," *Middle Eastern Studies* 42 (2006): 506.

2. On migration patterns of Ottoman and Turkish Jewry in the twentieth century, see McCarthy, "Jewish Population in the Late Ottoman Period," and Toktaş, "Turkey's Jews and Their Immigration to Israel."

3. The prolific research and publications of Rıfat Bali have reversed this trend, with a focus on Jews in the first decades of the Republic. Marcy Brink-Danan's work contributes to our understandings of the contemporary community in Turkey. See Marcy Brink-Danan, *Jewish Life in Twenty-first-Century Turkey: The Other Side of Tolerance*, Indiana Series in Sephardi and Mizrahi Studies (Bloomington: Indiana University Press, 2012).

4. See the scholarship of André Levy for anthropological research on the Moroccan Jewish community and its unique structures and strategies for survival, which have remained understudied owing to the small numbers and assumed decline of the community; for example, André Levy, "Notes on Jewish-Muslim Relationships: Revisiting the Vanishing Moroccan Jewish Community," *Cultural Anthropology* 18, no. 3 (2003): 365–97.

5. A roundtable, "The Spacial Turn in Middle East Studies: Interdisciplinary Methods and Approaches," organized by Amy Mills, articulated this interdisciplinary turn among geographers and others through questions of space, place, and landscape related to diverse topics of research in Middle East studies. Middle East Studies Association Annual Meeting, December 1–4, 2011, Washington, DC.

6. Past scholarship referring to cosmopolitanism in the Ottoman capital and port cities successfully challenged long-standing historical assumptions about segregated ethno-religious communities and limited intercommunality in the empire. For recent scholarship seeking to fine-tune, retheorize, or dispense with the term in the area of Ottoman, Turkish, and Jewish Studies, see Brink-Danan, *Jewish Life in Twenty-first-Century Turkey*; Maureen Jackson, "'Cosmopolitan Smyrna': Illuminating or Obscuring Cultural Histories?" *Geographical Review* 102, no. 3 (2012): 337–49; Amy Mills, *Streets of Memory: Landscape, Tolerance, and National Identity in Istanbul* (Athens: University of Georgia Press, 2010); and Sibel Zandi-Sayek, *Ottoman Izmir: The Rise of a Cosmopolitan Port, 1840–1880* (Minneapolis: University of Minnesota Press, 2012).

7. For the seminal critical analysis of the so-called millet system, see Benjamin Braude, "Foundation Myths of the Millet System," in *Christians and Jews in the Ottoman Empire: The Functioning of a Plural Society*, ed. Benjamin Braude and Bernard Lewis (New York: Holmes & Meier, 1982), 1:69–90. For subsequent scholarship and responses, see Michael Ursinas, "Millet," in *Encyclopedia of Islam*, ed. C. E. Bosworth (Leiden: A. J. Brill, 1993), 61–64; Daniel Goffman, "Ottoman Millets in the Early Seventeenth Century," *New Perspectives on Turkey*, no. 1 (1994): 1; and Benjamin Braude, "The Strange History of the Millet System," in *The Great Ottoman-Turkish Civilisation*, ed. Kemal Çiçek et al. (Ankara: Yeni Türkiye, 2000), 409–18.

8. Sephardic immigrant congregations in the United States, for example, have been categorized as Orthodox according to American Jewish congregational divisions (Orthodox, Conservative, Reform). However, the term's usage is problematic for Ottoman and Turkish Jews whose history of religious reform was not characterized by the same divisions. See Norman A. Stillman, *Sephardi Religious Responses to Modernity* (Luxembourg: Harwood Academic Publishers, 1995).

9. For an introduction to a collection of articles tangling with "Sephardi" as a term of Jewish identity, see Matthias B. Lehmann, "Introduction: Sephardi Identities," *Jewish Social Studies: History, Culture, Society* 15, no. 1 (2008): 1–9.

10. *Dönme* refers to a follower of the heterodox rabbi Sabetay Sevi (d. 1676). Well-represented in Salonika, the diverse community appeared in public as Muslim, while continuing to follow Sabetay Sevi's precepts and practices. For the most comprehensive study to date, see Marc David Baer, *The Dönme: Jewish Converts, Muslim Revolutionaries, and Secular Turks* (Stanford, CA: Stanford University Press, 2010).

11. The memoir of Sa'adi Besalel a-Levi, a printer, singer, and composer in Salonika, reflects the tensions experienced by an Ottoman Jewish musician in conflict with rabbinical authority in the mid-nineteenth century. See Aron Rodrigue and Sarah Abrevaya Stein, eds., *A Jewish Voice from Ottoman Salonica: The Ladino Memoir of Sa'adi Besalel a-Levi* (Stanford, CA: Stanford University Press, 2012).

12. For scholarship on the history of Ottoman music, see Cem Behar, "The Ottoman Musical Tradition," in *The Cambridge History of Turkey*, Vol. 3: *The*

Later Ottoman Empire, 1603–1839, ed. Suraiya N. Faroqhi (Cambridge: Cambridge University Press, 2006), 393–407; Walter Feldman, *Music of the Ottoman Court: Makam, Composition and the Early Ottoman Instrumental Repertoire*, Intercultural Music Studies 10 (Berlin: Verlag für Wissenschaft und Bildung, 1996); Walter Feldman, "Music in Performance: Who Are the Whirling Dervishes?" in *The Garland Encyclopedia of World Music: The Middle East* (New York: Routledge, 2002), 107–11; and Maureen Jackson, "Music," in *Encyclopedia of the Ottoman Empire*, ed. Gábor Ágoston and Bruce Masters (New York: Facts on File, 2009), 404–9.

13. See, in particular, the work of Edwin Seroussi, with related studies by Aaron Kohen, Walter Feldman, and Owen Wright (see the References).

14. Shabbat begins at sundown on Friday and ends after dusk on Saturday. Maftirim singers historically gathered on Saturday morning before prayer services. According to religious law, no instruments are allowed in the synagogue on Shabbat.

15. See Sam Lévy, *Salonique à la fin du XIXe siècle: Mémoires* (Istanbul: Isis, 2000), 21; Edwin Seroussi, "The Peşrev as a Vocal Genre in Ottoman Hebrew Sources," *Turkish Music Quarterly* (Summer 1991): 1–2; Edwin Seroussi, "From the Court and Tarikat to the Synagogue: Ottoman Art Music and Hebrew Sacred Songs," in *Sufism, Music and Society in Turkey and the Middle East*, ed. Anders Hammarlund, Tord Olsson, and Özdalga Elisabeth (Istanbul: Swedish Research Institute, 2001), 91; and Edwin Seroussi, *Mizimrat Qedem: The Life and Music of R. Isaac Algazi from Turkey* (Jerusalem: Renanot Institute for Jewish Music, 1989), 33.

16. There is evidence that historically Ottoman mosques were similarly multifunctional, for example as a venue for the Mevlevi ceremony and a variety of music-making that in contemporary orthodox understandings are not appropriate for the mosque.

17. For a detailed review of Hebrew song-text collections, see Edwin Seroussi, "Introduction," in *Maftirim* (Istanbul: Gözlem, 2009).

18. Şarkı is a vocal work that became a prominent and popular part of *gazino* (nightclub) music. The composer Hacı Arif Bey (1831–1885) is heralded in Turkish music history as one of the first and most prolific composers of the genre.

Chapter One

1. *Meşk* is a process of oral teaching and learning of Ottoman music in master-pupil relationships. See Chapter One, page 36.

2. Necdet Yaşar, personal interview, August 8, 2006. Necdet Yaşar mistakenly refers to Tekirdağ, not Edirne, as Benaroya's hometown. Both cities are in Thrace, the region to the west of Istanbul.

3. Ibid.

4. Judith Amiel (daughter of Samuel Benaroya), personal interview, November 14, 2006.

5. M. Selim Gökçe, "Necdet Yaşar: 'Yahya Kemal Bana "Küçük Cemil'im" Derdi,'" *Türk Edebiyatı* 34, no. 393 (2006): 51–52; and Bülent Aksoy, "Necdet Yaşar'la

görüşme," *Necdet Yaşar* (Istanbul: Kalan Müzik, CD 102, 1998), 18. In some sources the year of birth of Tanburi Cemil Bey is 1873.

6. See Note 15 in the Introduction.

7. Walter Feldman, *Music of the Ottoman Court: Makam, Composition and the Early Ottoman Instrumental Repertoire*, Intercultural Music Studies 10 (Berlin: Verlag für Wissenschaft und Bildung, 1996). See also the following albums: Feldman, scholarly notes, *Lalezar: Music of the Sultans and Seraglios*, Vol. III: *Minority Composers* (New York: Traditional Crossroads, CD 4303, 2001); and *Tanburi Isak: Bezmara Music Ensemble* (Thessaloniki: En Chordais, Musical Traditions of the Mediterranean, CD 1918, 2004).

8. Hazan Aaron Kohen, "Osmanlı İmparatorluğunun Kuruluş Yıllarından Günümüze Yahudi Dini Musikisi," *Folklor/Edebiyat* 6, no. 21 (2000–2001): 81–114. *Haham* (plural, *hahamim*) is a religious scholar as well as the head of a congregation who fulfills multiple roles, such as prayer leader, religious teacher, shohet (ritual slaughterer), and visitor of the sick and dying.

9. Among local histories exploring Ottoman social relations in Istanbul, see Cem Behar, *A Neighborhood in Ottoman Istanbul: Fruit Vendors and Civil Servants in the Kasap Ilyas Mahalle* (Albany: State University of New York Press, 2003), and Cengiz Kırlı, "The Struggle over Space: Coffeehouses of Ottoman Istanbul, 1780–1845," Ph.D. dissertation (State University of New York, 2001).

10. See Note 11 in the Introduction.

11. The word "secular" is problematic as an attribute for nonreligious music and performance spaces in the Ottoman context, because of its Eurocentric social and political meanings as well as its reference here to music performed outside of religious contexts but often set to Ottoman love poetry with ambiguous meanings related to earthly or divine love.

12. *Haham, hahambaşı,* and *hazan* are titles for religious positions among Ottoman and Turkish Jewry, which, in practice, involve fluidity of responsibilities, religious education, or musical expertise, depending on the individual as well as the size, needs, and economic status of the Jewish community or a particular congregation. *Hahambaşı* is the head *haham,* or chief rabbi, of a city, region, empire, or nation, serving as administrator over numerous congregations and liaison with the government; a *hazan* is the prayer leader of a single congregation performing religious liturgies. On *haham,* see Note 8 above.

13. An ud is a short-necked fretless lute, the ancestor of the European lute.

14. Such contrafacta include Hebrew texts set to compositions by Jewish or non-Jewish composers of Ottoman court music. For a study of Ottoman-Hebrew contrafacta by Israel Najara based on contemporaneous Ottoman Turkish and other songs, see Andreas Tietze and Joseph Yahalom, *Ottoman Melodies Hebrew Hymns: A 16th Century Cross-Cultural Adventure* (Budapest: Akademiai Klado, 1995).

15. For example, neither musician appears in the standard encyclopedia of Turkish music, Yılmaz Öztuna, *Büyük Türk Musikisi Ansiklopedisi,* 2 vols. (Ankara: Başbakanlık Basımevi, 1990), or in biographical dictionaries of musicians, such as

İbnülemin Mahmut Kemal İnal, *Hoş Sada* (Istanbul: Türkiye İş Bankası Kültür Yayınları, 1958).

16. "Osmanlının Son Cumhuriyetin İlk Hahambaşısı Rabbi Hayim Moşe Becerano (1846–1931)," *Tiryaki* 3 (March 1998): 12–22. The entry for Becerano ("Bejerano, Bekhor Hayyim ben Moses"), which reflects non-Turkish spelling, in the *Encyclopaedia Judaica* records a different date for his birth (1850) and appointment as chief rabbi in Istanbul (1922). S.v. "Bejerano," in Fred Skolnik and Michael Berenbaum, *Encyclopaedia Judaica*, 2nd ed., 22 vols. (Farmington Hills, MI: Keter, 2007), 3:272–73.

17. Zvi Keren, *The Jews of Rusçuk: From Periphery to Capital of the Tuna Vilayeti* (Istanbul: Isis, 2005), 236–38. The Alliance Israélite Universelle, founded in Paris in 1860, established French-Jewish schools in North Africa and the Middle East to promote European post-Enlightenment education, religious reform, and the integration of Jews into their respective societies. Based on collaboration with local Sephardic intellectuals, the first Ottoman schools were built in the Balkans in the 1860s and in Istanbul, Izmir, and Salonika in the 1870s. See Esther Benbassa and Aron Rodrigue, *Sephardi Jewry: A History of the Judeo-Spanish Community, 14th to 20th Centuries* (Berkeley: University of California Press, 2000 [1993]), 83–89; and Aron Rodrigue, *French Jews, Turkish Jews: The Alliance Israélite Universelle and the Politics of Jewish Schooling in Turkey, 1860–1925* (Bloomington: Indiana University Press, 1990).

18. "Osmanlının Son Cumhuriyetin İlk Hahambaşısı Rabbi Hayim Moşe Becerano (1846–1931)," 20; and Oral Onur, *1492'den Günümüze Edirne Yahudi Cemaati* (Istanbul: Oral Onur, 2005), 137. *Şeyh* (sheikh) is the spiritual leader of a Sufi brotherhood. Atatürk, the first president of the Turkish Republic, reportedly stayed with Becerano during his trips between Sofia and Salonika, and spent an extended time with him after the Gallipoli campaign in 1915 during World War I. In a later interview with a journalist, Becerano spoke of Atatürk as a very old and close friend, who visited him in Edirne at least twenty times. In the same interview he used the Arabic numerology of "Gazi Mustafa Kemal" to calculate the year of victory in the War of Independence: 1338, or 1922 (Behçet Kami, "Hahambaşı Becerano İle Mulakat," *İleri*, nr. 1685, 14 Teşrin-i evvel 1338/1922, in Onur, *1492'den Günümüze Edirne Yahudi Cemaati*, 141).

19. See Note 14 in the Introduction. Here the author is referring to prayer services on Saturday in the synagogue.

20. Karabetyan Bedros, *Kirkor Çulhayan Otobiografik Eser*, 1937 (Armenian), as quoted in Hazan Aaron Kohen, "Kirkor Çulhayan Efendi (1868–1938)," *Tiryaki* 1 (October 1994): 23.

21. For example, see Becerano's endorsement in the preface of *Shire Yisrael be-Erets ha-kedem* (Songs of Israel in the Land of the East) (Istanbul: Benjamin Raphael B. Joseph, circa 1921).

22. The Maftirim piece by Becerano is entitled "Hag Amakabim" (Yürük semai usul; Uşşak makam) and is sung for the holiday of Hanukkah.

23. Kohen, "Kirkor Çulhayan Efendi (1868–1938)," 23. See also "Kirkor Çulhayan [Kemani ve Nısfiyezen]," in Öztuna, *Büyük Türk Musikisi Ansiklopedisi,* 1:447.

24. In 1902 Kirkor Çulhayan had established a music store in Bahçekapı where he gave private music lessons, notated music, and met with composers and other musical friends. In 1910 he made his first record, in the same period that İsak Varon and İsak Algazi were making records. Kohen, "Kirkor Çulhayan Efendi (1868–1938)," 19.

25. "Osmanlının Son Cumhuriyetin İlk Hahambaşısı Rabbi Hayim Moşe Becerano (1846–1931)," 12.

26. Ibid., 21.

27. Ibid., 22.

28. Ibid.

29. Kohen, "Kirkor Çulhayan Efendi (1868–1938)," 22.

30. See the recording of Benaroya: Edwin Seroussi, *Ottoman Hebrew Sacred Songs* (Jerusalem: Jewish Music Research Center, 1998).

31. Judith Amiel, personal interview, March 7, 2007.

32. See Note 15 in the Introduction for historical evidence of Mevlevi-Jewish encounters.

33. Biographical information about Reverend Samuel Benaroya is drawn from three sources: personal interviews with Eric Offenbacher (January 17, 1988) and Edwin Seroussi (October 24, 1992); and my personal interviews with his daughter, Judith Amiel (September 11, 2005; November 14, 2006; and March 7, 2007).

34. Samuel Benaroya, interview with Eric Offenbacher, January 17, 1988. The Alliance school in Edirne was founded in 1867. Aron Rodrigue, *Jews and Muslims: Images of Sephardi and Eastern Jewries in Modern Times* (Seattle: University of Washington Press, 2003).

35. Ottoman teachers often evaluated prospective students' ear and memory before accepting them as pupils. For examples from late Ottoman composers, see Cem Behar, *Aşk Olmayınca Meşk Olmaz: Geleneksel Osmanlı/Türk Müziğinde Öğretim ve Intikal,* 2nd ed. (Istanbul: Yapı Kredi Yayınları, 2003 [1998]), 54–56.

36. The exact nature of these learning relationships, whether through indirect exposure or lessons, is not known. Judith Amiel, personal interview, September 11, 2005.

37. Ibid.

38. Ibid., March 7, 2007.

39. *Tarikat* is a Sufi order or brotherhood.

40. Benaroya refers to the Mevlevi performance in the mosque; he is likely referring to the Mevlevi lodge in Edirne.

41. Benaroya is referring to the songbook of Maftirim compositions *Shire Yisrael be-Erets ha-kedem.* See Chapters Two and Five.

42. Samuel Benaroya, interview with Edwin Seroussi, October 24, 1992. Video recording provided by Judith Amiel.

43. *Sema* is the Mevlevi ceremony, a religious choreography. The *ayin* is the accompanying musical suite.

44. Cem Behar, "The Ottoman Musical Tradition," in *The Cambridge History of Turkey*, Vol. 3: *The Later Ottoman Empire, 1603–1839*, ed. Suraiya N. Faroqhi (Cambridge: Cambridge University Press, 2006), 402.

45. Judith Amiel, personal interview, September 11, 2005.

46. Samuel Benaroya, interview with Eric Offenbacher, January 17, 1988.

47. Ibid.

48. Samuel Benaroya, interview with Edwin Seroussi, October 24, 1992.

49. Samuel Benaroya, interview with Eric Offenbacher, January 17, 1988. According to Benaroya, the choir was composed of students he knew from the Alliance school. Though qualified to attend a special school in Istanbul for Hebrew liturgical music, he was unable to go due to lack of funds. Judith Amiel, personal interview, September 11, 2005.

50. The *Trakya Olayları* (Thrace Incidents) in 1934 involved anti-Jewish violence in border cities in Thrace, such as Edirne. See Chapter Two.

51. Samuel Benaroya, interview with Eric Offenbacher, January 17, 1988.

52. Judith Amiel, personal interview, March 7, 2007. After 1972 Benaroya became known among Sephardic-American congregations beyond Seattle for his four-part "Birkat Hamazon" (Grace after Meals).

53. Judith Amiel, personal interview, November 14, 2006.

54. Ibid., September 11, 2005. A *taksim* is an improvisatory, performance-generated composition introducing the makam of the upcoming piece or transitioning between pieces in different makams.

55. See biographical entries for both composers in Öztuna, *Büyük Türk Musikisi Ansiklopedisi*. The compositions of Mısırlı İbrahim Efendi are routinely included in books of lyrics and sets of scores of Turkish classical music. According to his daughter, Mısırlı İbrahim Efendi died of a heart attack in his Galata apartment in 1948. Cem Behar, personal communication, January 19, 2010. Yılmaz Öztuna mistakenly indicates the death date as 1933, s.v. "İbrahim Efendi [Mısırlı Udi Avram]," Öztuna, *Büyük Türk Musikisi Ansiklopedisi*, 1:379–80. Mısırlı İbrahim Efendi should not be confused with Hanende İbrahim (1881–?), who recorded as a vocalist on the Odeon, Orfeon, Favorite, and Columbia labels. For a biography of Hanende İbrahim, see Cemal Ünlü, *Git Zaman Gel Zaman: Fonograf, Gramofon, Taş Plak* (Istanbul: Pan Yayıncılık, 2004), 518.

56. Hazan Aaron Kohen, "Osmanlı İmparatorluğunun Kuruluş Yıllarından Günümüze Yahudi Dini Musikisi," *Folklor/Edebiyat* 6, no. 21 (2000–2001): 81–114; and Hazan Aaron Kohen, "Müziğe Aşık Bir Bestekar Haham Nesim Sevilya Efendi," *Tiryaki* 8–9 (March–April, 1995): 65–70. For a brief period, Nesim Sevilya directed a Maftirim ensemble at Knesset Israel synagogue in Galata-Şişhane, where he moved after his position in Kasturiya in the 1920s. David Sevilya (grandson), in Kohen, "Müziğe Aşık Bir Bestekar Haham Nesim Sevilya Efendi," 68.

57. "İsmail Hakkı Bey [Kaymakam, Hoca, Muallim, ser-hanende]," in Öztuna,

186   Notes to Chapter One

Büyük Türk Musikisi Ansiklopedisi, 402–3. In some sources the year of birth for İsmail Hakkı Bey is 1865. He performed in the Mızıka-yı Hümayun, the imperial band he joined as a youth.

58. David Behar, interview with Jak Esim (date not indicated). Audio recording provided by interviewer.

59. İsmail Hakkı Bey founded Musıki-yi Osmani Mektebi with the composer İzzeddin Hümayi Elçioğlu (1875–1950) in Şehzadebaşı, a district in central Istanbul not far from the mouth of the Golden Horn and present-day Eminönü. Both Darülelhan and his own school were part of the turn-of-the-century trend toward private schools and music societies that commercialized music learning while simultaneously widening its public availability. Cem Behar, *Zaman, Mekan, Müzik: Klasik Türk Musıkisinde Eğitim (Meşk), Icra ve Aktarım* (Istanbul: AFA Yayıncılık, 1993), 36–40.

60. Kohen, "Müziğe Aşık Bir Bestekar Haham Nesim Sevilya Efendi," 68.

61. *Solfège* is the application of European sol-fa syllables to musical scales or melodies, often as an exercise. For differing perspectives on the impact of Western influences on Ottoman music in this period, see Ursula Reinhard, "Turkey: An Overview," in *The Garland Encyclopedia of World Music: the Middle East*, ed. Marcus and Reynolds Danielson (New York: Routledge, 2002), 759–77, and Behar, "The Ottoman Musical Tradition," 406–7.

62. Kohen, "Müziğe Aşık Bir Bestekar Haham Nesim Sevilya Efendi," 66. It is not known exactly how a young Jewish singer came to the attention of the sultan. The timing of the first invitation (1871) coincides with one of Hasköy's cholera epidemics, when Sevilya and his family moved to tents in Okmedanı. It is possible that channels to the palace opened up through the emergency services of a growing imperial public health ministry, provided during the epidemic to the community, through the chief rabbi. The second invitation possibly arose once more through court-community connections via the then chief rabbi Moşe Benhabib or even from Sevilya's developing musical reputation outside the synagogue.

63. Ibid., 66; and Kohen, "Osmanlı İmparatorluğunun Kuruluş Yıllarından Günümüze Yahudi Dini Musikisi," 96. Performing in Hebrew or Ladino for official imperial occasions may not have been unusual in this period. In his memoir, Sa'adi Besalel a-Levi discusses composing and performing three songs (two in Hebrew and one in Ladino) in honor of Sultan Abdülmecid's visit to Salonika in 1859. Aron Rodrigue and Sarah Abrevaya Stein, eds., *A Jewish Voice from Ottoman Salonica: The Ladino Memoir of Sa'adi Besalel a-Levi* (Stanford, CA: Stanford University Press, 2012), 91, 142. Such public multilingual performances for sultans would have served imperial aims in the period of Tanzimat reforms of the nineteenth century when legislation sought to unify Ottoman citizenry across ethno-religious communities. See Chapter Three, Note 24. Some reports about singers performing in Hebrew for the sultan follow folk narratives about the ethical dilemma of a Jewish musician forced to sing, against religious law, on a Jewish holiday. In order to avoid punishment or death, the musician would perform a

Hebrew song for the holiday, impressing and being rewarded by the ruler. For an example involving the Ottoman and Turkish singer Hayim Efendi (1853–1938), see Edwin Seroussi and Rivka Havassy, *An Early Twentieth-Century Sephardi Troubadour: The Historical Recordings of Haim Effendi of Turkey* (Jerusalem: Jewish Music Research Center, CD, 2008), 12.

64. "Nesim Sevilya [Haham]," in Öztuna, *Büyük Türk Musikisi Ansiklopedisi*, 1:107. These fasıl genres are included in the İsmail Hakkı Bey and Arel notated collections.

65. Interview with Moşe Niyego, as reported in Kohen, "Müziğe Aşık Bir Bestekar Haham Nesim Sevilya Efendi," 67–68.

66. Rav Leon Yeuda Adoni, personal interview, June 19, 2006.

67. It is uncertain how Mısırlı İbrahim Efendi acquired his nickname, which appears in performance announcements of late Ottoman newspapers. He reportedly spent time making music in Egypt before 1923; however, according to his daughter he visited the Egyptian royal family later in the 1930s to give a concert series (Cem Behar, personal communication, June 28, 2011). It is possible that he adopted the name as a recording and stage name in his late Ottoman career. On naming among Turkish gazino musicians today, see Münir Nurettin Beken, "Ethnicity and Identity in Music—a Case Study: Professional Musicians in Istanbul," in *Manifold Identities: Studies on Music and Minorities*, ed. Ursula Hemetek et al. (London: Cambridge Scholars Press, 2004), 188. On names in the life of an early republican minority woman singer, see John Morgan O'Connell, "The Mermaid of the Meyhane: The Legend of a Greek Singer in a Turkish Tavern," in *Music and the Sirens*, ed. Linda Austern and Inna Naroditskaya, 273–93 (Bloomington: Indiana University Press, 2006).

68. "İbrahim Efendi [Mısırlı Udi Avram]," in Öztuna, *Büyük Türk Musikisi Ansiklopedisi*, 1:379–80.

69. On the Lonca neighborhood, see Jak Deleon, *Ancient Districts on the Golden Horn* (Istanbul: Gözlem, 1991), and Ahmet F. Özbilge, *Fener Balat Ayvansaray* (Istanbul: Bağlam Yayıncılık, 2005).

70. Münir Nurettin Beken, "Musicians, Audience and Power: The Changing Aesthetics in the Music at the Maksim Gazino of Istanbul," Ph.D. dissertation (University of Maryland, 1998), 45.

71. On the changing structure and contexts of fasıl programs, see ibid., and Karl L. Signell, *Makam: Modal Practice in Turkish Art Music* (Seattle: University of Washington/Asian Music Publications, 1977).

72. For a detailed history of the gazino and its predecessors, see Beken, "Musicians, Audience and Power," 42–48. Historical businesses, informants, and scholars often make flexible use of Turkish terms for a variety of socializing spaces (*meyhane, kahvehane, gazino,* etc.), with a resulting lack of clarity about their exact daily activities. For a discussion of diverse definitions, see ibid., 42–46. Although accurate statistics on coffeehouses and gazinos in Istanbul are difficult to compile, a combination of memoirs and censuses yields an estimated growth from 2,500 cafés in

1840 to thousands after World War I and 227 gazinos in 1925. François Georgeon, "Osmanlı İmparatorluğu'nun Son Döneminde İstanbul Kahvehaneleri," in *Doğu'da Kahve ve Kahvehaneler*, ed. Hélène Desmet-Grégoire and François Georgeon (Istanbul: Yapı Kredi, 1999), 59.

73. Walter Feldman, album notes, *Lalezar: Music of the Sultans and Seraglios*, Vol. III: *Minority Composers* (New York: Traditional Crossroads, CD 4303, 2001), 12.

74. According to Yılmaz Öztuna, the first Turkish Muslim-owned gazino, Sarayburnu Gazinosu, opened in Istanbul in 1928. Beken, "Musicians, Audience and Power" 48.

75. A concert announcement for Mısırlı İbrahim Efendi appears in "Divanyolu'nda Arif'in Kıraathanesi'nde," *Ikdam*, September 9, 1910. For descriptions of gazinos in Istanbul neighborhoods, see Georgeon, "Osmanlı İmparatorluğu'nun Son Döneminde İstanbul Kahvehaneleri," 60.

76. Georgeon, "Osmanlı İmparatorluğu'nun Son Döneminde İstanbul Kahvehaneleri," 59–60.

77. Ibid., 64. On the urban history of new modes of urban land and water transport in Istanbul, see Zeynep Çelik, *The Remaking of Istanbul: Portrait of an Ottoman City in the Nineteenth Century* (Seattle: University of Washington Press, 1986), 82–103.

78. "Beyoğlu Taksim Bahçesi Aynalı Gazino'da Ramazan Bayramının," *Ikdam*, October, 15, 1909. "Ramazan" is Turkish for the Muslim holiday of Ramadan.

79. The semai kahvehanesi replaced Janissary-run coffeehouses after the dissolution of the Janissaries (1826) and became popular for such events as poetic competitions and performances connected with the holiday of Ramazan.

80. François Georgeon, "İmparatorluktan Cumhuriyete İstanbul'da Ramazan," in *Osmanlı İmparatorluğu'nda Yaşamak*, ed. François Georgeon and Paul Dumont (Istanbul: İletişim Yayınları, 2000), 113.

81. Ibid., 111–12.

82. *Yalılar* (singular, *yalı*) were waterside mansions or summer homes of the Ottoman aristocracy.

83. Öztuna, *Büyük Türk Musikisi Ansiklopedisi*, 2:42. The Mehterhane was closed in 1826, when the Janissaries were dissolved, after which the palace supported instruction in and performance of European military band music.

84. Sanayi-i Nefise Mektebi was founded in 1882 under the directorship of the painter Osman Hamdi Bey. Its name was changed to Güzel Sanatlar Akademisi (1928) and later to Mimar Sinan Güzel Sanatlar Üniversitesi (1982).

85. Şemtov (Santo) Şikari (1840–1920) taught music at the Hamidiye Sanayi Mektebi (Hamidian Trade School) in Izmir.

86. A number of testimonies from the turn of the twentieth century give extensive evidence of interurban musical contact. According to Isaac Maimon, hazanim from Edirne and Istanbul came to Tekirdağ to teach new songs. Isaac Maimon, personal interview, November 14, 2001. According to Benaroya, knowledgeable teachers from Istanbul joined Maftirim sessions in Edirne. Samuel Benaroya,

interview by Eric Offenbacher, January 17, 1988, audio recording and transcription from University of Washington Libraries, Special Collections. Aaron Kohen notes Izmir-to-Bursa musical migration via the Jewish composer and teacher Santo Şikari. Kohen, "Osmanlı İmparatorluğunun Kuruluş Yıllarından Günümüze Yahudi Dini Musikisi," 88.

87. Musicians invited to sing for the sultan often received mementos, such as medals, prayer rugs, or vases, which they could then display in their homes. For examples in the lives of musicians Santo Şikari, Bohoraçi Levi, Karakaş and Jozef Kohen Paraci, see Kohen, "Osmanlı İmparatorluğunun Kuruluş Yıllarından Günümüze Yahudi Dini Musikisi," 88–110.

88. The term "music world" conveys a boundedness not applicable to Ottoman society; however, the concept assists in understanding economic and political underpinnings of music-making.

89. On patronage, aesthetics, and professional conventions in art worlds, see Howard S. Becker, *Art Worlds* (Berkeley: University of California Press, 1982).

90. Behar, *Aşk Olmayınca Meşk Olmaz*, 69. Behar's work on Ottoman and Turkish meşk is the most comprehensive to date. See also Cem Behar, "Transmission musicale et mémoire textuelle dans la musique classique ottomane/turque," *Revue de Monde Musulman et de la Méditerranée* 75–76 (1996): 91–102. A typical Ottoman song-text collection, or *güfte mecmuası*, documented lyrics and minimal musical cues, such as usul and makam. They were used as a mnemonic tool in oral transmission. For a comparative study of Arab-Persian and Ottoman song-text collections, see Owen Wright, *Words without Songs: A Musicological Study of an Early Ottoman Anthology and Its Precursors* (London: SOAS, 1992).

91. On social codes of conduct in meşk, see Behar, *Aşk Olmayınca Meşk Olmaz*, 69–129.

92. Beken, "Musicians, Audience and Power," 165. See also "Meşk Silsilesi," in Öztuna, *Büyük Türk Musikisi Ansiklopedisi*, 2:47–52.

93. Behar, *Aşk Olmayınca Meşk Olmaz*, 92.

94. In the nineteenth century, notation was referred to as the "fenn-i musıki düşmanı," or the enemy of the science of music. Ibid., 15.

95. For a sociological, cultural, and political study on the construction of genealogies, see Eviatar Zerubavel, *Ancestors and Relatives: Genealogy, Identity, and Community* (Oxford: Oxford University Press, 2011).

96. "Santo Şikari," in Öztuna, *Büyük Türk Musikisi Ansiklopedisi*, 2:262; and "Elkutlu [Rakım, İzmirli Neyzen Hoca Mehmet]," in ibid., 1:253. 'Şikari' appears in Ottoman and Turkish sources. Cf. Spanish, Chiquiar.

97. "Elkutlu [Rakım, İzmirli Neyzen Hoca Mehmet]," in ibid., 1:253–54.

98. "Santo Şikari," in ibid., 2:262; and "Şenozan [Neyzen Dr. Albay Osman Şükrü]," in ibid., 2:351.

99. "Varon [İsak]," in ibid., 2:475; and "Refik Bey [Manyasi-zade]," in ibid., 2:223.

100. Samuel Benaroya, interview with Edwin Seroussi, October 24, 1992.

101. Judith Amiel, personal interview, November 14, 2006. The Maftirim piece is entitled "Yeme Levavi Biroti" (poetry by Israel Najara; music by Yusuf Paşa; Devri Kebir usul; Segah makam).

102. On Yusuf Paşa, see "Yusuf Paşa [Ferik Neyzen]," in Öztuna, *Büyük Türk Musikisi Ansiklopedisi*, 2:503–4.

Chapter Two

1. Synagogues in Istanbul are commonly referred to by their neighborhoods, for example Şişli synagogue (Bet Israel) and Ortaköy synagogue (Etz Ahayim).

2. A kanun is a Middle Eastern plucked dulcimer of the zither family.

3. For the historical practices before and after Maftirim singing, see Edwin Seroussi, "Introduction," in *Maftirim* (Istanbul: Gözlem, 2009), 59.

4. For example, by Yusuf Paşa, İsmail Hakkı Bey, and Dede Efendi.

5. While David Sevi brings scores of notated Maftirim compositions completed by Fatih Salgar in the 1980s, the singers have booklets copied from approximately 75 pages of *Shire Yisrael be-Erets ha-kedem*. See Chapter Five.

6. David Sevi, personal interview, January 6, 2006.

7. For critical discussions of the general periodization of Turkish history, see Erik J. Zürcher, *Turkey: A Modern History* (London: I. B. Taurus, 1997 [1993]), 1–6; and Reşat Kasaba, "Dreams of Empire, Dreams of Nation," in *Empire to Nation: Historical Perspectives on the Making of the Modern World*, ed. Joseph W. Esherick, Hasan Kayalı, and Eric Van Young (Lanham, MD: Rowman and Littlefield, 2006), 198–225. Whereas Zürcher argues for a periodization emphasizing transitions from the Ottoman to the republican periods, Kasaba proposes a reconsideration of the rupture narrative, distinguished from nationalist historiographies marginalizing an Ottoman past. For histories of Turkish minorities that implicitly or explicitly propose alternative periodizations accommodating minority-related policies, events, and experiences, see Alexis Alexandris, *The Greek Minority of Istanbul and Greek-Turkish Relations, 1918–1974* (Athens: Centre for Asia Minor Studies, 1992 [1983]); and the work of Rıfat Bali, for example, Rıfat N. Bali, *Cumhuriyet Yıllarında Türkiye Yahudileri: Bir Türkleştirme Serüveni 1923–1945* (Istanbul: İletişim Yayınları, 2005 [1999]).

8. *Alaturka* and *alafranga* refer to musical as well as other sociocultural practices in the Ottoman-Turkish and European styles respectively. John Morgan O'Connell, "In the Time of Alaturka: Identifying Difference in Musical Discourse," *Ethnomusicology* 49 (2005): 184–87.

9. Kemal H. Karpat, *Ottoman Population 1830–1914: Demographic and Social Characteristics* (Madison: University of Wisconsin Press, 1985), 86, 102–3. See chapter 5, "The Population and the Social and Economic Transformation of Istanbul: An Ottoman Microcosm," 86–106, for a fuller discussion of the late nineteenth- and early twentieth-century socioeconomic changes in the city, including a discussion of its European (Pera) and Muslim (old city) spacial divide.

10. Justin McCarthy, "Jewish Population in the Late Ottoman Period," in

The Jews of the Ottoman Empire, ed. Avigdor Levy (Princeton, NJ: Darwin Press; Washington, DC: Institute of Turkish Studies, c. 1994), 386.

11. Ibid., 387–88. After World War I, the Jewish community in Bursa likewise amounted to only a third of its prewar population.

12. For example, Çana and Sirkeci synagogues were made available to World War I Jewish refugees from Izmit and the Balkans; Ashkenazi synagogue Tofre Begadim (currently Schneider Temple) became known as the Edirneli synagogue. Naim Güleryüz, *İstanbul Sinagogları* (Istanbul: Ajans Class, 1992), 25, 30, 85. Apollon and later Neve Şalom synagogues were both built to accommodate the rising Jewish population in Galata.

13. Ibid., 69.

14. Pamela J. Dorn, "Change and Ideology: The Ethnomusicology of Turkish Jewry," Ph.D. dissertation (Indiana University, 1991), 176.

15. Vittorio Levy's almanac 1926–1927, as reported in Hazan Aaron Kohen, "Osmanlı İmparatorluğunun Kuruluş Yıllarından Günümüze Yahudi Dini Musikisi," *Folklor/Edebiyat* 6, no. 21 (2000–2001): 93.

16. Kohen, "Osmanlı İmparatorluğunun Kuruluş Yıllarından Günümüze Yahudi Dini Musikisi," 93. Sources on Maftirim leaders sometimes contradict each other; for example, according to Maçoro, Benatar was the Maftirim şef (conductor), while Kordova came only occasionally (İsak Maçoro, interview with Karen Gerson Şarhon, March 27, 2004). I suspect such contradictions can be explained as issues of memory and changing leadership at a time of high emigration. It is also possible that, in times of highly musical and experienced membership, leadership was shared.

17. Seroussi, "Introduction," 55.

18. Publications of notated scores increased in the context of music societies (*cemiyets*), record production, concerts in private homes, and other amateur music-making in the early twentieth century. John Morgan O'Connell, "Alaturka Revisited: Style as History in Turkish Vocal Performance," Ph.D. dissertation (UCLA, 1996), 257–58.

19. Seroussi, "Introduction," 54–63.

20. Several song-text collections of Ottoman Hebrew music published in Salonika beginning in the mid-nineteenth century were predecessors to *Shire Yisrael*. Published earlier in a city with a long-established print culture, these texts similarly sought to preserve and motivate the singing of historical Jewish religious song in music guilds organized in Salonika at the time and were interwoven with aspects of Maftirim music and musicians in other cities, such as Istanbul. For a detailed history, see Edwin Seroussi, "Musika osmanit klasit be-kerev yehudei saloniki (Ottoman Classical Music among the Jews of Saloniki)," in *Ladinar: Mehkarim ba-sifrut, ba-musika uba-historia shel dovrei ladino*, ed. Judith Dishon and Shmuel Refael (Tel Aviv: Ha-Makhon Le-Heker Ha-Tefutsot, 1998), 79–92 (Hebrew).

21. Seroussi, "Introduction," 59. Seroussi suggests that some of the songs may not have been performed, but included as part of Wissenschaft des Judentums

Notes to Chapter Two

(Science of Judaism), a philosophy, beginning in the late eighteenth and early nineteenth centuries, of precise, historical documentation of Jewish history and culture.

22. Ibid., 54–63.
23. Paul Vernon, "Odeon Empire," *Folkroots* 19, nos. 2–3 (1997): 33–37, 170–71.
24. These business patterns accompanied a post-1850s boom in European commercial interests in the empire as a whole, and Istanbul in particular. Karpat, *Ottoman Population 1830–1914*, 104.
25. Cemal Ünlü, *Git Zaman Gel Zaman: Fonograf, Gramofon, Taş Plak* (Istanbul: Pan Yayıncılık, 2004), 110, 175–92; and Kohen, "Osmanlı İmparatorluğunun Kuruluş Yıllarından Günümüze Yahudi Dini Musikisi," 106.
26. Ünlü, *Git Zaman Gel Zaman*, 83–119.
27. Yılmaz Öztuna, *Büyük Türk Musikisi Ansiklopedisi*, 2 vols. (Ankara: Başbakanlık Basımevi, 1990), 2:475, and 1:171. Varon reportedly served as an agent for His Master's Voice, Pathé, and Polydor in Salonika. Kohen, "Osmanlı İmparatorluğunun Kuruluş Yıllarından Günümüze Yahudi Dini Musikisi," 104.
28. Bülent Aksoy, album notes, *İsak Algazi Efendi* (Istanbul: Kalan Müzik, CD 333, 2004), 64.
29. Cemal Ünlü, personal communication, October 5, 2011.
30. Yossef Burgana, interview with Edwin Seroussi, December 20, 1988, as reported in Edwin Seroussi, *Mizimrat Qedem: The Life and Music of R. Isaac Algazi from Turkey* (Jerusalem: Renanot Institute for Jewish Music, 1989), 42.
31. Dorn, "Change and Ideology," 155–56.
32. Seroussi, *Mizimrat Qedem*, 40–41; and Walter Feldman, album notes, *Lalezar: Music of the Sultans and Seraglios*, Vol. III: *Minority Composers* (New York: Traditional Crossroads, CD 4303, 2001), 18.
33. Seroussi, *Mizimrat Qedem*, and Kohen, "Osmanlı İmparatorluğunun Kuruluş Yıllarından Günümüze Yahudi Dini Musikisi," 103–4; Bülent Aksoy, album notes, *İsak Algazi Efendi* (Istanbul: Kalan Müzik, CD 333, 2004), 40.
34. Kohen, "Osmanlı İmparatorluğunun Kuruluş Yıllarından Günümüze Yahudi Dini Musikisi," 109–10.
35. Ibid., 99–101, 104–5.
36. For a detailed history of the gazino and its predecessors, see Münir Nurettin Beken, "Musicians, Audience and Power: The Changing Aesthetics in the Music at the Maksim Gazino of Istanbul," Ph.D. dissertation (University of Maryland, 1998), 42–48.
37. Münir Nurettin Beken, "Ethnicity and Identity in Music—a Case Study: Professional Musicians in Istanbul," in *Manifold Identities: Studies on Music and Minorities*, ed. Ursula Hemetek et al. (London: Cambridge Scholars Press, 2004), 183.
38. *Cumhuriyet*, December 30, 1925, as cited in François Georgeon, "Osmanlı İmparatorluğu'nun Son Döneminde İstanbul Kahvehaneleri," in *Doğu'da Kahve ve Kahvehaneler*, ed. Hélène Desmet-Grégoire and François Georgeon (Istanbul: Yapı Kredi, 1999), 59.

39. Sermet Muhtar Alus, "Kırk Yıl Evvelkiler," *Akşam gazetesi*, April 1939, as reprinted in Ünlü, *Git Zaman Gel Zaman*, 129–30.

40. Münir Nurettin Beken, "Globalization vs Tradition: Commercial Music in Early 20th Century Istanbul," in *Urban Music in the Balkans: Drop-out Ethnic Identities or a Historical Case of Tolerance and Global Thinking? (in Honorem Ramadan Sokoli)*, ed. Sokol Shupo (Tirana: Documentation and Communication Center for Regional Music, 2006), 59.

41. The new imperial band, Mızıka-yı Hümayun, was established circa 1826 to reform Ottoman military music. Its first director was Giuseppe Donizetti (1788–1856), the elder brother of Gaetano Donizetti, the Italian composer. Emre Aracı, "Giuseppe Donizetti at the Ottoman Court: A Levantine Life," *Musical Times* 143, no. 1880 (2002): 49.

42. The *şeyh*s are Celaleddin Efendi at Yenikapı (1848–1907), Ataullah Efendi at Galata (1842–1910), and Hüseyin Fahreddin Dede at Bahariye (1854–1911). Sonometers were used, particularly by Ataullah Efendi, to measure musical intervals. O'Connell, "Alaturka Revisited," 148.

43. Cem Behar, *Zaman, Mekan, Müzik: Klasik Türk Musıkisinde Eğitim (Meşk), Icra ve Aktarım* (Istanbul: AFA Yayıncılık, 1993), 36–40.

44. During his fieldwork in Istanbul, Dane Kusić heard rumors that the Cerrahi Tekkesi never closed down, possibly because Atatürk's mother was a Cerrahi dervish or sympathizer. Dane Kusić, "Discourse on Three Teravih Namazi-s in Istanbul: An Invitation to Reflexive Ethnomusicology," Ph.D. dissertation (University of Maryland, 1996), 174. See also Kudsi Erguner's memoir of a practicing Mevlevi family and lodge operating clandestinely in republican Istanbul: Kudsi Erguner, *Journeys of a Sufi Musician* (London: Saqi Books, 2005).

45. Visits of Mevlevis to Algazi's synagogue in Izmir and Istanbul are documented. See Seroussi, *Mizimrat Qedem*, 33; Bülent Aksoy, album notes, *İsak Algazi Efendi* (Istanbul: Kalan Müzik, CD 333, 2004), 41.

46. Bülent Aksoy, album notes, *İsak Algazi Efendi* (Istanbul: Kalan Müzik, CD 333, 2004), 38 and 41.

47. David Behar, personal communication, November 2005.

48. Oral Onur, personal interview, June 21, 2006.

49. Ibid. See also Oral Onur, *1492'den Günümüze Edirne Yahudi Cemaati* (Istanbul: Oral Onur, 2005), 72.

50. Seroussi, "Introduction."

51. Bali, *Cumhuriyet Yıllarında Türkiye Yahudileri*, 206–28. Senem Aslan, "'Citizen, Speak Turkish!': A Nation in the Making," *Nationalism and Ethnic Politics* 13, no. 2 (2007): 245–72.

52. For a full discussion of this discursive development, see Howard Eissenstat, "Metaphors of Race and Discourse of Nation: Racial Theory and the Beginnings of Nationalism in the Turkish Republic," in *Race and Nation: Ethnic Systems in the Modern World*, ed. Paul Spickard (New York: Routledge, 2005), 239–56.

53. Seroussi, *Mizimrat Qedem*, 21–22.

54. Music by Algazi and lyrics by İsak Ferrera. Naim Güleryüz, *500. Yıl Vakfı Türk Musevileri Müzesi/The Quincentennial Foundation Museum of Turkish Jews (Jewish Museum of Turkey)* (Istanbul: Gözlem Gazetecilik, 2004), 31. Reproduction of 1927 publication of piece in Bülent Aksoy, album notes, *İsak Algazi Efendi* (Istanbul: Kalan Müzik, CD 333, 2004), 32.

55. On Algazi's performance for Atatürk, see Seroussi, *Mizimrat Qedem*, 19; Halil Erdoğan Cengiz, ed., *Yaşanmış Olaylarla Atatürk ve Müzik: Riyaset-i Cumhur Ince Saz Hey'eti Şefi Binbaşı Hafız Yaşar Okur'un Anıları (1924–1938)* (Ankara: Müzik Ansiklopedisi Yayınları, 1993); and Avram Galante, *Histoire des Juifs de Turquie*, 9 vols. (Istanbul: Isis, 1985). For a discussion of the dramatically different accounts of Algazi's performance for Atatürk, see Maureen Jackson, "Mixing Musics: The Urban Landscape of Late Ottoman and Turkish Synagogue Music," Ph.D. dissertation (University of Washington, 2008), 77–78. Communal sources indicate that Algazi impressed Atatürk with his musical lecture and performance, leaving with a signed copy of the Qu'ran; see Galante, *Histoire des Juifs de Turquie*, 3:122; Moşe Grosman, *Vittorio Levi, Dr. Markus (1870–1944)* (Istanbul: 1 AS Matbaacılık AŞ, 1992), 381; Kohen, "Osmanlı İmparatorluğunun Kuruluş Yıllarından Günümüze Yahudi Dini Musikisi," 103; and Seroussi, *Mizimrat Qedem*, 19. By contrast, Hafız Yaşar, the head of the state music ensemble, who was present at the meeting, asserts that, based on increasing preferences for European musical presentation, Atatürk insulted Algazi for his high-volume, musically flawed, and informal presentation; see: Cengiz, ed., *Yaşanmış Olaylarla Atatürk ve Müzik*, 76–80. Such accounts of Algazi's official relationships likely conflict because of differing interpretive lenses: the pride of community members at a distance from events, on the one hand, and, on the other, the critical view of a musician-appointee at a time of changing republican musical tastes and cultural agendas. However, other accounts of Atatürk's criticism and correction of singers' diction lend some credence to Hafız Yaşar's account. See Vasfi Rıza Zobu's testimony, as reported in Orhan Tekelioglu, "The Rise of a Spontaneous Synthesis: The Historical Background of Turkish Popular Music," in *Turkey: Identity, Democracy, Politics*, ed. Sylvia Kedourie (London: Frank Cass, 1996), 202.

56. Bülent Aksoy, album notes, *İsak Algazi Efendi* (Istanbul: Kalan Müzik, CD 333, 2004), 40 and 46.

57. Algazi is listed in the Istanbul Radio program of July 4, 1928, together with musicians Udi Izmirli Cemal Bey, Hanende Hikmet Hanım, and Artaki Candan. Ünlü, *Git Zaman Gel Zaman*, 301.

58. Uygur Kocabaşoğlu, *Şirket Telsizinden Devlet Radyosuna (TRT Öncesi Dönemde Radyonun Tarihsel Gelişimi ve Türk Siyasal Hayatı İçindeki Yeri)*, Ankara Üniversitesi Siyasal Bilgiler Fakültesi Yayınları No. 442 (Ankara: SBF Basın ve Yayın Yüksek Okulu Basımevi, 1980), 122.

59. A temporary ban on broadcasting alaturka music on Turkish state radio resulted in listeners tuning into Arab music broadcasts outside Turkey. Payami Safa, "Mısır Radyosu," *Cumhuriyet*, August 6, 1936, 3. See also Murat Ergin,

"On Humans, Fish, and Mermaids: The Republican Taxonomy of Tastes and Arabesk," *New Perspectives on Turkey* 33 (2005): 72. A contemporary Turkish news article outlines the cultural and political role of national radio stations around the world; see "Radyo bugün sade bir eğlence vasıtası değildir," *Cumhuriyet*, January 15, 1936.

60. According to a cantorial colleague, Moşe Vital, as reported in Seroussi, *Mizimrat Qedem*, 20–21. Although Öztuna records that Ankara Radio was founded in 1934, after Algazi's departure from Turkey (Öztuna, *Büyük Türk Musikisi Ansiklopedisi*, 1:418), other scholars, based on primary source material, claim its first broadcasts were the same year that Istanbul Radio was founded (1927). These sources lend credence to Vital's testimony. A possible reason for Öztuna's misinformation is that Ankara Radio broadcasts were initially more intermittent than Istanbul's and its programs were not printed in local newspapers until 1930. See Kocabaşoğlu, *Şirket Telsizinden Devlet Radyosuna*.

61. See Note 51 above. On Algazi's newspaper, see Seroussi, *Mizimrat Qedem*, 21.

62. The Treaty of Lausanne, signed in July 1923, included articles protecting linguistic, religious, and legal rights of non-Muslim minorities. However, subsequent legislation eroded these rights, for example the adoption of the Swiss civil code in 1925–1926 established universal personal and family law, distinct from non-Muslim religious laws protected in Article 42 of the treaty. For a discussion of the renunciation of rights by non-Muslim communities, see Alexandris, *The Greek Minority of Istanbul and Greek-Turkish Relations, 1918–1974*, 135–39. Aron Rodrigue argues that Turkish Jews experienced social and political losses in the shift from millet to minority, because of sociopolitical continuities with the late Ottoman empire. These include incomplete reforms related to universal citizenship, French rather than Turkish acculturation through Alliance schools, and the ongoing perception of Jews as European economic and political allies. Losing their protected Ottoman status, Turkish Jews relinquished communal cultural institutions without gaining national acceptance and integration. Aron Rodrigue, "From Millet to Minority: Turkish Jewry," in *Paths of Emancipation: Jews, States, and Citizenship*, ed. Pierre Birnbaum and Ira Katznelson (Princeton, NJ: Princeton University Press, 1995), 238–61.

63. Andrew Mango, biographer of Atatürk, uses the phrase "measured terror" in his discussion of the role of Independence Tribunals (1920–1927) in repressing political opposition and trying suspects in such incidents as the Şeyh Said rebellion (1925) and the assassination attempt on the president (1926). See Andrew Mango, *Atatürk* (London: John Murray, 1999), 442–53. Established during the War of Independence, these political tribunals tried, sentenced, and sometimes executed suspected traitors and opponents before and after the founding of the Republic. The Law on the Maintenance of Order (1925–1929) allowed the government to ban organizations and publications, including newspapers, considered disruptive of law and order. See Zürcher, *Turkey: A Modern History*, 172; and Mango, *Atatürk*, 426–27. For statistics on executions based on this law, see Mete Tunçay,

T.C.'nde Tek-Parti Yönetimi'nin Kurulması (1923–1931) (Istanbul: Cem, 1989), 169. Some minority papers feared prosecution under the law against insulting Turkishness and at least one minority (Greek) journalist, Eugenopoulos, was executed (1926) and a newspaper owner (Mlle Eleni) was imprisoned (1929). See Alexandris, *The Greek Minority of Istanbul and Greek-Turkish Relations, 1918–1974*, 140. It goes without saying that as a newspaper owner himself, Algazi would have been cognizant of these police actions.

64. Economic fluctuations also interacted with taste and technology. For example, with manufacturing plants outside Turkey, commonly in Germany (Odeon) or Britain (Columbia and Gramophone), record production often fluctuated with changes in the European political economy, whether competition with new film and radio technology, global economic depression, or, later, Nazi controls on trade with "non-Aryan" nations. Ali Jihad Racy, "Record Industry and Egyptian Traditional Music: 1904–1932," *Ethnomusicology* 20 (1976): 45–46; Vernon, "Odeon Empire"; and Vernon, "Sans Border Radio," *Folkroots* 130 (1994), www.bolingo.org/audio/texts/fr130radio.html (accessed August 15, 2011). For further discussion of changing vocal aesthetics in the early Republic, see O'Connell, "Alaturka Revisited," 322–25. Algazi's recording career lasted from 1909 to 1929, with his last commercial recording on Pathé. "Isaac Algazi," *Sephardic Music: A Century of Recordings*, www.sephardicmusic.org (accessed August 15, 2011).

65. John Morgan O'Connell, "Song Cycles: The Life and Death of the Turkish Gazel: A Review Essay," *Ethnomusicology* 47 (2003): 404. In the area of musical instrumentation, the electrical mike favored quieter, less sonorous instruments (Racy, "Record Industry and Egyptian Traditional Music," 28). On the radio, the electrical mike, which preceded electrical gramophone recording, likewise altered musical instrumentation. For an example from Cuban music, see Vernon, "Sans Border Radio."

66. Algazi's recordings include Hebrew and Ladino liturgical song, Maftirim music, and Ladino folksongs.

67. Beken, "Musicians, Audience and Power," 99–101. Münir Nurettin Selçuk's concert at the Fransız Tiyatrosu on February 22, 1930, is considered seminal in promoting these artistic changes. For a comparative analysis of his vocal style before and after his sojourn in Paris, see O'Connell, "Alaturka Revisited," 204–9.

68. Beken, "Globalization vs Tradition," 60.

69. For further discussion of the loss of diverse musical genres in the recording industry, see ibid., 60–61.

70. Falih Rıfkı Atay recalls the music Atatürk enjoyed was alaturka, whereas the music he believed in was Western. See Falih Rıfkı Atay, *Çankaya: Atatürk Devri Hatıraları* (Istanbul: Dünya Yayınları, 1958). See also Ergin, "On Humans, Fish, and Mermaids," 68.

71. Cemal Ünlü, personal communication, October 5, 2011.

72. Eric Bernard Ederer, "The *Cümbüş* as Instrument of 'The Other' in Mod-

ern Turkey," masters thesis (University of California Santa Barbara, 2007). The cümbüş is a fretless, plucked banjo-like instrument.

73. Among the women vocalists who recorded Mısırlı İbrahim Efendi's songs are Hamiyet Yüceses (1915–1996), Vedia Rıza (1903–?), Müşerref Hanım (1905–?), Nezihe (1897–?), and Muzaffer (dates not known).

74. For a critical analysis of Hafız Yaşar's poor review of Algazi's performance, see John Morgan O'Connell, "A Staged Fright: Musical Hybridity and Religious Intolerance in Turkey (1923–38)," *Twentieth-Century Music* 7, no. 1 (2011): 1–26.

75. For an ethnographic study of individual stories related to the Family Name Law of 1934, see Meltem Türköz, "Surname Narratives and the State-Society Boundary: Memories of Turkey's Family Name Law of 1934," *Middle Eastern Studies* 43, no. 6 (2007): 893–908.

76. Ibid., 902–3.

77. For a contemporaneous critique of popular Arab-Persian understandings of Turkish culture, see Payami Safa, "Mısır Radyosu," *Cumhuriyet*, August 6, 1936, 3. In the 1930s the Turkish state favored alliances and reconciliation with Middle Eastern and Balkan nations as well as the Soviet Union over European occupiers of the recent past, specifically through the Balkan Pact (with Greece, Yugoslavia, and Romania in 1934) and Sadabad Pact (with Iran, Iraq, and Afghanistan in 1937). Its formal alliances with European nations and the United States increased later, during and after World War II.

78. For further discussion, see Rıfat N. Bali, *1934 Trakya Olayları* (Istanbul: Kitabevi, 2008), and Leyla Neyzi, "Strong as Steel, Fragile as a Rose: A Turkish Jewish Witness to the Twentieth Century," *Jewish Social Studies: History, Culture, Society* 12, no. 1 (2005): 172, 188n23.

79. Samuel Benaroya, interview with Eric Offenbacher, January 17, 1988. According to this interview, Benaroya left Edirne in 1933.

80. The Capital Tax (1942–1944) was ostensibly levied on those profiting from the war; however, research has shown that it was enforced in a discriminatory way against non-Muslims in Turkey, often dispossessing small business people of their entire assets. See Rıfat N. Bali, *The "Varlık Vergisi Affair": A Study of Its Legacy—Selected Documents* (Istanbul: Isis, 2005); Bali, *Varlık Vergisi: Hatıralar-Tanıklıklar* (Istanbul: Libra, 2012). Several recent studies have investigated other anti-minority policies and incidents affecting Jews in the early Republic. See, for example, Senem Aslan, "'Citizen, Speak Turkish!': A Nation in the Making," *Nationalism and Ethnic Politics* 13, no. 2 (2007): 245–72; and Bali, *1934 Trakya Olayları*.

81. For a Jewish student's memories of the Turkish press during World War II, see Erol Haker, *From Istanbul to Jerusalem: The Itinerary of a Young Turkish Jew* (Istanbul: Isis, 2003), 89–91.

82. On Jewish emigration from Turkey, see Esther Benbassa and Aron Rodrigue, *Sephardi Jewry: A History of the Judeo-Spanish Community, 14th to 20th Centuries* (Berkeley: University of California Press, 2000 [1993]), 186–88; and Şule

Toktaş, "Turkey's Jews and Their Immigration to Israel," *Middle Eastern Studies* 42 (2006): 505–19. Although Zionism made inroads among Ottoman and Turkish Jews beginning in the late empire, Jewish emigration from the Turkish Republic was primarily motivated by a concern for security and economic betterment. Because of the republican platform for national unity and against affiliation with foreign institutions, Zionist groups operated clandestinely in the early Republic. Benbassa and Rodrigue, *Sephardi Jewry*, 130–34. For historical studies of cultural and political Zionism in the Ottoman empire and Turkey, see Esther Benbassa, "Zionism in the Ottoman Empire at the End of the 19th and Beginning of the 20th Century," *Studies in Zionism* 11, no. 2 (1990): 27–40; Benbassa and Rodrigue, *Sephardi Jewry*, 116–58; Michelle U. Campos, "Between 'Beloved Ottomania' and 'The Land of Israel': The Struggle over Ottomanism and Zionism among Palestine's Sephardi Jews, 1908–13," *International Journal of Middle East Studies* 37, no. 4 (2005): 461–83; and Minna Rozen, "The Istanbul Community between the Hatt-ı Şerif of Gülhane and the Treaty of Lausanne (1839–1923)," in *The Last Ottoman Century and Beyond: The Jews in Turkey and the Balkans, 1808–1945* (Tel Aviv: Tel Aviv University, 2005), 77–130.

83. These approximate population figures are based on state statistics cited in Toktaş, "Turkey's Jews and Their Immigration to Israel," 506, and in Rıfat N. Bali, *Aliya: Bir Toplu Göçün Öyküsü (1946–1949)* (Istanbul: Iletişim Yayınları, 2003), 432. In this period, the Turkish Jewish population was increasingly concentrated in Istanbul, and secondarily in Izmir (for regional distribution, see Bali, *Aliya*, 433–44).

84. On the life of Giuseppe Donizetti at court, see Aracı, "Giuseppe Donizetti at the Ottoman Court." On changing classical vocal style in the context of alaturka and alafranga musical debates in Turkey, see O'Connell, "Alaturka Revisited." See John Morgan O'Connell, "Fine Art, Fine Music: Controlling Turkish Taste at the Fine Arts Academy in 1926," *Yearbook for Traditional Music* 32 (2000), 117–42, for a discourse analysis of alaturka and alafranga debates, and the resulting emergence of a "national synthesis" music. On the history of the terms *alaturka* and *alafranga*, see O'Connell, "In the Time of Alaturka."

85. For an overview of music-related republican reforms, see Ahmet Say, *Türkiye'nin Müzik Atlası* (Istanbul: Ofset Yapımevi, 1998), 32–36; and Orhan Tekelioğlu, "An Inner History of 'Turkish Music Revolution'—Demise of a Music Magazine," in *Sufism, Music and Society in Turkey and the Middle East*, ed. Anders Hammarlund, Tord Olsson, and Elisabeth Özdalga (Istanbul: Swedish Research Institute, 2001), 111–16.

86. For an English translation of Atatürk's speech at Sarayburnu Gazinosu (1928) and an overview of the record of Atatürk's remarks on music, see O'Connell, "Alaturka Revisited," 187–92.

87. On artists' multiethnicity and criticism, see ibid., 185.

88. Ziya Gökalp, *Türkçülüğün Esasları* (Principles of Turkism, 1923). See also Tekelioğlu, "An Inner History," 112.

89. The Turkish Five were Cemal Reşit Rey (1904–1985), Ahmed Adnan Saygun (1907–1991), Ulvi Cemal Erkin (1906–1972), Hasan Ferit Alnar (1906–1978), and Necil Kazım Akses (1908–1999). Most of them studied music in European conservatories in the 1920s. They take their name from the Russian Five (lit. "Mighty Handful" in Russian), a group of nineteenth-century composers seeking an authentic Russian classical music. Likewise, in the 1920s, a music critic dubbed a contemporary group of French composers the French Six (Les Six) after the Russian Five. On Ahmed Adnan Saygun, see Emre Aracı, "Reforming Zeal," *Musical Times* 138, no. 1855 (1997): 12–15.

90. Tekelioğlu, "An Inner History," 114. The radio ban lasted from November 2, 1934, to September 6, 1935. Kusić, "Discourse on Three Teravih Namazi-s in Istanbul," 169. People's Houses (Halk Evleri) were cultural institutions active in Turkish cities and towns between 1932 and 1951. With close ties to the ruling Republican People's Party, they were built to spread nationalist ideas through educational programs.

91. Cornelia Zimmermann-Kalyoncu, *Deutsche Musiker in der Türkei im 20. Jahrhundert* (Frankfurt: Peter Lang Verlag, 1985), 138.

92. Within six months of Hitler's appointment as Chancellor (January 1933), German Jewish citizens lost public sector and attorney jobs through the Law for the Restoration of the Professional Civil Service and the Law Regulating Admission to the Bar (April 1933). The national book-burning of works considered "un-German" (May 1933) likewise marginalized Jewish and some non-Jewish artists and intellectuals. Wolfgang Benz, *A Concise History of the Third Reich* (Berkeley: University of California Press, 2006), 32–33, 141–42.

93. The émigrés to Turkey were part of a larger migration of Jewish musicians from Germany to the United States, Britain, and Palestine, contributing to the establishment of music programs, orchestras, and performance series. See Michael H. Kater, *The Twisted Muse: Musicians and Their Music in the Third Reich* (Oxford: Oxford University Press, 1997), 105–19. Three universities were slated for restructuring according to German models: University of Istanbul, Istanbul Technical University, and Ankara University. Arnold Reisman, *Turkey's Modernization: Refugees from Nazism and Atatürk's Vision* (Washington, DC: New Academia, 2006), 7–8.

94. The uneasy relationship with the Nazi regime is evident in the embassy's effort to promote German cultural influence in Turkey as fulfilling the claims made in German propaganda, while addressing Nazi concerns about the consequent protection of Jewish musicians. Zimmermann-Kalyoncu, *Deutsche Musiker in der Türkei im 20. Jahrhundert*, 78, 95.

95. In the world of opera, Jewish librettists and themes were also targeted by Nazi arts policies. See Kater, *The Twisted Muse*, 85–86.

96. In 1937 and 1938 the Nazi regime presented exhibits of art and music it considered degenerate. The 1938 exhibit included the work of Paul Hindemith. See ibid., 178, 181.

97. Frank Tachau, "German Jewish Emigrés in Turkey," in *Jews, Turks, Ottomans*, ed. Avigdor Levy (Syracuse, NY: Syracuse University Press, 2002), 240. According to Tachau, twenty-six Austro-German performing artists were employed in Turkey, representing 18 percent of the total pool of émigrés from all fields (medicine, natural and social sciences, humanities and law).

98. Gönül Paçacı, "Belediye Konservatuvarı," in *Dünden Bugüne İstanbul Ansiklopedisi*, 8 vols. (Istanbul: Ana Basım, 1993–1994), 2:142.

99. Paul Hindemith's correspondence contains letters regarding his consulting work in Turkey. Geoffrey Skelton, ed., *Selected Letters of Paul Hindemith* (New Haven, CT: Yale University Press, 1995). Hindemith outlines his proposal in *Vorschläge für den Aufbau des Türkischen Musiklebens* (Suggestions for the Development of Turkish Music Life), 1935–1936. For a Turkish/German bilingual version, see Hindemith, *Türk Kuğ Yaşamının Kalkınması İçin Öneriler: 1935/36* (Izmir: Kuğ Yayını, 1983). See also Reisman, *Turkey's Modernization*, 87–88.

100. On German and Austrian musicians emigrating to Turkey during the Third Reich, see Kater, *The Twisted Muse*; Reisman, *Turkey's Modernization*; and Zimmermann-Kalyoncu, *Deutsche Musiker in der Türkei im 20. Jahrhundert*.

101. Zimmermann-Kalyoncu, *Deutsche Musiker in der Türkei im 20. Jahrhundert*, 35. In 1935, on his first trip to Turkey, Hindemith participated in ethnographic research trips to gather information on Turkish folk music. Ibid., 24.

102. In the early 1930s unemployment among musicians owing to the economic crisis was 20 percent, twice the national average. Kater, *The Twisted Muse*, 9.

103. Say, *Türkiye'nin Müzik Atlası*, 278–79, 33–34; and Reisman, *Turkey's Modernization*, 88–94. Praetorius had divorced his Jewish wife and remarried. According to other sources, Praetorius himself was Jewish. See Zimmermann-Kalyoncu, *Deutsche Musiker in der Türkei im 20. Jahrhundert*, 76. From the beginning of the Nazi regime, having a Jewish spouse could jeopardize the career of German musicians, some of whom divorced to reduce the risk. Kater, *The Twisted Muse*, 82.

104. On Licco Amar's biography, see Zimmermann-Kalyoncu, *Deutsche Musiker in der Türkei im 20. Jahrhundert*, 142; on his Turkish students, see Say, *Türkiye'nin Müzik Atlası*, 205–8; 300; and Reisman, *Turkey's Modernization*, 91. Additional instrumentalists and vocalists who came from Germany and Austria to Turkey in the 1930s include Gilbert Back (violinist), Teodoro Fuchs (composer), Walter Gerhard (violinist), A. Haendschke (violinist), Heinrich Jacoby (violinist, composer), Max and Steffi Klein (opera), Walter Schlosenger (pianist), Wolfgang Schocken (violinist), Friedrich Schonfeld (flutist, musicologist), Adolf Winkler (violinist), and Walter Wunsch (violinist). Say, *Türkiye'nin Müzik Atlası*, 279; Reisman, *Turkey's Modernization*, 90–91.

105. German and Austrian Jewish musicians and composers emigrating to Britain, Palestine, and the United States likewise participated in establishing and maintaining educational and arts programs in their respective countries. For example, the Palestine Symphony Orchestra, founded by the visiting Polish Jewish violinist Bronislaw Huberman as a deliberate anti-Nazi initiative in the mid-1930s, was

composed almost entirely of German Jewish émigré instrumentalists. Nearly five hundred musicians and composers, mostly Jewish, emigrated to the United States during the Nazi era, the most notable being Arnold Schoenberg, who became a professor of music at UCLA. See Kater, *The Twisted Muse*, 107, 109–12.

106. For example, Reisman and Tachau link the safe haven for German Jews with earlier Ottoman hospitality to the Sephardic Jews (Reisman, *Turkey's Modernization*, 11–13; Tachau, "German Jewish Emigrés in Turkey," 245) and the film *Desperate Hours*, directed by Victoria Barrett (Turkey, 2001, 64 min) represents Turkey as a national anomaly in the World War II era. In contrast, the exhibit *Haymatloz—Exile in Turkey from 1933 to 1945* at the Aktives Museum at the Akademie der Künste, Berlin, January–June 2000, takes a more critical position. See a review of the exhibit by Regine Erichsen, "Haymatloz—Exile in Turkey from 1933 to 1945. An Exhibition of the Aktives Museum at the Akademie der Künste in Berlin and the Viadrina University in Frankfurt/Oder (January to June 2000) and German-Turkish Relations," *Electronic Journal of Oriental Studies/Utrecht University* 3, no. 1 (2000): 1–4, http://web.archive.org/web/20050510090623/http://www2.let.uu.nl/Solis/anpt/ejos/pdf/Regine.pdf (accessed August 15, 2011).

107. For an alternative historical discussion integrating these two migrations, see Jackson, "Mixing Musics."

108. Zimmermann-Kalyoncu, *Deutsche Musiker in der Türkei im 20. Jahrhundert*, 148.

109. Unofficial musical activity spanning decades (see Chapter Two, pages 77–85) in the end contributed to state funding of classical Turkish music education. Whether or not Jewish musicians had direct involvement, beginning in the 1950s several classical musicians and teachers initiated plans to establish an official curriculum. In the late 1960s this musical enterprise gained the necessary political support, and the first conservatory, the Türk Musıkisi Devlet Konservatuarı, opened in 1976. On the politics involved in establishing the conservatory, see Öztuna, *Büyük Türk Musikisi Ansiklopedisi*, 2:431–32.

110. According to Şaul Palaçi, as reported in Hazan Aaron Kohen, "Değerli Bir Bestekar: Udi Mısırlı İbrahim Efendi (1878–1948)," *Tiryaki*, 1 (December, 1994): 38–39.

111. Ibid., 107–8. Taragano's dates are unknown.

112. For example, during my fieldwork in Istanbul (2005–2006), a senior Jewish instrumentalist confirmed during an informal conversation that he had worked as a gazino musician, but later denied it during a formal interview about religious music.

113. See the testimony of Yossef Burgana in Seroussi, *Mizimrat Qedem*, 42.

114. For a comparative phenomenon in Nazi Germany, see Kater, *The Twisted Muse*, 86–87.

115. An amateur in classical Turkish music denoted a potentially very well-trained musician who did not make money through performing but had a profession outside the music marketplace.

116. For information about Maçoro's musical life I am indebted to an interview with him by Karen Gerson Şarhon, March 27, 2004. Details about David Behar's biography are taken from conversations with him, as well as knowledgeable members of the community, 2005–2006.

117. David Behar, personal communication, December 17, 2005.

118. A series of traditionalist şefs conducted this ensemble until the appointment of Münir Nurettin Selçuk in the early 1950s (Paçacı, "Belediye Konservatuvarı," 2:143).

119. After 1954, as şef of the conservatory's Türk Musıkisi İcra Heyeti, Selçuk presented concerts, broadcast live on state radio, every Sunday morning. Ibid., 2:144. Safiye Ayla, a prominent singer of Turkish art music, became a popular gazino and recording artist in the Republic. See Öztuna, *Büyük Türk Musikisi Ansiklopedisi*, 2:376–77. Personal interviews report Maçoro's invitation from Münir Nurettin Selçuk (Selin Maçoro, personal communication, January 19, 2006) and his performance with Safiye Ayla (İsak Maçoro, interview by Karen Gerson Şarhon, March 27, 2004).

120. David Sevi, personal interview, January 6, 2006. Composer Erol Sayan (b. 1936) confirmed Behar as an usul master.

121. Beken, "Musicians, Audience and Power," 24–27. Beken usefully conceptualizes the *ev toplantısı* as a civil-society development, asserting and supporting social interests in opposition to those of the state. Beken, "Globalization vs Tradition," 57.

122. Abdurrahman Nevzat Tırışkan, personal interview, Keşan Yayla, Turkey, July 23, 2006. Yomtov Sulam, the Maftirim conductor at Kasturiya synagogue in the 1930s, reportedly attended music sessions in homes to learn classical Turkish music. Viki Behar, personal communication, November 2005.

123. Abdurrahman Nevzat Tırışkan, personal interview, July 23, 2006.

124. According to Kudsi Erguner, his grandfather, Süleyman Erguner, and father, Ulvi Erguner, held musical gatherings at their family home, which after his death took place at the home of Cahit Gözkan. Kudsi Erguner, *Journeys of a Sufi Musician* (London: Saqi Books, 2005), 21–22. See also album notes, *Ud: Türk Müziği Ustaları—Masters of Turkish Music* (Istabul: Kalan Müzik, CD 324–325, 2004), 72–73.

125. *Hafiz* is an individual who can recite the Qur'an from memory.

126. The dates of David Asseo are unknown.

127. Abdurrahman Nevzat Tırışkan, personal interview, July 23, 2006.

128. Yavuz Yekta, personal communication, April 4, 2006.

129. David Sevi, personal interview, July 12, 2006. Kani Karaca informally recorded two Maftirim compositions in Konya upon the request of friends.

130. Emin Ongan (1906–1985) was a composer, Istanbul Radio artist, and long-standing director of Üsküdar Musıki Cemiyeti, 1927–1985. In 1987 the school was renamed Emin Ongan Üsküdar Musıki Cemiyeti. See Orhan Nasuhioğlu, "Geçmişten Günümüze Üsküdar Musiki Cemiyeti," *Musiki Mecmuası* 461 (1998): 7–9.

131. Victor Beruhiel, personal interview, April 12, 2006.
132. Fatih Salgar, personal communication, April 28, 2006.
133. Bülent Aksoy, album notes, *İsak Algazi Efendi* (Istanbul: Kalan Müzik, CD 333, 2004), 33; and observations of the author, 2005–2006.

Chapter Three

1. According to Janti Behar, there was a *beit midrash* (house of study) on the grounds that may correspond to what this informant is referring to as the gatekeeper's house.
2. Janti Behar, personal interview, April 7, 2006.
3. Marie-Christine Varol, *Balat: Faubourg juif d'Istanbul* (Istanbul: Isis, 1989), 1. By the late nineteenth century, the two Golden Horn neighborhoods of Balat and Hasköy were the principal Jewish neighborhoods in Istanbul. Ibid.
4. For an extensive discussion of Kasturiya, based on ethnographic research, see ibid., 20–22. Varol's informants include Jews born before 1921, and Jews, Turks, Greeks, and Armenians born between 1921 and 1940. For historical background on the synagogue, see Naim Güleryüz, *İstanbul Sinagogları* (Istanbul: Ajans Class, 1992), 22–23. There are brief references to the neighborhood as a section of Balat in Jak Deleon, *Ancient Districts on the Golden Horn* (Istanbul: Gözlem, 1991), 29, and Eli Şaul, *Balat'tan Bat-Yam'a* (Istanbul: İletişim, 1999), 43.
5. Recent scholarly literature seeks to redress this conceptual invisibility through detailed research into minority neighborhoods and histories of Istanbul. For empirical and archival detail, see the monographs of Orhan Türker, published by Sel Yayıncılık in Istanbul: Orhan Türker, *Mega Revma'dan Arnavutköy'e: Bir Boğaziçi Hikayesi* (1999); *Galata'dan Karaköy'e: Bir Liman Hikayesi* (2000); *Fanari'den Fener'e: Bir Haliç Hikayesi* (2001); *Halki'den Heybeli'ye: Bir Ada Hikayesi* (2003); *Nihori'den Yeniköy'e: Bir Boğaziçi Köyünün Hikayesi* (2004). See also Ahmet F. Özbilge, *Fener Balat Ayvansaray* (Istanbul: Bağlam Yayıncılık, 2005); Marie-Christine Bornes-Varol, "The Balat Quarter and Its Image: A Study of a Jewish Neighborhood in Istanbul," in *The Jews of the Ottoman Empire*, ed. Avigdor Levy (Princeton, NJ: Darwin Press; Washington, DC: Institute of Turkish Studies, 1994), 633–44; Varol, *Balat*; and Deleon, *Ancient Districts on the Golden Horn*. For an analysis of minority histories of Kuzguncuk in the context of Turkish nationalism, collective memory, and contemporary cultural change, see Amy Mills, *Streets of Memory: Landscape, Tolerance, and National Identity in Istanbul* (Athens: University of Georgia Press, 2010), and Amy Mills, "Narratives in City Landscapes: Cultural Identity in Istanbul," *Geographical Review* 95, no. 3 (2005): 441–62.
6. Naim Güleryüz explains the criteria and process for restoring Ahrida synagogue in 1992 in Deleon, *Ancient Districts on the Golden Horn*, 51–53.
7. For early scholarship on the concept of soundscape, see R. Murray Schafer, *The Soundscape: Our Sonic Environment and the Tuning of the World* (Rochester, VT: Destiny Books, 1994 [1977]). Recent urban studies include M. Bull, *Sounding out the City: Personal Stereos and the Management of Everyday Life* (Oxford: Berg,

2000); Rowland Atkinson, "Ecology of Sound: The Sonic Order of Urban Space," *Urban Studies* 44, no. 10 (2007): 1905–17; and M. Bull and L. Back, eds., *The Auditory Culture Reader* (Oxford: Berg, 2003). For an analysis of understudied architectural soundscapes, see Nina Ergin, "The Soundscape of Sixteenth-Century Istanbul Mosques: Architecture and Qur'an Recital," *Journal of the Society of Architectural Historians* 67 (2008): 204–21.

8. The commonly cited source for this injunction is Talmud Bavli Berakhot 24a, with the normative interpretation at Shulchan Arukh, Even Ha-Ezer 21:2. For references to the law in literature on women and music, see Irene Heskes, "Miriam's Sisters: Jewish Women and Liturgical Music," *Notes* 48, no. 4 (1992): 1193; and Edwin Seroussi, "De-Gendering Jewish Music: The Survival of the Judeo-Spanish Folksong Revisited," *Music and Anthropology* 3 (1998): 1.

9. According to Matthias Lehmann, the gendering of space and roles in Ottoman rabbinical literature was based not on assumptions of female sexuality or impurity, but on assumptions that males could not control their own sexual desire. In this conceptualization of gender, women's roles were defined as keeping a home that supported men's Torah study and as staying at home to prevent male sexual arousal. Matthias B. Lehmann, *Ladino Rabbinic Literature and Ottoman Sephardic Culture*, Jewish Literature and Culture (Bloomington: Indiana University Press, 2005), 124. For Lehmann's full discussion of gender in Ladino rabbinical texts, see chap. 7, "The Representation of Gender," 121–34.

10. Since the 1970s ethnomusicological scholarship on Ladino song has situated the genre in its local contexts through textual, musical, and social analyses. This approach challenges previous studies drawing an unbroken link between medieval Spanish and Ottoman Jewish compositions based on text-only analyses. Contemporary studies by women ethnomusicologists, in particular, have focused attention on individual female performers. See Samuel G. Armistead, *El romancero judeo-español en el Archivo Menendez Pidal (Catálogo-índice de romances y canciones)*, 3 vols. (Madrid: Catedra Seminario Menendez Pidal, 1978); Samuel G. Armistead, Joseph Silverman, and Israel Katz, *Judeo-Spanish Ballads from Oral Tradition*, vol. 2 (Berkeley: University of California Press, 1986, 1993); Judith Cohen, "Women's Roles in Judeo-Spanish Song Traditions," in *Active Voices: Women in Jewish Culture*, ed. Maurie Sacks (Urbana: University of Illinois Press, 1995), 182–200; Judith Cohen, "Sephardic Song," *Midstream* 49, no. 5 (2003): 12–16; Susana Welch-Shahak, "Adaptations and Borrowings in the Balkan Sephardic Repertoire," *Balkanista* 11 (1998): 87–125; Seroussi, "De-Gendering Jewish Music"; and Edwin Seroussi and Susana Welch-Shahak, "Judeo-Spanish Contrafacts and Musical Adaptations: The Oral Tradition," *Orbis Musicae* 10 (1990): 164–94. Two dated, but still relevant, bibliographies are Judith Cohen, "Sonography of Judeo-Spanish Song (Cassettes, LPs, CD's, Video, Film)," *Jewish Folklore and Ethnology Review/Special Issue: Sephardic Folklore: Exile and Homecoming* 15, no. 2 (1993): 49–55; and Edwin Seroussi, "Sephardic Music: A Bibliographical Guide with a Checklist of Notated Sources," *Jewish Folklore and Ethnology Review/Special Issue:*

Sephardic Folklore: Exile and Homecoming 15, no. 2 (1993): 56–61. For a critique of scholarship assuming unchanging Spanish origins of Ladino song, see Kay Kaufman Shelemay, "Mythologies and Realities in the Study of Jewish Music," in *Enchanting Powers: Music in the World's Religions*, ed. Lawrence E. Sullivan (Cambridge, MA: Harvard University Press, 1997), 299–318. Turkish Jewry is explored in the CD and liner notes to Hadass Pal-Yarden, *Yahudice: Ladino Şehir Müziği* (Istanbul: Kalan Müzik, CD 272, 2003), a compilation based on ethnomusicological research of urban Ladino music in Istanbul, Izmir, Thessaloniki, and Jerusalem.

11. Seroussi, "De-Gendering Jewish Music," 3.

12. Seroussi and Welch-Shahak, "Judeo-Spanish Contrafacts," analyzes the adaptation of Ladino melodies for Hebrew liturgical pieces. For a discussion of "backward" contrafacts, including the use of liturgical melodies and Hebrew phrases in Ladino songs, see ibid., 186–87.

13. For an overview of Jewish women's manuscript songbooks, see Edwin Seroussi, "Archivists of Memory: Written Folksong Collections of Twentieth-Century Sephardi Women," in *Music and Gender: Perspectives from the Mediterranean*, ed. Tullia Magrini (Chicago: University of Chicago Press, 2003), 197–200. See also Cohen, "Women's Roles in Judeo-Spanish Song Traditions," 191–92, and Barbara C. Johnson, "'Hen noseot et mahberoteihen itan': shirei nashim Yehudiot mi-Kochin be-sfat ha-makom" ("'They Carry Their Notebooks with Them': Women's Vernacular Jewish Songs from Cochin"), *Pe'amim* 82 (2000): 64–80 (Hebrew).

14. Seroussi, "De-Gendering Jewish Music," 12–13.

15. Judith Cohen, "Judeo-Spanish Songs in Montreal and Toronto," *Jewish Folklore and Ethnology Review/Special Issue: Jewish Women* 12, no. 1–2 (1990): 26.

16. According to Pamela Dorn's informants, preadolescent girls were allowed to sit with their fathers in the main body of the synagogue and participate vocally as much as boys. Many such daughters of rabbinical families reportedly remember words and melodies clearly from their childhood experience. Pamela J. Dorn, "Change and Ideology: The Ethnomusicology of Turkish Jewry," Ph.D. dissertation (Indiana University, 1991), 191.

17. Among Ottoman musical theater performances in the second half of the nineteenth century were dancing and singing women and girls, including "canto girls," who sang between acts. The Ottoman press and aristocrats criticized these performers, who were predominantly minorities, especially Armenians, as immoral. Pioneer Women on Stage in Istanbul, *Women's Library and Information Center Foundation Diary* (2008). Roza Eskenazi (c. 1885–1980), a Jewish vocalist and recording artist, performed rebetika music (a popular urban genre flourishing in Smyrna and Athens) primarily in Greece in the early twentieth century, and later toured outside the country. Born in Istanbul, but living in Salonika from an early age, Eskenazi was linked to late Ottoman music through her vocal style and performance with Ottoman-born Greek instrumentalists from Asia Minor. However, in the area of gender issues, Eskenazi requires a separate study, because of her distinctive popular genre and unique sociohistorical context. Her rebetika

music-making took place within the Hellenization of the Balkans after the Balkan Wars (1912–1913), as well as within an exile Greek community following the Izmir fire (1922) and population exchange between Greece and Turkey (1923–1924). According to Gail Holst-Warhaft, rebetika as a socially marginalized music promoted gender flexibility in performance, as did Eskenazi's status as a double (Jewish and immigrant) outsider. Gail Holst-Warhaft, "The Female Dervish and Other Shady Ladies of the Rebetika," in *Music and Gender: Perspectives from the Mediterranean*, ed. Tullia Magrini (Chicago: University of Chicago Press, 2003), 9–10, 189n10. Moreover, Eskenazi's discography operated within the market forces of Greek, Turkish, and other diaspora communities, with some recordings made in Greece for American audiences. Steve Frangos, "Portraits in Modern Greek Music: Roza Eskenazi," *Resound: Archives of Traditional Music* 12, no. 1–2 (1993): 5–8.

18. For a discussion of changes in meşk in this period, see Cem Behar, *Zaman, Mekan, Müzik: Klasik Türk Musıkisinde Eğitim (Meşk), Icra ve Aktarım* (Istanbul: AFA Yayıncılık, 1993), 36–40.

19. A comparative observation has been made in ethnomusicological research of other regions. In her study of amateur musicians in a British town, Ruth Finnegan contends that inheritances such as family support and musical home environments, rather than gender, constitute "the most striking characteristic of musical transmission." Ruth Finnegan, *The Hidden Musicians: Music-Making in an English Town* (Cambridge: Cambridge University Press, 1989), 320. Erynn Marshall shows how musical family members, especially men, facilitated the learning and performing opportunities for women in communities with male-only performance norms. Erynn Marshall, *Music in the Air Somewhere: The Shifting Borders of West Virginia's Fiddle and Song Traditions* (Morgantown: West Virginia University Press, 2006), 112.

20. Bornes-Varol, "The Balat Quarter and Its Image," investigates the disparity between the self-perception of Balat Jewry and historical reports by outsiders.

21. Deleon, *Ancient Districts on the Golden Horn*, 19, 58–59.

22. On the Alliance Israélite Universelle schools during the Ottoman period, see Chapter One, Note 17. A chronological list of dates for school openings in Istanbul appears in Aron Rodrigue, *French Jews, Turkish Jews: The Alliance Israélite Universelle and the Politics of Jewish Schooling in Turkey, 1860–1925* (Bloomington: Indiana University Press, 1990), 185n60.

23. Varol, *Balat*, 3; and Rodrigue, *French Jews, Turkish Jews*, 109.

24. In the Tanzimat period of legal, military, educational, and bureaucratic reforms (1829–1876), the government generally appointed chief rabbis who supported reform. Norman A. Stillman, *Sephardi Religious Responses to Modernity* (Luxembourg: Harwood Academic Publishers, 1995), 36. For the effect of Tanzimat reforms on Ottoman Jews, see Esther Benbassa and Aron Rodrigue, *Sephardi Jewry: A History of the Judeo-Spanish Community, 14th to 20th Centuries* (Berkeley: University of California Press, 2000 [1993]), 68–72. Also see Chapter One, Note 63.

25. Nur Akın, "Balat," in *Dünden Bugüne İstanbul Ansiklopedisi*, 8 vols. (Istanbul: Ana Basım, 1993–1994), 2:10. These seven sections were based on nineteenth-

century Ottoman municipal mappings, which placed Balat within the boundaries of the sixth district. Jewish residents referred to their own related divisions with Ladino names. See Şaul, *Balat'tan Bat-Yam'a*, 43; and Varol, *Balat*, 6.

26. Deleon, *Ancient Districts on the Golden Horn*, 32. According to senior Maftirim conductor David Behar, İsmail Hakkı Bey gave lessons to a number of Jewish hazanim (David Behar, interview with Jak Esim, no date).

27. For related multireligious soundscapes in Ottoman Izmir and Salonika, see Sibel Zandi-Sayek, "Orchestrating Difference, Performing Identity: Urban Space and Public Rituals in Nineteenth-Century Izmir," in *Hybrid Urbanism: On the Identity Discourse and the Built Environment*, ed. Nezar Al-Sayyad (Westport, CT: Praeger, 2001), 42–66; and Leon Sciaky, *Farewell to Salonica: City at the Crossroads* (Philadelphia: Paul Dry Books, 2003 [1946]).

28. For instance, in the 1930s the Milli and Çiçek cinemas in Balat, as well as theaters in other districts, were frequented by Jewish residents. See Şaul, *Balat'tan Bat-Yam'a*, 35; and Niso Tiza's memories in Deleon, *Ancient Districts on the Golden Horn*, 48–49. During the summer a theater tent, pitched in a soccer field, showcased tightrope walkers, dancers, and theatrical shows. Niso Tiza in Deleon, *Ancient Districts on the Golden Horn*, 50. Numerous Sephardic memoirs emphasize the ubiquity of Istanbul street vendors of diverse ethnicity, singing or calling out to sell their wares. See Varol, *Balat*, 31–32; Bornes-Varol, "The Balat Quarter and Its Image," 641–42; Şaul, *Balat'tan Bat-Yam'a*, 44; and Liz Behmoaras, *Kimsin Jak Samanon?* (Istanbul: Sel Yayıncılık, 1997), 59–60.

29. Quoted in Deleon, *Ancient Districts on the Golden Horn*, 69–70.

30. Verda Baruch, quoted in ibid., 42.

31. Varol, *Balat*, 1–2.

32. Salamon Bicerano, quoted in Deleon, *Ancient Districts on the Golden Horn*, 69.

33. Sciaky, *Farewell to Salonica*. Salonika refers to the Ottoman city and Thessaloniki to the present-day Greek city.

34. Bornes-Varol, "The Balat Quarter and Its Image," 641. These memories suggest subsequent pressures, at times resulting in violence, on non-Muslims to learn and speak Turkish as citizens of the new Turkish Republic. See Senem Aslan, "'Citizen, Speak Turkish!': A Nation in the Making," *Nationalism and Ethnic Politics* 13, no. 2 (2007): 245–72.

35. Janti Behar, personal interview, April 7, 2006; Varol, *Balat*, 27; and Behmoaras, *Kimsin Jak Samanon?*, 97, 127.

36. Cohen, "Sephardic Song," 13, 14.

37. Numerous Sephardic memoirs recollect children's weekly or monthly visits to the baths with their mothers, who socialized there with other Jewish, and sometimes non-Jewish, women, singing and eating together. Henry Benezra (b. Istanbul, 1899) describes these occasions as "indoor picnics," unique to women's baths. (Henry Benezra, interview by H. Droker, January 28 and February 4, 1982). See also Şaul, *Balat'tan Bat-Yam'a*, 38; Deleon, *Ancient Districts on the Golden Horn*,

48; and Erol Haker, *Once Upon a Time Jews Lived in Kırklareli* (Istanbul: Isis Press, 2003), 61–62.

38. Janti Behar, personal interview, April 7, 2006.

39. Varol suggests that Balat excelled in meyhanes (taverns) because of the legal authorization of Jews to produce wine for religious purposes, as well as vinegar for home use (Varol, *Balat*, 30). A comparison with other contemporaneous neighborhoods would be required to confirm Balat's exceptionalism in this area.

40. See Chapter One, pages 37–38.

41. Varol, *Balat*, 30. In general, Varol's informants were reluctant to discuss meyhanes, because of the latter's negative status in the neighborhood.

42. Şaul, *Balat'tan Bat-Yam'a*, 46.

43. Bornes-Varol, "The Balat Quarter and Its Image," 640–41. Coffeehouses were historically associated with the Janissaries and their Sufi order, the Bektaşi. After the dissolution of the Janissaries in 1826, these venues became bases for firefighting units (*tulumbacı* coffeehouses).

44. Ibid., 641.

45. Varol, *Balat*, 30.

46. Ibid., 27.

47. Ibid.

48. Şaul, *Balat'tan Bat-Yam'a*, 39.

49. Varol, *Balat*, 27.

50. Şaul, *Balat'tan Bat-Yam'a*, 40. In this passage Şaul lists different genres included in the popular fasıl of the gazino (peşrev, beste, şarkı, saz semaisi).

51. Vefa Zat, "Gazinolar," in *Dünden Bugüne İstanbul Ansiklopedisi*, 3:379.

52. For a discussion of such religious judgments by Ottoman Sephardic rabbis, see Lehmann, *Ladino Rabbinic Literature and Ottoman Sephardic Culture*. Specific examples include a general injunction against leisure activities ("passing time"), by Abraham Palachi (*Va-hokhiah Avraham*, Salonika, 1853, and Izmir, 1862); against visiting coffeehouses, as well as singing, dancing, and drinking at picnics (Elijah ha-Kohen, *Shevet Musar*, Izmir, 1860); against drinking, tavern-going, and eating "gentile" food on the Sabbath (Issac Badhab, *Nehemadim mi-Zahav*, Jerusalem, 1899); and against gambling in various places, including coffeehouses (Eli'ezer Papo, *Pele Yo'ets*, Vienna, 1870–1872). There is evidence of rabbinical complaints against the pervasive socializing in "gentile" coffeehouses in Salonika and Izmir in the eighteenth century. See Lehmann, *Ladino Rabbinic Literature and Ottoman Sephardic Culture*, 226n43.

53. Ibid., 86.

54. Bornes-Varol, "The Balat Quarter and Its Image," 639.

55. Testimony about Purim by Marko Kastoriyano is reported in Güleryüz, *İstanbul Sinagogları*, 22. Purim is a festival commemorating the rescue of the Persian Jews from massacre, according to the Book of Esther. The Ladino song "Ermoza sos en Kantida" appears in Varol, *Balat*, 27.

56. Zat, "Gazinolar," 3:379.

57. Janti Behar, personal interview, April 17, 2008.

58. Avni Bey probably refers to the udi and composer of the early twentieth century, Hüseyin Avni Bey. See Yılmaz Öztuna, *Büyük Türk Musikisi Ansiklopedisi*, 2 vols. (Ankara: Başbakanlık Basımevi, 1990), 1: 357.

59. Şaul, *Balat'tan Bat-Yam'a*, 40.

60. Cem Behar discusses how the commercialization of meşk introduced two elements, notation and payment for services, that had not characterized historical oral transmission and master-pupil relations. Behar, *Zaman, Mekan, Müzik*, 36–40.

61. Hayim Nahum was chief rabbi (hahambaşı) of Ottoman Jewry from 1908–1909 to 1920, the candidate of Alliancist notables in the community. Esther Benbassa, "Associational Strategies in Ottoman Jewish Society in the Nineteenth and Twentieth Centuries," in *The Jews of the Ottoman Empire*, ed. Avigdor Levy (Princeton, NJ: Darwin Press; Washington, DC: Institute of Turkish Studies, 1994), 466.

62. Behmoaras, *Kimsin Jak Samanon?*, 47–48.

63. Dede Efendi is no relation to the teacher Leon Efendi, referred to in the preceding quotation. "Efendi" is an Ottoman honorific title, not a surname.

64. Behmoaras, *Kimsin Jak Samanon?*, 48.

65. During this period, Jews expanded their communities in such Bosphorus neighborhoods as Ortaköy, Beşiktaş, Arnavutköy, Kuzguncuk, and Haydarpaşa. Ilan Karmi, *The Jewish Community of Istanbul in the Nineteenth Century: Social, Legal and Administrative Transformations* (Istanbul: Isis, 1996), 4, 51–52.

66. Behmoaras, *Kimsin Jak Samanon?*, 53

67. European-oriented neighborhoods, such as Galata and Pera, where significant Jewish populations lived, provided popular European musical entertainment, and Alliance schools included instruction in European musical genres. The rise of the recording industry further globalized musical exposure and tastes. On the influence of dance from Europe and the Americas, as well as the recording industry, on Ladino song repertoires, see Welch-Shahak, "Adaptations and Borrowings in the Balkan Sephardic Repertoire," 101–3; and Edwin Seroussi, "New Directions in the Music of the Sephardic Jews," in *Modern Jews and Their Musical Agendas*, ed. Ezra Mendelsohn (Oxford: Oxford University Press, 1993), 70–71.

68. Şaul, *Balat'tan Bat-Yam'a*, 38. Many hazanim I interviewed in Istanbul made this point, in addition to Janti Behar, personal interview, April 7, 2006.

69. According to Janti, Kasturiya's Turkish name was Tekfur Sarayı. The other village in upper Balat was Ichtipol (also referred to as İstipol or İştipol); the neighborhood and its synagogue were named after immigrants from İchtip, Macedonia. Güleryüz, *İstanbul Sinagogları*, 24–25. The wealthy families included the Paltis, who manufactured fezzes and lived opposite the synagogue. Varol, *Balat*, 21.

70. Varol, *Balat*, 20, 22, 30.

71. Ibid., 22.

72. Janti Behar, personal interview, April 7, 2006.

73. Ibid.

74. Material about Yomtov Sulam is drawn from conversations with his granddaughter, Viki Behar, during 2006, and an interview with Janti Behar, April 7, 2006. Yomtov was a manager at a local cigarette factory.

75. It is likely that he learned the Maftirim repertoire under the direction of composer-haham Nesim Sevilya, who led a youth group at Kasturiya synagogue in the 1920s. Hazan Aaron Kohen, "Müziğe Aşık Bir Bestekar Haham Nesim Sevilya Efendi," *Tiryaki* 8–9 (March–April 1995): 67–68.

76. Varol, *Balat*, 21.

77. Janti Behar, personal interview, April 7, 2006. The teva is the raised platform/lectern in the synagogue from which the hazan leads the prayer service.

78. Here Janti is including a broader set of Hebrew song in Maftirim music than actually appears in this art-music-based repertoire. When she mentions the Maftirim later in her testimony, however, it is clear that she is correctly representing the music through her comparisons with fasıl music and ensembles, as well as with gazino programs. "Pithu li" is, in fact, from the Hallel psalms ("Pithu li sha'areh tsedek, avo vam odeh Ya . . .") sung in Sephardic synagogues on Rosh Hodesh (New Moon), Festival Holidays (Pesah, Shavuot, and Sukkot), and Hanukkah.

79. According to several hazanim and congregants attending Turkish synagogues in this period, girls were never seen at the teva, although they were allowed to sing from the balcony during congregational group singing (personal communications, January 2011).

80. Janti Behar, personal interview, April 7, 2006.

81. For an ethnographic example of a beautiful voice winning out over religious precepts, see an oral interview of a Syrian Jewish woman in Kay Kaufman Shelemay, "The Power of Silent Voices: Women in the Syrian Jewish Musical Tradition," in *Music and the Play of Power in the Middle East, North Africa and Central Asia*, ed. Laudan Nooshin (Farnham, Surrey: Ashgate, 2009), 285.

82. Bornes-Varol, "The Balat Quarter and Its Image," 639.

83. Janti Behar, personal interview, April 7, 2006.

84. Ibid.

85. Judith Cohen discusses the partiality of musical knowledge of Sephardim in the diaspora, based on gendered musical practices. Cohen, "Judeo-Spanish Songs in Montreal and Toronto," 26.

86. Janti Behar, personal interview, April 7, 2006.

87. Münir Nurettin Beken, "Musicians, Audience and Power: The Changing Aesthetics in the Music at the Maksim Gazino of Istanbul," Ph.D. dissertation (University of Maryland, 1998), 65.

88. Münir Beken, personal communication, September 2008. Since the 1930s there has been a trend toward simplification of usuls and makams of gazino music (Beken, "Musicians, Audience and Power," 243).

89. Janti Behar, personal interview, April 17, 2008.

90. Janti Behar, personal interview, April 7, 2006. "Farığ Olmam" is a composition by Sadettin Kaynak (1893–1961) in Isfahan makam.

91. Comments by Viki Behar during the personal interview with her mother, Janti Behar, April 7, 2006.

92. One of Kay Shelemay's informants among Syrian Jewish women experienced a similar shift at adolescence, away from Hebrew religious music and toward the Arab songs representing the source of the Hebrew songs. See Shelemay, "The Power of Silent Voices," 283.

93. Janti Behar, personal interview, April 7, 2006.

94. By the 1930s the Blumenthal Brothers were agents for Columbia in Turkey, Syria, and Albania. Their factory had been sold to Columbia under the directorship of Julius Blumenthal's son Marcel (1907–1993), and their business relationship with Columbia continued to the mid-1960s. Sevengül Sönmez, *Istanbul'un 100 Ailesi* (Istanbul: Istanbul Büyükşehir Belediyesi Kültür A.S. Yayınları, 2010) 54–56. On the Blumenthal Brothers' recording company, see Chapter Two, and Cemal Ünlü, *Git Zaman Gel Zaman: Fonograf, Gramofon, Taş Plak* (Istanbul: Pan Yayıncılık, 2004), 110, 175–92; and Hazan Aaron Kohen, "Osmanlı İmparatorluğunun Kuruluş Yıllarından Günümüze Yahudi Dini Musikisi," *Folklor/Edebiyat* 6, no. 21 (2000–2001): 106.

95. Viki Behar, personal interview, April 17, 2008.

96. Janti Behar, personal interview, April 7, 2006.

97. As Mathias Lehmann has argued, Sephardi rabbinical literature distinguishes not between public and private spaces but rather between the sacred and the profane. In this religious worldview, the home and the synagogue could be considered continuous spaces (as sacred or not profane), rather than distinguished from each other as public and private, a framing that further challenges distinct male/public and female/private conceptual divides. Lehmann, *Ladino Rabbinic Literature and Ottoman Sephardic Culture*.

98. Seroussi, "Archivists of Memory," 204–6. According to Seroussi, Sene's collection reflects "new Sephardi song" popular among Jews in the interwar period inside and outside Turkey, becoming standards by the 1950s and contrasting with academic constructions of "museumized" Ladino repertoires (ibid., 197). Also see Rivka Havassy, "The Ladino Song in the 20th Century: A Study of the Collections of Emily Sene and Bouena Sarfatty-Garfinkle," Ph.D. dissertation (Bar-Ilan University, 2007) (Hebrew).

99. Seroussi, "Archivists of Memory," 205.

100. Judith Amiel, personal interview, March 7, 2007.

101. Reported by Leon Hakim (a member of the Izmir Maftirim group as a youth), personal interview, July 3, 2010.

102. For example, Yusuf Paşa's "Segah peşrev" and Ismail Hakkı Bey's "Seni Hükm-i Ezel Aşub-ı Devran Etmek İstermiş."

103. See Dorn, "Change and Ideology," 191n21.

104. Concerning modernizing North African and Middle Eastern Jewish women, Rachel Simon has made the point that "overall, concepts regarding one's

place in the world were slower to change than individual achievements. Consequently, 'New Women' often found themselves continuing to live in a conceptually old world, despite their spiritual metamorphosis and external evidence to the contrary." Rachel Simon, "Between the Family and the Outside World: Jewish Girls in the Modern Middle East and North Africa," *Jewish Social Studies: History, Culture, Society* 7, no. 1 (2000): 94.

105. *Maftirim* (Istanbul: Gözlem, 2009). See Chapter Five.

106. Robert Abudara, personal interview, January 16, 2006.

107. Such progressive expansion of linguistic knowledge and participation in urban life is probably based on social pressures to learn and speak Turkish, a burgeoning entertainment life through film, radio, and gazinos, and the increasing ability of women to participate in such events, particularly Jewish women of means who chose to remain in Turkey.

108. Interviews with numerous hazanim in Istanbul, 2006.

109. An Istanbul hazan, personal interview, July 12, 2006.

Chapter Four

1. Ilan Karmi, *The Jewish Community of Istanbul in the Nineteenth Century: Social, Legal and Administrative Transformations* (Istanbul: Isis, 1996), 4, 51–52. On changing occupational and residential patterns among individuals of diverse ethno-religious affiliation in Istanbul at the turn of the twentieth century, see Edhem Eldem, "Istanbul 1903–1918: A Quantitative Analysis of a Bourgeoisie," *Boğaziçi Journal: A Review of Social, Economic and Administrative Studies* 11, no. 1–2 (1997): 53–98.

2. Ilan Karmi, *Jewish Sites of Istanbul: A Guide Book* (Istanbul: Isis, 1992), 86.

3. Selihot are the penitential poems and prayers recited during early morning services during the High Holidays.

4. For news reports on the 1986 synagogue attack, see Alan Cowell, "Jews in Istanbul Reopen Synagogue," *New York Times*, May 21, 1987; Clyde Haberman, "Istanbul Journal: Where 16 Synagogues Stand among the Minarets," *New York Times*, July 30, 1990; and Judith Miller, "The Istanbul Synagogue Massacre," *New York Times*, January 4, 1987. On the 2003 synagogue attack, see Yigal Schleifer, "Bombers Kill 20 in Attacks on Synagogues," *Telegraph Media Group*, November 16, 2003; Yigal Schleifer, "Turkish Jews Dig out after Bombs," *Jewish Telegraphic Agency/Jewishjournal.com*, November 21, 2003; and "Seven Jailed for Turkey Bombings," *BBC*, February 17, 2007, http://news.bbc.co.uk/2/hi/europe/6370117.stm (accessed December 1, 2012).

5. Robert Abudara, personal interview, January 16, 2006.

6. Personal communication, congregation member, 2006.

7. Although "community" is a contested term among academics, its use for this observant minority within a minority is warranted because of members' close affiliation with each other and local Jewish religious institutions. For an incisive study of the history of the term and a proposal for interdisciplinary scholarly use,

see Kay Kaufman Shelemay, "Musical Communities: Rethinking the Collective in Music," *Journal of the American Musicological Society* 64, no. 2 (2011): 349–90.

8. Ruth Gruber's work suggests there is a distinction between "culture" and "cultural product" in the contemporary European construction and reconstruction of things Jewish. These terms are useful in elucidating broad differences in the interests and performances of the two Maftirim groups in order to understand their political context. However, the dichotomy is problematic in its implication of purity on the one hand and impurity on the other as well as in its assumption that only pure forms should and do participate in cultural heritage and change. Ruth Ellen Gruber, *Virtually Jewish: Reinventing Jewish Culture in Europe* (Berkeley: University of California Press, 2002), 61–71. Alternatively, scholarship on culture, heritage, and tourism has argued for the constructedness of all cultural heritage, an approach that avoids the thorny question of authenticity, but risks overlooking the historical continuities that authenticate music like the Maftirim for its music-makers and listeners as well as the role of commodification and profit motives in cultural construction and change. See, for example, Barbara Kirshenblatt-Gimblett, "Theorizing Heritage," *Ethnomusicology* 39, no. 3 (1995): 367–80.

9. On migration patterns, see Chapter Two, pages 53–54 and 69–70.

10. For example, the neighborhoods of Ulus, Şişli, Nişantışı, and Kurtuluş. See Şule Toktaş, "Turkey's Jews and Their Immigration to Israel," *Middle Eastern Studies* 42 (2006): 511.

11. Çağlar Keyder, ed., *Istanbul between the Global and the Local* (Lanham, MD: Rowman & Littlefield, 1999). See the editor's introduction for a historical overview of the city through the 1990s.

12. For further discussion of the reclamation of Istanbul as an Islamic city and historic imperial capital, see Ayfer Bartu, "Who Owns the Old Quarters? Rewriting Histories in a Global Era," and Tanıl Bora, "Istanbul of the Conqueror: The 'Alternative Global City' Dreams of Political Islam," both in Keyder, ed., *Istanbul between the Global and the Local*; and Alev Çınar, *Modernity, Islam, and Secularism in Turkey: Bodies, Places, and Time* (Minneapolis: University of Minnesota Press, 2005).

13. David Sevi, personal interview, January 5, 2006.

14. According to attendee Rıfat Dana, the Maftirim ensemble met in the Selaniko synagogue of Balat at least until 1955. Rıfat Dana, personal interview, July 6, 2006. Most scholarship and some Maftirim attendees outside Balat do not recognize the length of time the repertoire was regularly performed in that neighborhood.

15. David Sevi, personal interview, January 5, 2006.

16. Descriptions of the Maftirim sessions at Şişli synagogue are based on observations of the author, November 2005–May 2006.

17. See Chapter Two.

18. David Sevi, personal interview, February 23, 2006.

19. Ibid., January 5, 2006.

20. *İstanbul Müziğin Renkleri* (Istanbul: the Colors of Music) (Istanbul: Boyut Müzik, CD, 1996). For other CD releases sponsored by the city in 1996 (*İstanbul Şarkıları* and *İstanbul Türküleri*), see Martin Stokes, "Sounding Out: The Culture Industries and the Globalization of Istanbul," in Keyder, ed., *Istanbul between the Global and the Local*, 127. For CDs and other productions of the municipality for Habitat II, see also Çınar, *Modernity, Islam, and Secularism in Turkey*, 120.

21. David Sevi, personal interview, January 5, 2006.

22. Ibid., February 23, 2006.

23. Ibid., January 5, 2006.

24. David Sevi, personal interviews, 2006.

25. Liner notes, *Maftirim: Judeo-Sufi Connection* (Istanbul: Kalan Müzik, CD 234, 2001), 60; and Menahem Eskenazi, personal interview, April 4, 2006.

26. Taşkın Savaş, personal interview, March 29, 2008. Dhimmi ("protected people") are non-Muslim ethno-religious communities that, under Islamic law, were administered separately from Muslim communities.

27. This selection is based on my research in Istanbul in 2005–2006. Members of this chorus have performed and recorded at least since 1999, and have continued to perform at various public events since 2006. The Rumi Project, or "Mevlana ve Hoşgörü" (Rumi and Tolerance) concert, occurred on October 2, 2005, at Cemal Reşit Rey concert hall, Istanbul, and interpreted the philosophy of thirteenth century Sufi poet Celaleddin Rumi through verse, music, and film. The production has been staged in New York and Berlin as well. The "Hatay Medeniyetler Buluşması" took place in Hatay-Antakya on September 26, 2005 to commemorate the Abrahamic faith communities that historically resided there.

28. Yahudi Kültürü Avrupa Günü (European Day of Jewish Culture), September 4, 2005. This annual festival began in Europe in 1996 and in Istanbul in 2003, shortly before the synagogue attacks that year. Marcy Brink-Danan insightfully points out the political and social significance of the repetition of, rather than retreat from, the European Day of Jewish Culture each year after the attacks, allowing the Jewish community to maintain a political and social presence "beyond what their numbers might predict." Brink-Danan, *Jewish Life in Twenty-first-Century Turkey*, 104–5.

29. Bensi Elmas, personal communication, November 15, 2005.

30. General information about the group's activities is based on attendance at their concerts and rehearsals, as well as interviews with the conductor and conversation with members, 2005–2006.

31. *Maftirim: Judeo-Sufi Connection* (Istanbul: Kalan Müzik, CD 234, 2001).

32. The concerts have continued annually at least through June 2011. The 2011 concert included two Jewish groups, the Sinagog Maftirim Korosu and Los Paşaros Sefardis, a longtime folk ensemble in Istanbul performing in Ladino.

33. For a description of the 1953 commemorations, see Gavin D. Brockett, *How Happy to Call Oneself a Turk: Provincial Newspapers and the Negotiation of a Muslim*

National Identity, Modern Middle East Series (Austin: University of Texas Press, 2011), 195–200.

34. For a study of the role of multiparty politics and a burgeoning provincial press in these debates between 1945 and 1954, conceptualized as a renegotiation of national identity, see ibid. On the 1953 commemorations and their social and political significance, see ibid., 195–200.

35. Revised representations and the popularization of Ottoman history in literature, film, and news media between 1945 and 1954 appear in ibid., 190–95.

36. As Brockett persuasively argues, Erdoğan's political platform reasserted previous political accommodations to public religious life, for example the platform and policies of the Democratic Party (1950–1960), as well as the "Turkish-Islamic synthesis" of 1960s and 1970s intellectuals and Turgut Özal (prime minister, 1983–1989). Ibid., 223, 226.

37. For a cultural politics analysis of the celebration of Conquest Day, see Çınar, *Modernity, Islam, and Secularism in Turkey*, chap. 4 (138–67). Electoral successes of Islamist parties in Turkey include winning 28 of 72 municipal governments in 1994 (including Istanbul and Ankara) and heading the national government in 1996–1997 and after 2002. For recent scholarship on the AKP, see the review article, Alev Çınar, "The Justice and Development Party: Turkey's Experience with Islam, Democracy, Liberalism, and Secularism," *International Journal of Middle East Studies* 43 (2011): 529–41. Among extensive social science scholarship on the Refah (Welfare) and AK (Justice and Development) parties, see Ümit Cizre, ed., *Secular and Islamic Politics in Turkey: The Making of the Justice and Development Party*, Routledge Studies in Middle Eastern Politics (New York: Routledge, 2008); Spyridon Kotsovilis, "Between Fedora and Fez: Modern Turkey's Troubled Road to Democratic Consolidation and the Pluralizing Role of Erdogan's Pro-Islam Government," in *Turkey and the European Union: Internal Dynamics and External Challenges*, ed. Joseph S. Joseph (New York: Palgrave Macmillan, 2006); Nilufer Narli, "The Rise of the Islamist Movement in Turkey," in *Revolutionaries and Reformers: Contemporary Islamist Movements in the Middle East*, ed. Barry Rubin (New York: State University of New York Press, 2003); and M. Hakan Yavuz, ed., *The Emergence of a New Turkey: Democracy and the AK Parti*, Utah Series in Turkish and Islamic Studies (Salt Lake City: University of Utah Press, 2006). For scholarship on Islamist-secularist debates in Turkey from a cultural studies perspective, see Esra Özyürük, "Public Memory as Political Battleground," in *The Politics of Public Memory in Turkey*, ed. Esra Özyürük (Syracuse, NY: Syracuse University Press, 2007), and Esra Özyürük, *Nostalgia for the Modern: State Secularism and Everyday Politics in Turkey* (Durham, NC: Duke University Press, 2006).

38. Brockett, *How Happy to Call Oneself a Turk*, 200–201.

39. Çınar, *Modernity, Islam, and Secularism in Turkey*, 172. According to Çınar, as mayor of Istanbul, Recep Tayyip Erdoğan invested in public fora to dialogue and debate with secularist perspectives, in contrast to the adversarial position of the more conservative wing of the Refah (Welfare) Party.

40. Ibid., 154.

41. Ibid., 157–58. Çınar compares divergent framings of the event: one as a prophesized Islamic conquest (by a representative of the Islamist municipal government), the other as a Turkish victory (in an official national history text).

42. Ahmed Tohumcu, "A Metamorphosis Story: Sema," unpublished paper, ICTM Study Group on Music and Dance in Southeastern Europe Symposium, April 7–11, 2010, Ege University, Izmir, Turkey.

43. For example, in 1994 proposals to build a mosque and Islamic cultural center in Taksim, as well as to tear down ruined Byzantine (read Greek) city walls coincided with a tour by the new Beyoğlu mayor (N. Bayraktar) of all synagogues and churches of the district. Bartu, "Who Owns the Old Quarters? Rewriting Histories in a Global Era," 40–43.

44. Concert organizer, personal interview, March 29, 2008.

45. Ibid.

46. Cengiz Bektaş, *Kuzguncuk* (Istanbul: Literatür, 2003). See also Cengiz Bektaş, *Hoşgörünün Öteki Adı: Kuzguncuk* (Istanbul: Tasarım Yayın Grubu, 1996).

47. The Kuzguncuk concert was sponsored by the municipality, but was directed not by an employee of the administration, but by a classical musician, Mehmet Güntekin, with an interest in minority music.

48. Concert organizer, personal interview, March 29, 2008.

49. As Beyoğlu mayor N. Bayraktar, who toured his district's synagogues and churches before his election in 1994, later asserted, "The first thing I ordered was to clean the garbage around the Armenian church. Now how can you say that Refah is the party of Islam alone?" Bartu, "Who Owns the Old Quarters? Rewriting Histories in a Global Era," 41.

50. Choir members, personal communications, 2006.

51. On the 1892 commemorations, see Julia Phillips Cohen, "Fashioning Imperial Citizens: Sephardi Jews and the Ottoman State, 1856–1912," Ph.D. dissertation (Stanford University, 2008), chap. 2. Whereas the 1992 celebrations took place within a political context of a unique, mutually favorable Turkish state–Jewish community relationship, the 400-year commemorations celebrated an Ottomanism in which diverse ethno-religious populations participated. Michelle U. Campos provides an in-depth study of multiethnic politics and Ottoman citizenship after the 1908 Constitutional Revolution in *Ottoman Brothers: Muslims, Christians, and Jews in Early Twentieth-Century Palestine* (Stanford, CA: Stanford University Press, 2011).

52. On the Capital Tax, see Chapter Two, Note 80. For an extensive discussion of the filming of *Salkım Hanım'ın Taneleri* (Mrs. Salkım's Beads) about the Capital Tax, see Rıfat N. Bali, *The "Varlık Vergisi Affair": A Study of Its Legacy—Selected Documents* (Istanbul: Isis, 2005), 133–80. The Jewish protagonists in the novel were changed to Armenian characters in the film, in part because the filmmaker could not receive permission to film at Jewish sites in the city. Therefore, the public perception is that Armenians were the primary victims of the tax.

53. Turkish armed forces invaded Cyprus in July 1974 in response to a Greek military coup and following a decade of rising political tensions over the status of the Turkish minority on Cyprus. The invasion initiated massive movements of Greek Cypriots from northern to southern Cyprus as well as Turkish Cypriots from southern to northern Cyprus. The first of a series of attacks on Turkish diplomats worldwide through the 1980s took place in 1973 in Los Angeles when Gourgen Yanikian killed Turkish Consul General Mehmet Baydar and Vice Consul Bahadır Demir. In the 1980s ASALA (Armenian Secret Army for the Liberation of Armenia) and JCAG (Justice Commandos of the Armenian Genocide) claimed responsibility for a number of attacks. On the changing relationship between the Turkish state and the Turkish Jewish community as a result of these external events, see: Rıfat N. Bali, "The 1934 Thrace Events: Continuity and Change within Turkish State Policies Regarding Non-Muslim Minorities: An Interview with Rıfat Bali," http://ejts.revues.org/index2903.html (2008) (accessed April 1, 2012).

54. National holidays in Turkey are related to events in which Mustafa Kemal Atatürk was involved between 1919 and 1938. On the significance of extending Turkish nationalist commemoration into the Ottoman centuries, see Çınar, *Modernity, Islam, and Secularism in Turkey*, chap. 4 (138–67).

55. In fact, Ali Bulaç, an Islamist intellectual who influenced Recep Tayyip Erdoğan's policies as mayor of Istanbul, advocated the adoption of separate, millet systems of justice. Ibid., 10.

56. Şule Toktaş, "The Conduct of Citizenship in the Case of Turkey's Jewish Minority: Legal Status, Identity, and Civic Virtue Aspects," *Comparative Studies of South Asia, Africa and the Middle East* 26, no. 1 (2006): 132.

57. Brink-Danan, *Jewish Life in Twenty-first-Century Turkey*, 58–59.

58. In the 1990s, films and literature on the Capital Tax, population exchange, Armenian, Greek, and Kurdish issues began to be produced. Since the publication of *Anneannem* (My Grandmother) by Fethiye Çetin in 2004, at least eight books of autobiography and fiction have been published in Turkish on the Armenian genocide, and an academic conference on the genocide took place at Istanbul Bilgi University in September 2005. For details, see Ayşe Gül Altınay and Yektan Türkyılmaz, "Unravelling Layers of Gendered Silencing: Converted Armenian Survivors of the 1915 Catastrophe," in *Untold Histories of the Middle East: Recovering Voices from the 19th and 20th Centuries*, ed. Amy Singer, Christoph K. Neumann, and Selçuk Akşin Somel (London: Routledge, 2011), 36–37, 51. Following the assassination of Armenian journalist Hrant Dink in January 2007, the foundation established in his name has sponsored conferences, publications, exhibits, and awards related to Armenian, Turkish, and minority culture and coexistence. See the website of the Hrant Dink Vakfı (Hrant Dink Foundation): www.hrantdink.org. For critical scholarship about Turkish Jewish social history, see the work of Rıfat Bali and the review article, Marc David Baer, "Turkish Jews Rethink '500 Years of Brotherhood and Friendship,'" *Turkish Studies Association Bulletin* 24, no. 2 (2000): 63–74.

59. As André Levy argues about Moroccan Jews in Casablanca, self-confinement may generate a vicious cycle of fear and security because disengagement with the surrounding society may confirm and thus increase rather than decrease fear. Moreover, financial support, for example from the American Joint Distribution Committee, requires the maintenance of a distinct community of Moroccan Jews, as Levy argues, through boundaries and controls exerted by this centralized institution. André Levy, "Notes on Jewish-Muslim Relationships: Revisiting the Vanishing Moroccan Jewish Community," *Cultural Anthropology* 18, no. 3 (2003): 372–73.

60. Gruber, *Virtually Jewish*, chap. 2 (esp. 25, 29).

61. Judith Cohen, "Constructing a Spanish Jewish Festival: Music and the Appropriation of Tradition," *World of Music* 41, no. 3 (1999): 85–113; and Judith Cohen, "Music and the Re-Creation of Identity in Imagined Iberian Jewish Communities," *Revista de dialectología y tradiciones populares* 54, no. 2 (1999): 125–44.

62. Gruber, *Virtually Jewish*, analyzes multiple faces of "things Jewish" in Europe, focusing on a cultural study of non-Jewish engagement with "Jewish culture."

63. Ibid., chap. 7 (131–54).

64. During my research year in Istanbul, 2005–2006, I met a Jewish tour guide who noted a dramatic shift in his tours after 1992, from sites of regional and multi-civilizational interest in the past, including the pilgrimage sites of Saint Paul, to local Jewish structures. Personal communication, December 13, 2005. On the Quincentennial celebrations, including officially sponsored tours, see Brink-Danan, *Jewish Life in Twenty-first-Century Turkey*, 33–62.

65. For an overview of scholarship arising from the 1992 celebrations, see Daniel Goffman, "The Quincentennial of 1492 and Ottoman-Jewish Studies: A Review Essay," *Shofar* 11, no. 4 (1993): 57–67; and Laurent-Olivier Mallet, *La Turquie, Les Turcs et Les Juifs: Histoire, représentations, discours et stratégies* (Istanbul: Isis, 2008), 473–74.

66. Gruber, *Virtually Jewish*, 61–62.

67. Cohen, "Constructing a Spanish Jewish Festival."

68. In Turkish, "ucuz, kolay, çabuk." Personal interview, April 11, 2008. It goes without saying that musical borrowing is common in music-making across space, time, and ethno-religious affiliations.

69. Ruth Gruber's term. Gruber, *Virtually Jewish*, 10. Historian Diana Pinto uses the term "Jewish space" to denote European space filled with present-day Jewish phenomena. Diana Pinto, "Potsdamer Platz versus Aschenbach: Two Paradigms of Jewish Life in Europe," European Association for Jewish Culture, 2002, http://jewish-theatre.com/visitor/article_display.aspx?articleID=265 (accessed December 4, 2012).

70. For example, the villages of Ribadavia and Hervas, discussed in Cohen, "Constructing a Spanish Jewish Festival," and Maribor, Slovenia, in Gruber, *Virtually Jewish*, 118–21.

71. Factors prompting emigration included linguistic and sociocultural pres-

sures, such as the "Citizen, Speak Turkish!" campaign, economic discrimination in the civil service, and the Varlık Vergisi (Capital Tax). See Chapter Two.

72. Choir and community members, personal communications, 2006.

73. Bali, *The "Varlık Vergisi Affair,"* 139. In my own research, informants have given this reason to justify their silence about violent or discriminatory experiences in their families.

74. Gruber, *Virtually Jewish*, chap. 1 (3–24).

75. Cohen uses the term "pseudomitologia" for the religious inaccuracies she encountered at Sephardic festivals in Spain. Cohen, "Constructing a Spanish Jewish Festival," 104. Like Cohen, here I am referencing not cultural authenticity, but rather the self-representational character of the community choir and its avoidance, as such, of egregious errors in representing, for example, broadly accepted interpretations of Jewish religious law.

Chapter Five

1. Lag B'Omer is a feast day and celebration in the spring commemorating the death of Rabbi Shimon Bar Yohai, who is traditionally believed to have authored the Kabbalistic text the *Zohar*.

2. Izi Eli produced the instrumental arrangement from the group's scores. Bensi Elmas, personal communication, May 10, 2006.

3. Perkey Avot (Turkish spelling) or Pirké Avot, popularly known as "The Ethics of the Fathers," is customarily read between the holidays of Passover and Shavuot.

4. Cem Behar, *Aşk Olmayınca Meşk Olmaz: Geleneksel Osmanlı/Türk Müziğinde Öğretim ve Intikal*, 2nd ed. (Istanbul: Yapı Kredi Yayınları, 2003 [1998]), 15, 96.

5. "Traditional" is used here as a fluid academic term that in specific, real-life contexts often refers to fixed notions of authentic heritage.

6. For a detailed review of historical song-text collections for Ottoman Hebrew music, see Edwin Seroussi, "Introduction," in *Maftirim* (Istanbul: Gözlem, 2009), the Maftirim project of the Ottoman-Turkish Sephardic Culture Research Center.

7. *Shire Yisrael be-Erets ha-kedem* (Istanbul: Benjamin Raphael B. Joseph, circa 1921).

8. See Chapter Two, pages 49–50.

9. For a comparative case regarding contemporary Moroccan Jews, see André Levy, "Notes on Jewish-Muslim Relationships: Revisiting the Vanishing Moroccan Jewish Community," *Cultural Anthropology* 18, no. 3 (2003): 365–97. On the consolidation of the Turkish Jewish community today, see Marcy Brink-Danan, *Jewish Life in Twenty-first-Century Turkey: The Other Side of Tolerance*, Indiana Series in Sephardi and Mizrahi Studies (Bloomington: Indiana University Press, 2012).

10. Yusuf Altıntaş, personal interview, January 31, 2006. Hazan Victor Beruhiel also described David Behar teaching with usuls (Victor Beruhiel, personal interview, April 12, 2006).

11. See Chapter Two, page 79 and Note 120.

12. Behar, *Aşk Olmayınca Meşk Olmaz*, 20. Each usul has a pattern of light and heavy beats of different number and length. Because this pattern is in a direct relationship with the melodic structure, beating the usul makes it easier to learn and remember the piece (ibid., 17). On the centrality of usuls in meşk, see "Meşk ve Usul" in ibid., chap. 1 (16–25). In other oral art forms and performance it is generally understood that rhythm serves as an important memory device.

13. Selim Behar, long-standing hazan at Yeniköy synagogue, first heard and learned Maftirim pieces as a youth at David Behar's home, where Behar also played the kanun (Selim Behar, personal communication, January 31, 2006). Nesim Sevilya also organized a Maftirim group for youth at Kasturiya synagogue in the late 1920s, and taught boys through meşk methods at Haydarpaşa synagogue in the late 1940s (see Chapter One).

14. Rav Leon Adoni, personal interview, June 19, 2006. See quote by Samuel Benaroya, Chapter One, page 30.

15. Behar, *Aşk Olmayınca Meşk Olmaz*, 39. On the history and use of Ottoman song-text collections, see "Güfte Mecmuaları," in ibid., chap. 2 (39–41).

16. *Shire Yisrael be-Erets ha-kedem*, paraphrase of Rosanes.

17. Julia Phillips Cohen and Sarah Abrevaya Stein, "Sephardic Scholarly Worlds: Toward a Novel Geography of Modern Jewish History," *Jewish Quarterly Review* 100, no. 3 (2010): 349–84, traces understudied multigenerational Sephardic intellectuals, their publications and transnational networks to enlarge Jewish intellectual history.

18. Rosanes refers specifically to musical expertise in the cities of Constantinople and Izmir, and the island of Rhodes, and the loss of these Ottoman possessions to other countries. Indeed, at the time of the songbook's publication (circa 1921), these areas were occupied by European powers and Greece (Constantinople and Izmir respectively) or incorporated into Italy (Rhodes).

19. See Chapter Two, pages 54–55.

20. See Chapter One, Note 59; Chapter Three, page 103 and Note 60.

21. Behar, *Aşk Olmayınca Meşk Olmaz*, 86. On the difference in notational philosophies between Darülelhan and Darüttalim-i Musıki, see "Bir İstisna: Darüttalim-i Musıki," in ibid., chap. 3 (85–95). Whereas Darülelhan sought to notate "authentic" original compositions, Darüttalim-i Musıki made no such claims, following an Ottoman concept of compositional versions, legitimized by performers through the masters who taught them.

22. Algazi published a few scores in Izmir and Istanbul, including two Hebrew fasıls, which he notated (Istanbul, c. 1925) and which were part of the same classical musical trends. Pamela J. Dorn, "Change and Ideology: The Ethnomusicology of Turkish Jewry," Ph.D. dissertation (Indiana University, 1991).

23. See Seroussi, "Introduction," 62.

24. Behar discusses the ongoing use of notation as musical reminder in Turkey,

as well as early republican use of notation in modern visual representations (Behar, *Aşk Olmayınca Meşk Olmaz*, 15, 96, 139–40, 177).

25. In the 1940s and 1950s many vocal and instrumental apprentices employed by Istanbul and Ankara Radio learned music through meşk methods from more experienced artists. These informal "radio schools" came to an end in 1954 (ibid., 143–44).

26. David Sevi, personal interview, February 23, 2006.

27. Rav Leon Adoni, personal interview, January 16, 2006, and David Sevi, personal interview, February 23, 2006.

28. Victor Beruhiel, personal interview, April 12, 2006.

29. Ibid.

30. Menahem Eskenazi, personal interview, April 4, 2006.

31. Behar, *Aşk Olmayınca Meşk Olmaz*.

32. Menahem Eskenazi, personal interview, April 4, 2006.

33. David Sevi, personal interview, February 23, 2006.

34. Ibid.

35. Behar, *Aşk Olmayınca Meşk Olmaz*, 54. There are numerous examples of composers who tested prospective students' ability to memorize a piece before accepting them as a student. Hafiz Süleyman is an example of someone with a beautiful voice for reciting the Qu'ran and singing *gazels* (a vocal improvisation using a text and meter-free music), but because of a poor memory was considered incapable of learning music (ibid., 55–58). Meşk had a dual function of teaching vocal or instrumental technique and transmitting an entire repertoire (ibid., 14); therefore, memory was an important ability.

36. Victor Beruhiel, personal interview, April 12, 2006.

37. Menahem Eskenazi, personal interview, April 4, 2006.

38. These are current or past suburbs of Istanbul; Sarıyer and Beykos are on opposite sides of the northern Bosphorus and Avcılar is outside the historical core of the city.

39. Here the interviewee uses "İspanyolca" ("Spanish" in Turkish) for the Judeo-Spanish language spoken by Turkish Jews.

40. Victor Beruhiel, personal interview, April 12, 2006.

41. Ibid.

42. David Sevi, personal interview, February 23, 2006.

43. Victor Beruhiel, personal interview, April 12, 2006.

44. Rıfat Dana, personal interview, July 6, 2006.

45. On audiences, co-creation, and oral art forms, see John Miles Foley, *The Singer of Tales in Performance* (Bloomington: Indiana University Press, 1995).

46. See Seroussi, "Introduction," 62–63.

47. Victor Beruhiel, personal interview, April 12, 2006.

48. Maftirim member, personal communication, November 2005.

49. Yusuf Altıntaş, personal interview, January 31, 2006.

50. Victor Beruhiel, personal interview, April 12, 2006.

51. On knowledge of makam in Turkish society and a game show in the 1970s with "makam" as a category, see Münir Nurettin Beken, "Musicians, Audience and Power: The Changing Aesthetics in the Music at the Maksim Gazino of Istanbul," Ph.D. dissertation (University of Maryland, 1998), 85.

52. Victor Beruhiel, personal interview, April 12, 2006.

53. Ibid.

54. Ibid.

55. Ibid.

56. On the urban consolidation of Moroccan Jews in Casablanca and Turkish Jews in Istanbul, see Note 9 above.

57. Naim Güleryüz, *İstanbul Sinagogları* (Istanbul: Ajans Class, 1992). Despite depletion of neighborhoods and synagogue closures, some historical synagogues have been renovated (e.g., Ahrida and Yanbol in Balat) and are attended by Jewish residents coming in from outlying districts.

58. Rıfat Dana, personal interview, July 6, 2006.

59. Menahem Eskenazi, personal interview, April 4, 2006.

60. Declining religious observance today is confirmed by hazan David Sevi of Şişli synagogue, officials in the chief rabbi's offices, and observations of the author. In her research in the Turkish Jewish community, Marcy Brink-Danan counters recent statistics about Turkish Jewish religious observance with the example of her own informants, whom she describes as "devoutly secular." Brink-Danan, *Jewish Life in Twenty-first-Century Turkey*, 20.

61. Victor Beruhiel, personal interview, April 12, 2006, and Menahem Eskenazi, personal interview, April 4, 2006.

62. David Sevi, personal interview, July 12, 2006.

63. Beken, "Musicians, Audience and Power," 225.

64. David Sevi, personal interview, January 5, 2006.

65. Ibid.

66. Rav Leon Adoni, personal interview, January 16, 2006.

67. Beken, "Musicians, Audience and Power," 226.

68. For example, the songbook used by David Sevi's Maftirim group contains approximately seventy pieces from over 250 compositions in *Shire Yisrael be-Erets ha-kedem*.

69. *Maftirim: Judeo-Sufi Connection* (Istanbul: Kalan Müzik, CD 234, 2001).

70. David Sevi, personal interview, July 12, 2006.

71. Observations of the author at Maftirim sessions at Şişli synagogue, November 2005–May 2006.

72. Scholarship on orality and textuality has argued that an older generation raised in oral art forms and methods may use new textual media in ways different from those of a younger generation, thus challenging assumptions of losses in oral transmission. Albert B. Lord, *The Singer of Tales*, 2nd ed. (Cambridge, MA: Harvard University Press, 2000 [1960]), 129–30.

73. On orality and literacy as forms of communication (face-to-face and within

hearing vs. production/dissemination beyond the range of the human voice), see Brian Stock, *The Implications of Literacy: Written Language and Models of Interpretation in the Eleventh and Twelfth Centuries* (Princeton, NJ: Princeton University Press, 1983).

74. Bruno Nettl makes the point that mixtures of oral and textual technologies often shape musical transmission: oral and handwritten media can promote learning versions or variant copies, whereas printed and audio-recorded documentation may standardize single compositions. Bruno Nettl, *Heartland Excursions* (Urbana: University of Illinois Press, 1995), 37. It is also necessary to take into account practical use: manuscripts ("written") can be photocopied and distributed, and recordings can remain unduplicated.

75. Karen Gerson Şarhon, personal communication, July 17, 2006.

76. For a comparative analysis of selective collecting of oral art forms for different audiences, see John Miles Foley, "Textualization as Mediation: The Case of the Traditional Oral Epic," in *Voice, Text, Hypertext: Emerging Practices in Textual Studies*, ed. Raimonda Modiano, Leroy F. Searle, and Peter Shillingsburg (Seattle: University of Washington Press, 2004), 101–20.

77. Lord describes the potential for a collector of songs to create "the song," or apparent originals, for new (academic, literate) audiences. In his words, "Proteus was photographed." Lord, *The Singer of Tales*, 124–25.

78. Musical archives collected, organized, and arranged for research purposes can become the basis for future traditions. For example, a collection by the Sephardic journalist, singer, and music collector Isaac Levy (1919–1977), entitled *Chants judéo-espagnols* (1959), helped to shape Sephardic music in the second half of the twentieth century. Edwin Seroussi, "Reconstructing Sephardic Music in the 20th Century: Isaac Levy and His 'Chants Judeo-Espagnols,'" *World of Music* 37, no. 1 (1995): 39–58. A revivalist music group in Portugal relied on harmonized transcriptions from collections published in the 1890s by Neves and Campos, in part because published sources were considered authoritative. Salwa El-Shawan Castelo-Branco, "Safeguarding Traditional Music in Contemporary Portugal," in *World Musics–Musics of the World: Aspects of Documentation, Mass Media and Acculturation*, ed. Max Peter Baumann (Berlin: Florian Noetzel Verlag, 1992), 179–80.

79. Behar, *Aşk Olmayınca Meşk Olmaz*, 92. On differing notions of fidelity (*sadakat*) and the impossibility of determining authentic originals in Ottoman music, see ibid., 88–95.

80. Ibid., 90, 92.

81. Ibid., 15, 89–90, 93–94. See Behar's appendix for examples of variant copies of the same composition. For an in-depth discussion of the issue of Ottoman "originals" and versions, see "Eserin Aslı," in ibid., chap. 3 (88–95). Musicians continue to modify compositions through *kalem oynatma* or *keriz*, slang for making nuanced alterations to compositions (ibid., 95–97).

82. Ibid., 97.

83. With few exceptions, my interviewees showed high respect for notation, while acknowledging to one degree or another the importance of ear learning.

84. Descriptive transcription is the scoring of a particular performance, whereas prescriptive transcription refers to a score considered autonomously authoritative and not drawn from a particular instantiation of the piece.

85. Religious law prohibits the recording of music on Shabbat as part of the prohibition of certain kinds of work on the Sabbath.

86. According to Cem Behar, audio and video recording of masters, such as Cemil Bey, Münir Nurettın Selçuk, Hafiz Sami, and Hafiz Şaşı Osman, can serve as *sanal* (virtual) meşk, allowing musicians today to learn the performance style of past masters (Behar, *Aşk Olmayınca Meşk Olmaz*, 152–53). On meşk today, see "Bugün ve Yarın," in ibid., chap. 4 (144–53).

87. Listening to recordings differs from face-to-face meşk sessions, because of the absence of an ongoing master-apprentice relationship and the multiple sensory awareness of memory arts, which would be reduced to the auditory. Yosihiko Tokumaru, *Musics, Signs and Intertextuality: Collected Papers* (Tokyo: Academia Music, 2005), 57.

Epilogue

1. Judith Amiel, personal interview, September 11, 2005.

2. For ethnomusicological studies of Syrian Jewish diaspora communities in the United States, see Kay Kaufman Shelemay, *Let Jasmine Rain Down: Song and Remembrance among Syrian Jews* (Chicago: University of Chicago Press, 1998), and Mark Kligman, *Maqam and Liturgy: Ritual, Music, and Aesthetics of Syrian Jews in Brooklyn* (Detroit: Wayne State University Press, 2009).

3. Samuel Benaroya, interview with Edwin Seroussi, October 24, 1992.

4. Edwin Seroussi, *Mizimrat Qedem: The Life and Music of R. Isaac Algazi from Turkey* (Jerusalem: Renanot Institute for Jewish Music, 1989), 23; and Edwin Seroussi, "Musika osmanit klasit be-kerev yehudei saloniki (Ottoman Classical Music among the Jews of Saloniki)," in *Ladinar: Mehkarim ba-sifrut, ba-musika uba-historia shel dovrei ladino*, ed. Judith Dishon and Shmuel Refael (Tel Aviv: 1998), 88.

5. İsak Maçoro, interview with Karen Gerson Şarhon, March 2004.

6. Judith Amiel, personal communication, May 8, 2012.

7. Ibid., September 11, 2005.

8. Kay Kaufman Shelemay, "Musical Communities: Rethinking the Collective in Music," *Journal of the American Musicological Society* 64, no. 2 (2011): 373–75.

Glossary

This glossary is intended as an easy reference for pertinent religious and musical terms. Some words may have changing historical usages or meanings that are not covered here.

Ar = Arabic
Fr = French
Heb = Hebrew
Tk = Turkish

alafranga [Tk; *adj*]: European-style music. Its usage widened to include social practices and habits of thought considered European.

alaturka [Tk; *adj*]: Turkish-style music. Its usage widened to include social practices and habits of thought considered Turkish.

ark: The receptacle at the front of the synagogue that houses the Torah scrolls.

ayin [Tk]: A suite of music that accompanies the Mevlevi religious choreography (*see* sema).

beit din [Heb]: A rabbinical court.

beit midrash [Heb]: A house of study.

bestekar [Tk]: A composer.

birkat hamazon [Heb]: Grace after meals.

cümbüş [Tk]: A fretless, plucked, banjo-like instrument that first appeared in the early twentieth century and was associated with popular urban music performed by minority musicians.

dervish: A mystic or religious devotee of a Sufi order. *See* Mevlevi.

dhimmi ("Protected people" or "People of the contract") [Ar; Tk, *zimmi*]: Non-Muslim ethno-religious communities that, under Islamic law, were administered separately from Muslim subjects. In the Ottoman era, Jews and Christians (Greek Orthodox and Armenian) were considered dhimmi and were granted communal autonomy without military obligations, while also paying an additional tax not levied on Muslim subjects. Jews and Christians were also called "People of the book" (Ar, *ahl al-kitab*) because their sacred texts were a part of Islamic heritage.

Enderun [Tk]: The Ottoman palace school, where music and a variety of other subjects were taught.

ev toplantısı ("home gathering") [Tk]: Salons meeting regularly between the 1920s and 1970s in the absence of official funding for classical Turkish music education. The sessions included, among other activities, meşk and musical performance, as well as intellectual conversation and religious observance, depending upon the patron and participants.

ezan [Tk]: The Muslim call to prayer.

fasıl ("suite") [Tk]: The classical Ottoman court suite, a collection of compositions of different genres in the same makam. In the nineteenth century the Ottoman court suite showcased compositions in more than one makam, and in the twentieth century, fasıl music progressively referred to the music of the gazino. Genres included in the classical fasıl include the peşrev (instrumental introduction), beste (vocal genre), ağır semai (vocal genre), and saz semaisi (instrumental postlude). In the nineteenth century performers began to include in the fasıl the şarkı (lit. "song"), a light vocal piece that became a prominent and popular part of gazino music.

gabay [Heb]: The lay leader of a Jewish congregation.

gazel [Tk]: A vocal improvisation utilizing a text and meter-free music.

gazino [Tk]: An entertainment venue that in the nineteenth century developed out of alafranga spaces and alaturka spaces, combining the elite clientele and alcohol service of the former with Turkish-style musical genres of the latter.

güfte mecmuası ("song-text collection") [Tk]: A collection of compositions that served as a record and mnemonic aid for the oral transmission of Ottoman court music. The collections generally provided lyrics and a variety of musical cues, such as makam, usul, and composer's name.

hafiz [Tk]: An individual who can recite the Qur'an from memory.

haham [Heb]: The head of a congregation, generally regarded as learned in religion and religious law. Depending on the congregation, he may fulfill a variety of duties, including religious teacher or scholar, prayer leader (hazan), shohet (ritual slaughterer), visitor of the sick and dying, among others.*

hahambaşı [Tk]: The chief rabbi (lit. "head haham") of a city, region, empire, or nation, generally serving as an administrator over numerous congregations and a liaison with the government. Hahambaşlığı is the office of the chief rabbinate.*

hazan [Heb]: A prayer leader who performs religious liturgy in a Jewish congregation.*

---

* Titles for religious positions among Ottoman and Turkish Jewry in practice reflected fluidity of responsibilities, religious education, or musical expertise, depending upon the individual, as well as the size, needs, and economic status of the congregation or broader Jewish community (for example, a religiously educated hazan of a small congregation would likely fulfill duties in addition to prayer services, while a musically adept haham likely performed in services).

Jewish religious holidays (selected) (listed chronologically according to the liturgical year; most holidays begin and end in the evening; the months represent the Hebrew names of the Jewish lunar calendar):

    Pesah ("Passover"): A commemoration of the Exodus of the Israelites from Egypt (eight days beginning on the 15th of the month of Nisan).

    Lag B'Omer: A feast day and celebration in the spring commemorating the death of Rabbi Shimon Bar Yohai, traditionally believed to be the author of the Kabbalistic text the *Zohar*.

    Shavuot: The Festival of Weeks commemorating receiving the Ten Commandments and the Torah on Mount Sinai (6th and 7th of the month of Sivan, or seven weeks after Pesah).

    Rosh Hashanah (lit., "head of the year"): The Jewish New Year (the 1st and 2nd of the month of Tishri).

    Selihot: Special penitential prayers that in Istanbul begin the month before Rosh Hashanah, continuing until Rosh Hashanah, and are included during the entire Yom Kippur service.

    Yom Kippur: The Day of Atonement, a day of fasting and prayer for repentance (the 10th of the month of Tishri). The prayer service on Yom Kippur includes an additional final service, Neila. The ten-day period encompassing Rosh Hashanah and Yom Kippur comprises the Jewish High Holy Days.

    Sukkot: The Festival of Huts or Booths, a seven-day autumn festival commemorating dwelling in the wilderness after the Exodus (15th of the month of Tishri).

    Simhat Torah: A celebration of completing and restarting the cycle of Torah readings (23rd of the month of Tishri).

    Hanukkah: An eight-day winter festival celebrating the rededication of the Temple in Jerusalem (25th of the month of Kislev through 2nd of the month of Tevet).

    Purim: A celebration of Queen Esther and the Jews' deliverance from Haman's plans to kill them (14th of the month of Adar).

kanun [Tk]: A Middle Eastern type of plucked dulcimer of the zither family. A kanuni is a kanun player.

Klasik Türk Müziği ("classical Turkish music") [Tk]: A twentieth-century term for court music forms both preserved and adapted in the Republic by traditionalist musicians.

Maftirim [Heb]: A Hebrew religious fasıl, or suite, paralleling the musical form of the Ottoman court suite.

makam [Tk]: Musical modes in a variety of Near Eastern and North African musics. Makams reflect intervallic and compositional or melodic tendencies, and thus are best demonstrated through performing a piece or taksim (improvisation).

meşk [Tk]: The oral learning process for acquiring Ottoman court music. Historically, meşk referred to learning a variety of Ottoman art forms, but its meaning eventually narrowed to encompass music and calligraphy alone.

mevlevihane [Tk]: A Mevlevi lodge.

Mevlevi [Tk]: A Muslim religious order, popularly known as the whirling dervishes, arising out of the spiritual leadership of Celaleddin Rumi in Konya in the thirteenth century. *See* tarikat.

mikveh [Heb]: A ritual bath.

muezzin [Tk]: The person making the Muslim call to prayer.

ney [Tk]: The principal wind instrument of Ottoman court music and Mevlevi music. A neyzen is a ney player.

Ottoman court music: Art music patronized by the Ottoman sultan, developed by multiethnic composers, and performed at court, in the homes of Ottoman aristocrats, and other urban venues.

pidyon [Heb]: Redemption of the first-born son.

Pirké Avot [Heb]: Perkey Avot (Tk), popularly known as "The Ethics of the Fathers," a text customarily read between the holidays of Passover and Shavuot.

piyasa [Tk]: The marketplace, or "commercial" as an attribute of music or musicians.

Ramazan [Tk]: A Muslim religious holiday (Ar, Ramadan) during the ninth month of the Islamic lunar calendar. The daily fast is broken by the *iftar* meal, with evening socializing and entertainment typical in Ottoman cities throughout the month.

rav [Heb]: A spiritual leader, teacher, or preacher of a congregation.

sema [Tk]: The religious choreography of the Mevlevi ceremony, accompanied by a suite of music. *See* ayin.

serbest okuma ("free singing") [Tk]: A term used by some hazanim to refer to meter-free vocal improvisation performed during prayer services.

se'uda [Heb]: The third Shabbat meal.

Shabbat [Heb]: The Jewish Sabbath. The 25-hour period begins Friday evening at sunset and ends Saturday evening after dusk. The three prayer services on Shabbat are Shaharit, Minha, and Arvit, with an additional Musaf service after Shaharit.

solfège [Fr]: The application of European sol-fa syllables to musical scales or melodies, especially as an exercise (Tk, *solfej*).

Sufi [*adj*]: Related to Sufism, a term used in Anglo-European scholarship to refer to mystical traditions in Islam. Amidst immense diversity, Sufi orders or brotherhoods are generally centered on master-disciple relationships aimed at developing a personal experience of the divine, sometimes through music, movement, and chant.

şamaz [Tk]: A beadle (Heb, *shamash*), or Jewish lay official responsible for a range of logistical support for the congregation.

şef [Tk]: A conductor.

şeyh [Tk]: The spiritual leader of a Sufi brotherhood (Eng, sheikh).

taksim [Tk]: A vocal or instrumental improvisation commonly employed to introduce the makam of an upcoming composition or to transition between pieces in different makams.

tanbur [Tk]: A long-necked lute with frets, plucked with a plectrum (*mızrap*). A tanburi is a tanbur player.

tarikat [Tk]: A Sufi order or brotherhood.

tekke [Tk]: The lodge of a Sufi order, including the Mevlevi.

teva [Heb]: The raised platform or lectern in the synagogue from which the hazan cantillates the Torah and leads the prayer service (*bimah* in Ashkenazi terminology).

Torah [Heb]: The five books of Moses (Pentateuch) inscribed on the Torah scrolls. The term is also used in a variety of ways to denote "teaching" or "law."

Torah scrolls: The scrolls (Heb, *Sefer Torah*) read during public worship, on which the five books of Moses are inscribed. The scrolls are kept in the ark in the synagogue.

Türk sanat müziği ("Turkish art music") [Tk]: Lighter classical genres developing in the course of the twentieth century.

ud [Tk; Ar, oud]: A short-necked fretless lute, plucked with a plectrum (*mızrap*). The ud is the ancestor of the European lute. An udi is an ud player.

usul [Tk]: The rhythm cycle in Ottoman and Turkish music.

Discography

An annotated discography of selected archival recordings.

İsak Algazi

Seroussi, Edwin. *Mizimrat Qedem: The Life and Music of R. Isaac Algazi from Turkey*. Jerusalem: Renanot Institute for Jewish Music, 1989.

Two cassettes of archival recordings accompanying this biography of Algazi include thirty-two songs: liturgical songs for the High Holidays, Shabbat, and Festivals; religious and folk songs in Ladino; the "Hatikvah"; and two Maftirim songs (an opening vocal taksim and "Yişlah Mişamayim").

Masters of Turkish Music. Massachusetts: Rounder Records, 1990.

Compact disc containing two Turkish selections by Algazi, a gazel in Hicaz makam ("Bi-karar olmaktı sevmekten muradı gönlümün") and a şarkı in Beyati makam by Şevki Bey ("Bir katre içen çeşme-i pür-hun-i fenadan").

Gazeller II: 78 Devirli Taş Plak Kayıları—Ottoman-Turkish Vocal Improvisations in 78 rpm Records. Istanbul: Kalan, 1997 (CD 072). Liner notes by Bülent Aksoy.

Compact disc of late Ottoman vocalists, including Algazi singing "Sana dil verdimse" in Beyati makam.

İsak Algazi Efendi—Rabbi Isaac Algazi from Turkey Singing Ottoman-Turkish and Ottoman-Jewish Music. Istanbul: Kalan, 2004 (CD 333).

Compact disc of twenty-four archival recordings including Ottoman gazels and şarkıs; Hebrew and Ladino religious songs; and Ladino folk songs. Liner notes by Bülent Aksoy.

David Behar, İsak Maçoro, and David Sevi

Maftirim. Istanbul: Gözlem, 2009.

A two-volume publication of archival recordings of sixty-three Maftirim compositions recorded in 1987 by David Behar, İsak Maçoro, and David Sevi. The compilation is arranged by makam and includes scores, lyrics, and a historical introduction by Edwin Seroussi. All texts and lyrics are translated into English, Ladino, and Turkish.

Samuel Benaroya

Ottoman Hebrew Sacred Songs. Jerusalem: Jewish Music Research Centre, 1998. Compiled, and with liner notes, by Edwin Seroussi.

Recordings of Benaroya singing twenty-four Maftirim songs, including three vocal taksims and the adaptation of the peşrev in Segah makam by Yusuf Paşa ("Yeme Levavi Biroti"). The selections were recorded in Seattle in 1983 and between 1989 and 1992.

Edirneli Hayim Efendi

An Early Twentieth-Century Sephardi Troubadour: The Historical Recordings of Haim Effendi of Turkey. Jerusalem: Jewish Music Research Centre, 2008.

A four-CD set of liturgical, paraliturgical, and Ladino songs, recorded between 1907 and 1922. Includes one Maftirim song in Muhayyer makam ("Rahum 'ad matai"). Notes by Edwin Seroussi and Rivka Havass.

Avram Karakaş

Turquie: Archives de la musique turque. Paris: Ocora Radio France, 1995. Liner notes by Christian Poché.

A two-volume compact disc of seventy-eight recordings of late Ottoman instrumentalists and vocalists, including a şarkı in Rast makam sung by Avram Karakaş from an original Zonophone 1904 recording: "Bilse bir kerre o şuh hali perişanımızı," by Ahmet Arifi Bey.

Yahudi Bestekarlar—Jewish Composers. Istanbul: Sony Music, 2001. Liner notes by Bülent Aksoy.

Compact disc includes one composition by Avram Karakaş ("Hüznüm kederim değil mi belli") in Hicaz makam, performed by contemporary Turkish vocalists and instrumentalists.

Maftirim İlahiler Korosu

Maftirim: Unutulan Yahudi-Sufi Geleneği—Judeo-Sufi Connection. Istanbul: Kalan, 2001 (CD 234).

Compact disc of the performing Maftirim ensemble under the direction of Aaron Kohen with accompaniment by Aziz Şenol Feliz (ney, bendir, kudüm) and Birol Yayla (tanbur). Includes eighteen Maftirim compositions and a vocal taksim.

Mısırlı İbrahim Efendi

Yahudi Bestekarlar—Jewish Composers. Istanbul: Sony Music, 2001. Liner notes by Bülent Aksoy.

Compact disc includes three compositions by Mısırlı İbrahim Efendi, performed by contemporary Turkish vocalists and instrumentalists.

Ud: Türk Müziği Ustaları—Masters of Turkish Music. Istanbul: Kalan, 2004 (CD 324 and 325). Liner notes by Osman Nuri Özpekel.

A two-CD set of archival recordings of late Ottoman and republican ud players, including four taksims by Mısırlı İbrahim Efendi. Also included are taksims by Yorgo Bacanos, Mehmet Fahri Kopuz, and Cahit Gözkan.

Nesim Sevilya

Yahudi Bestekarlar—Jewish Composers. Istanbul: Sony Music, 2001. Liner notes by Bülent Aksoy.

Compact disc includes two compositions by Nesim Sevilya, performed by contemporary Turkish vocalists and instrumentalists.

References

Akin, Nur. "Balat." In *Dünden Bugüne İstanbul Ansiklopedisi*, 2:10. Istanbul: Ana Basım, 1993–1994.
Alexandris, Alexis. *The Greek Minority of Istanbul and Greek-Turkish Relations, 1918–1974*. Athens: Centre for Asia Minor Studies, 1992 [1983].
Altınay, Ayşe Gül, and Yektan Türkyılmaz. "Unravelling Layers of Gendered Silencing: Converted Armenian Survivors of the 1915 Catastrophe." In *Untold Histories of the Middle East: Recovering Voices from the 19th and 20th Centuries*, edited by Amy Singer, Christoph K. Neumann, and Selçuk Akşin Somel, 25–53. London: Routledge, 2011.
Aracı, Emre. "Giuseppe Donizetti at the Ottoman Court: A Levantine Life." *Musical Times* 143, no. 1880 (2002): 49–56.
——. "Reforming Zeal." *Musical Times* 138, no. 1855 (1997): 12–15.
Armistead, Samuel G. *El romancero judeo-español en el Archivo Menendez Pidal (Catálogo-índice de romances y canciones)*. 3 vols. Madrid: Catedra Seminario Menendez Pidal, 1978.
Armistead, Samuel G., Joseph Silverman, and Israel Katz. *Judeo-Spanish Ballads from Oral Tradition*. 2 vols. Berkeley: University of California Press, 1986, 1993.
Aslan, Senem. "'Citizen, Speak Turkish!': A Nation in the Making." *Nationalism and Ethnic Politics* 13, no. 2 (2007): 245–72.
Atay, Falih Rıfkı. *Çankaya: Atatürk Devri Hatıraları*. Istanbul: Dünya Yayınları, 1958.
Atkinson, Rowland. "Ecology of Sound: The Sonic Order of Urban Space." *Urban Studies* 44, no. 10 (2007): 1905–17.
Baer, Marc David. *The Dönme: Jewish Converts, Muslim Revolutionaries, and Secular Turks*. Stanford, CA: Stanford University Press, 2010.
——. "Turkish Jews Rethink '500 Years of Brotherhood and Friendship.'" *Turkish Studies Association Bulletin* 24, no. 2 (2000): 63–74.
Bali, Rıfat N. "The 1934 Thrace Events: Continuity and Change within Turkish State Policies Regarding Non-Muslim Minorities: An Interview with Rifat Bali," 2008. http://ejts.revues.org/2903.

———. *1934 Trakya Olayları*. Istanbul: Kitabevi, 2008.
———. *Aliya: Bir Toplu Göçün Öyküsü (1946–1949)*. Istanbul: Iletişim Yayınları, 2003.
———. *Cumhuriyet Yıllarında Türkiye Yahudileri: Bir Türkleştirme Serüveni 1923–1945*. Istanbul: İletişim Yayınları, 2005 [1999].
———. *The "Varlık Vergisi Affair": A Study of Its Legacy—Selected Documents*. Istanbul: Isis, 2005.
———. *Varlık Vergisi: Hatıralar-Tanıklıklar*. Istanbul: Libra, 2012.
Bartu, Ayfer. "Who Owns the Old Quarters? Rewriting Histories in a Global Era." In *Istanbul between the Global and the Local*, edited by Çağlar Keyder, 31–45. Lanham, MD: Rowman & Littlefield, 1999.
Becker, Howard S. *Art Worlds*. Berkeley: University of California Press, 1982.
Behar, Cem. *Aşk Olmayınca Meşk Olmaz: Geleneksel Osmanlı/Türk Müziğinde Öğretim ve Intikal*. 2nd ed. Istanbul: Yapı Kredi Yayınları, 2003 [1998].
———. *A Neighborhood in Ottoman Istanbul: Fruit Vendors and Civil Servants in the Kasap Ilyas Mahalle*. Albany: State University of New York Press, 2003.
———. "The Ottoman Musical Tradition." In *The Cambridge History of Turkey*, Vol. 3: *The Later Ottoman Empire, 1603–1839*, edited by Suraiya N. Faroqhi, 393–407. Cambridge: Cambridge University Press, 2006.
———. "Transmission musicale et mémoire textuelle dans la musique classique ottomane/turque." *Revue de Monde Musulman et de la Méditerranée* 75–76 (1996): 91–102.
———. *Zaman, Mekan, Müzik: Klasik Türk Musıkisinde Eğitim (Meşk), Icra ve Aktarım*. Istanbul: AFA Yayıncılık, 1993.
Behmoaras, Liz. *Kimsin Jak Samanon?* Istanbul: Sel Yayıncılık, 1997.
Beken, Münir Nurettin. "Ethnicity and Identity in Music—a Case Study: Professional Musicians in Istanbul." In *Manifold Identities: Studies on Music and Minorities*, edited by Ursula Hemetek, Gerda Lechleitner, Inna Naroditskaya, and Anna Czekanowska, 181–89. London: Cambridge Scholars Press, 2004.
———. "Globalization vs Tradition: Commercial Music in Early 20th Century Istanbul." In *Urban Music in the Balkans: Drop-out Ethnic Identities or a Historical Case of Tolerance and Global Thinking? (in Honorem Ramadan Sokoli)*, edited by Sokol Shupo, 55–63. Tirana: Documentation and Communication Center for Regional Music, 2006.
———. "Musicians, Audience and Power: The Changing Aesthetics in the Music at the Maksim Gazino of Istanbul." Ph.D. dissertation, University of Maryland, 1998.
Bektaş, Cengiz. *Hoşgörünün Öteki Adı: Kuzguncuk*. Istanbul: Tasarım Yayın Grubu, 1996.
———. *Kuzguncuk*. Istanbul: Literatür, 2003.
Benbassa, Esther. "Associational Strategies in Ottoman Jewish Society in the Nineteenth and Twentieth Centuries." In *The Jews of the Ottoman Empire*, edited by Avigdor Levy, 457–84. Princeton, NJ: Darwin Press; Washington, DC: Institute of Turkish Studies, 1994.

———. "Zionism in the Ottoman Empire at the End of the 19th and Beginning of the 20th Century." *Studies in Zionism* 11, no. 2 (1990): 27–40.
Benbassa, Esther, and Aron Rodrigue. *Sephardi Jewry: A History of the Judeo-Spanish Community, 14th to 20th Centuries*. Berkeley: University of California Press, 2000 [1993].
Benz, Wolfgang. *A Concise History of the Third Reich*. Berkeley: University of California Press, 2006.
"Beyoğlu Taksim Bahçesi Aynalı Gazino'da Ramazan Bayramının." *Ikdam*, October 15, 1909.
Bora, Tanıl. "Istanbul of the Conqueror: The 'Alternative Global City' Dreams of Political Islam." In *Istanbul between the Global and the Local*, edited by Çağlar Keyder, 47–58. Lanham, MD: Rowman & Littlefield, 1999.
Bornes-Varol, Marie-Christine. "The Balat Quarter and Its Image: A Study of a Jewish Neighborhood in Istanbul." In *The Jews of the Ottoman Empire*, edited by Avigdor Levy, 633–44. Princeton, NJ: Darwin Press; Washington, DC: Institute of Turkish Studies, 1994.
Braude, Benjamin. "The Strange History of the Millet System." In *The Great Ottoman-Turkish Civilisation*, edited by Kemal Çiçek, Ercument Kuran, Nejat Göyünç, and Ilber Ortaylı, 409–18. Ankara: Yeni Türkiye, 2000.
Braude, Benjamin, and Bernard Lewis, eds. *Christians and Jews in the Ottoman Empire: The Functioning of a Plural Society*. New York: Holmes & Meier, 1982.
Brink-Danan, Marcy. *Jewish Life in Twenty-first-Century Turkey: The Other Side of Tolerance*. Indiana Series in Sephardi and Mizrahi Studies. Bloomington: Indiana University Press, 2012.
Brockett, Gavin D. *How Happy to Call Oneself a Turk: Provincial Newspapers and the Negotiation of a Muslim National Identity*. Modern Middle East Series. Austin: University of Texas Press, 2011.
Bull, M. *Sounding out the City: Personal Stereos and the Management of Everyday Life*. Oxford: Berg, 2000.
Bull, M., and L. Back, eds. *The Auditory Culture Reader*. Oxford: Berg, 2003.
Campos, Michelle U. "Between 'Beloved Ottomania' and 'The Land of Israel': The Struggle over Ottomanism and Zionism among Palestine's Sephardi Jews, 1908–13." *International Journal of Middle East Studies* 37, no. 4 (2005): 461–83.
———. *Ottoman Brothers: Muslims, Christians, and Jews in Early Twentieth-Century Palestine*. Stanford, CA: Stanford University Press, 2011.
Çelik, Zeynep. *The Remaking of Istanbul: Portrait of an Ottoman City in the Nineteenth Century*. Seattle: University of Washington Press, 1986.
Cengiz, Halil Erdoğan, ed. *Yaşanmış Olaylarla Atatürk ve Müzik: Riyaset-i Cumhur Ince Saz Hey'eti Şefi Binbaşı Hafız Yaşar Okur'un Anıları (1924–1938)*. Ankara: Müzik Ansiklopedisi Yayınları, 1993.
Çınar, Alev. "The Justice and Development Party: Turkey's Experience with Islam, Democracy, Liberalism, and Secularism." *International Journal of Middle East Studies* 43 (2011): 529–41.

———. *Modernity, Islam, and Secularism in Turkey: Bodies, Places, and Time.* Minneapolis: University of Minnesota Press, 2005.
Cizre, Ümit, ed. *Secular and Islamic Politics in Turkey: The Making of the Justice and Development Party.* Routledge Studies in Middle Eastern Politics. New York: Routledge, 2008.
Cohen, Judith R. "Constructing a Spanish Jewish Festival: Music and the Appropriation of Tradition." *World of Music* 41, no. 3 (1999): 85–113.
———. "Judeo-Spanish Songs in Montreal and Toronto." *Jewish Folklore and Ethnology Review/Special Issue: Jewish Women* 12, no. 1–2 (1990): 26.
———. "Music and the Re-Creation of Identity in Imagined Iberian Jewish Communities." *Revista de dialectología y tradiciones populares* 54, no. 2 (1999): 125–44.
———. "Sephardic Song." *Midstream* 49, no. 5 (2003): 12–16.
———. "Sonography of Judeo-Spanish Song (Cassettes, LPs, CD's, Video, Film)." *Jewish Folklore and Ethnology Review/Special Issue: Sephardic Folklore: Exile and Homecoming* 15, no. 2 (1993): 49–55.
———. "Women's Roles in Judeo-Spanish Song Traditions." In *Active Voices: Women in Jewish Culture*, edited by Maurie Sacks, 182–200. Urbana: University of Illinois Press, 1995.
Cohen, Julia Phillips. "Fashioning Imperial Citizens: Sephardi Jews and the Ottoman State, 1856–1912." Ph.D. dissertation, Stanford University, 2008.
Cohen, Julia Phillips, and Sarah Abrevaya Stein. "Sephardic Scholarly Worlds: Toward a Novel Geography of Modern Jewish History." *Jewish Quarterly Review* 100, no. 3 (2010): 349–84.
Cowell, Alan. "Jews in Istanbul Reopen Synagogue." *New York Times*, May 21, 1987.
Deleon, Jak. *Ancient Districts on the Golden Horn.* Istanbul: Gözlem, 1991.
"Divanyolu'nda Arif'in Kıraathanesi'nde." *Ikdam*, September 9, 1910.
Dorn, Pamela J. "Change and Ideology: The Ethnomusicology of Turkish Jewry." Ph.D. dissertation, Indiana University, 1991.
Dumont, Paul. "Jews, Muslims, and Cholera: Intercommunal Relations in Baghdad at the End of the Nineteenth Century." In *The Jews of the Ottoman Empire*, edited by Avigdor Levy, 353–72. Princeton, NJ: Darwin Press; Washington, DC: Institute of Turkish Studies, 1994.
Dünden Bugüne İstanbul Ansiklopedisi. 8 vols. Istanbul: Ana Basım, 1993–1994.
Ederer, Eric Bernard. "The Cümbüş as Instrument of 'The Other' in Modern Turkey." Masters thesis. University of California Santa Barbara, 2007.
Eissenstat, Howard. "Metaphors of Race and Discourse of Nation: Racial Theory and the Beginnings of Nationalism in the Turkish Republic." In *Race and Nation: Ethnic Systems in the Modern World*, edited by Paul Spickard, 239–56. New York: Routledge, 2005.
Eldem, Edhem. "Istanbul 1903–1918: A Quantitative Analysis of a Bourgeoisie." *Boğaziçi Journal: A Review of Social, Economic and Administrative Studies* 11, no. 1–2 (1997): 53–98.

El-Shawan Castelo-Branco, Salwa. "Safeguarding Traditional Music in Contemporary Portugal." In *World Musics–Musics of the World: Aspects of Documentation, Mass Media and Acculturation*, edited by Max Peter Baumann, 177–90. Berlin: Florian Noetzel Verlag, 1992.

Ergin, Murat. "On Humans, Fish, and Mermaids: The Republican Taxonomy of Tastes and Arabesk." *New Perspectives on Turkey* 33 (2005): 63–92.

Ergin, Nina. "The Soundscape of Sixteenth-Century Istanbul Mosques: Architecture and Qur'an Recital." *Journal of the Society of Architectural Historians* 67 (2008): 204–21.

Erguner, Kudsi. *Journeys of a Sufi Musician*. London: Saqi Books, 2005.

Erichsen, Regine. "Haymatloz—Exile in Turkey from 1933 to 1945. An Exhibition of the Aktives Museum at the Akademie der Künste in Berlin and the Viadrina University in Frankfurt/Oder (January to June 2000) and German-Turkish Relations." *Electronic Journal of Oriental Studies/Utrecht University* 3, no. 1 (2000): 1–4. http://web.archive.org/web/20050510090623/http://www2.let.uu.nl/Solis/anpt/ejos/pdf/Regine.pdf (accessed August 15, 2011).

Feldman, Walter. "Music in Performance: Who Are the Whirling Dervishes?" In *The Garland Encyclopedia of World Music: The Middle East*, 107–11. New York: Routledge, 2002.

———. *Music of the Ottoman Court: Makam, Composition and the Early Ottoman Instrumental Repertoire*. Intercultural Music Studies 10. Berlin: Verlag für Wissenschaft und Bildung, 1996.

Finnegan, Ruth. *The Hidden Musicians: Music-Making in an English Town*. Cambridge: Cambridge University Press, 1989.

Foley, John Miles. "Textualization as Mediation: The Case of the Traditional Oral Epic." In *Voice, Text, Hypertext: Emerging Practices in Textual Studies*, edited by Raimonda Modiano, Leroy F. Searle, and Peter Shillingsburg, 101–20. Seattle: University of Washington Press, 2004.

———. *The Singer of Tales in Performance*. Bloomington: Indiana University Press, 1995.

Frangos, Steve. "Portraits in Modern Greek Music: Roza Eskenazi." *Resound: Archives of Traditional Music* 12, no. 1–2 (1993): 5–8.

Galante, Avram. *Histoire des Juifs de Turquie*. 9 vols. Istanbul: Isis, 1985.

Georgeon, François. "İmparatorluktan Cumhuriyete İstanbul'da Ramazan." In *Osmanlı İmparatorluğu'nda Yaşamak*, edited by François Georgeon and Paul Dumont, 41–136. Istanbul: İletişim Yayınları, 2000.

———. "Osmanlı İmparatorluğu'nun Son Döneminde İstanbul Kahvehaneleri." In *Doğu'da Kahve ve Kahvehaneler*, edited by Hélène Desmet-Grégoire and François Georgeon, 43–85. Istanbul: Yapı Kredi, 1999.

Goffman, Daniel. "Ottoman Millets in the Early Seventeenth Century." *New Perspectives on Turkey*, no. 1 (1994): 1.

———. "The Quincentennial of 1492 and Ottoman-Jewish Studies: A Review Essay." *Shofar* 11, no. 4 (1993): 57–67.

Gökçe, M. Selim. "Necdet Yaşar: 'Yahya Kemal Bana "Küçük Cemil'im" Derdi.'" *Türk Edebiyatı* 34, no. 393 (2006): 48–52.

Grosman, Moşe. *Vittorio Levi, Dr. Markus (1870–1944)*. Istanbul: 1 AS Matbaacılık AŞ, 1992.

Gruber, Ruth Ellen. *Virtually Jewish: Reinventing Jewish Culture in Europe*. Berkeley: University of California Press, 2002.

Güleryüz, Naim. *500. Yıl Vakfı Türk Musevileri Müzesi/The Quincentennial Foundation Museum of Turkish Jews (Jewish Museum of Turkey)*. Istanbul: Gözlem Gazetecilik, 2004.

———. *İstanbul Sinagogları*. Istanbul: Ajans Class, 1992.

Haberman, Clyde. "Istanbul Journal: Where 16 Synagogues Stand among the Minarets." *New York Times*, July 30, 1990.

Haker, Erol. *From Istanbul to Jerusalem: The Itinerary of a Young Turkish Jew*. Istanbul: Isis, 2003.

———. *Once Upon a Time Jews Lived in Kırklareli*. Istanbul: Isis, 2003.

Havassy, Rivka. "The Ladino Song in the 20th Century: A Study of the Collections of Emily Sene and Bouena Sarfatty-Garfinkle." Ph.D. dissertation, Bar-Ilan University, 2007.

Heskes, Irene. "Miriam's Sisters: Jewish Women and Liturgical Music." *Notes* 48, no. 4 (1992): 1193–202.

Hindemith. *Türk Kuğ Yaşamının Kalkınması İçin Öneriler: 1935/36*. Izmir: Kuğ Yayını, 1983.

Holst-Warhaft, Gail. "The Female Dervish and Other Shady Ladies of the Rebetika." In *Music and Gender: Perspectives from the Mediterranean*, edited by Tullia Magrini, 169–94. Chicago: University of Chicago Press, 2003.

Inal, Ibnülemin Mahmut Kemal. *Hoş Sada*. Istanbul: Türkiye İş Bankası Kültür Yayınları, 1958.

Jackson, Maureen. "Crossing Musical Worlds: Ottoman Jewry, Music Making and the Rise of the Nation." *Comparative Studies of South Asia, Africa and the Middle East* 31, no. 3 (2011): 569–87.

———. "The Girl in the Tree: Gender, Istanbul Soundscapes and Synagogue Song." *Jewish Social Studies: History, Culture, Society* 17, no. 1 (2010): 31–66.

———. "Mixing Musics: The Urban Landscape of Late Ottoman and Turkish Synagogue Music." Ph.D. dissertation, University of Washington, 2008.

———. "Music." In *Encyclopedia of the Ottoman Empire*, edited by Gábor Ágoston and Bruce Masters, 404–9. New York: Facts on File, 2009.

———. "'Cosmopolitan Smyrna': Illuminating or Obscuring Cultural Histories?" *Geographical Review* 102, no. 3 (2012): 337–49.

Johnson, Barbara C. "'Hen noseot et mahberoteihen itan': shirei nashim Yehudiot mi-Kochin be-sfat ha-makom" ("'They Carry Their Notebooks with Them': Women's Vernacular Jewish Songs from Cochin"). *Pe'amim* 82 (2000): 64–80.

Karmi, Ilan. *The Jewish Community of Istanbul in the Nineteenth Century: Social, Legal and Administrative Transformations*. Istanbul: Isis, 1996.

———. *Jewish Sites of Istanbul: A Guide Book*. Istanbul: Isis, 1992.
Karpat, Kemal H. *Ottoman Population, 1830–1914: Demographic and Social Characteristics*. Madison: University of Wisconsin Press, 1985.
Kasaba, Reşat. "Dreams of Empire, Dreams of Nation." In *Empire to Nation: Historical Perspectives on the Making of the Modern World*, edited by Joseph W. Esherick, Hasan Kayalı, and Eric Van Young, 198–225. Lanham, MD: Rowman and Littlefield, 2006.
Kater, Michael H. *The Twisted Muse: Musicians and Their Music in the Third Reich*. Oxford: Oxford University Press, 1997.
Keren, Zvi. *The Jews of Rusçuk: From Periphery to Capital of the Tuna Vilayeti*. Istanbul: Isis, 2005.
Keyder, Çağlar, ed. *Istanbul between the Global and the Local*. Lanham, MD: Rowman & Littlefield, 1999.
Kırlı, Cengiz. "The Struggle over Space: Coffeehouses of Ottoman Istanbul, 1780–1845." Ph.D. dissertation, State University of New York, Binghamton, 2001.
Kirshenblatt-Gimblett, Barbara. "Theorizing Heritage." *Ethnomusicology* 39, no. 3 (1995): 367–80.
Kligman, Mark. *Maqam and Liturgy: Ritual, Music, and Aesthetics of Syrian Jews in Brooklyn*. Detroit: Wayne State University Press, 2009.
Kocabaşoğlu, Uygur. *Şirket Telsizinden Devlet Radyosuna (TRT Öncesi Dönemde Radyonun Tarihsel Gelişimi ve Türk Siyasal Hayatı İçindeki Yeri)*. Ankara Üniversitesi Siyasal Bilgiler Fakültesi Yayınları No. 442. Ankara: SBF Basın ve Yayın Yüksek Okulu Basımevi, 1980.
Koçu, Reşad Ekrem. *İstanbul Ansiklopedisi*. Istanbul, 1960.
Kohen, Hazan Aaron. "Kirkor Çulhayan Efendi (1868–1938)." *Tiryaki* 1 (October 1994): 22–24.
———. "Değerli Bir Bestekar: Udi Mısırlı İbrahim Efendi (1878–1948)." *Tiryaki* 1 (December 1994): 37–40.
———. "Müziğe Aşık Bir Bestekar Haham Nesim Sevilya Efendi." *Tiryaki* 8–9 (March–April 1995): 65–70.
———. "Osmanlı İmparatorluğunun Kuruluş Yıllarından Günümüze Yahudi Dini Musikisi." *Folklor/Edebiyat* 6, no. 21 (2000–2001): 81–114.
Kotsovilis, Spyridon. "Between Fedora and Fez: Modern Turkey's Troubled Road to Democratic Consolidation and the Pluralizing Role of Erdogan's Pro-Islam Government." In *Turkey and the European Union: Internal Dynamics and External Challenges*, edited by Joseph S. Joseph, 42–70. New York: Palgrave Macmillan, 2006.
Kusić, Dane. "Discourse on Three Teravih Namazi-s in Istanbul: An Invitation to Reflexive Ethnomusicology." Ph.D. dissertation, University of Maryland, 1996.
Lehmann, Matthias B. "Introduction: Sephardi Identities." *Jewish Social Studies: History, Culture, Society* 15, no. 1 (2008): 1–9.
———. *Ladino Rabbinic Literature and Ottoman Sephardic Culture*. Jewish Literature and Culture. Bloomington: Indiana University Press, 2005.

Levy, André. "Notes on Jewish-Muslim Relationships: Revisiting the Vanishing Moroccan Jewish Community." *Cultural Anthropology* 18, no. 3 (2003): 365–97.
Lévy, Sam. *Salonique à la fin du XIXe siècle: Mémoires*. Istanbul: Isis, 2000.
Lord, Albert Bates. *The Singer of Tales*. 2nd ed. Cambridge, MA: Harvard University Press, 2000 [1960].
Maftirim. Istanbul: Gözlem, 2009.
Mallet, Laurent-Olivier. *La Turquie, Les Turcs et Les Juifs: Histoire, Représentations, Discours et Stratégies*. Istanbul: Isis, 2008.
Mango, Andrew. *Atatürk*. London: John Murray, 1999.
Marshall, Erynn. *Music in the Air Somewhere: The Shifting Borders of West Virginia's Fiddle and Song Traditions*. Morgantown: West Virginia University Press, 2006.
McCarthy, Justin. "Jewish Population in the Late Ottoman Period." In *The Jews of the Ottoman Empire*, edited by Avigdor Levy, 375–97. Princeton, NJ: Darwin Press; Washington, DC: Institute of Turkish Studies, c. 1994.
Miller, Judith. "The Istanbul Synagogue Massacre." *New York Times*, January 4, 1987.
Mills, Amy. "Narratives in City Landscapes: Cultural Identity in Istanbul." *Geographical Review* 95, no. 3 (2005): 441–62.
———. *Streets of Memory: Landscape, Tolerance, and National Identity in Istanbul*. Athens: University of Georgia Press, 2010.
Narlı, Nilufer. "The Rise of the Islamist Movement in Turkey." In *Revolutionaries and Reformers: Contemporary Islamist Movements in the Middle East*, edited by Barry Rubin, 125–40. New York: State University of New York Press, 2003.
Nasuhioğlu, Orhan. "Geçmişten Günümüze Üsküdar Musiki Cemiyeti." *Musiki Mecmuası* 461 (1998): 7–9.
Nettl, Bruno. *Heartland Excursions*. Urbana: University of Illinois Press, 1995.
Neyzi, Leyla. "Strong as Steel, Fragile as a Rose: A Turkish Jewish Witness to the Twentieth Century." *Jewish Social Studies: History, Culture, Society* 12, no. 1 (2005): 167–89.
O'Connell, John Morgan. "Alaturka Revisited: Style as History in Turkish Vocal Performance." Ph.D. dissertation, UCLA, 1996.
———. "Fine Art, Fine Music: Controlling Turkish Taste at the Fine Arts Academy in 1926." *Yearbook for Traditional Music* 32 (2000): 117–42.
———. "In the Time of Alaturka: Identifying Difference in Musical Discourse." *Ethnomusicology* 49 (2005): 177–205.
———. "The Mermaid of the Meyhane: The Legend of a Greek Singer in a Turkish Tavern." In *Music and the Sirens*, edited by Linda Austern and Inna Naroditskaya, 273–93. Bloomington: Indiana University Press, 2006.
———. "Song Cycles: The Life and Death of the Turkish Gazel: A Review Essay." *Ethnomusicology* 47 (2003): 399–414.
———. "A Staged Fright: Musical Hybridity and Religious Intolerance in Turkey (1923–38)." *Twentieth-Century Music* 7, no. 1 (2011): 1–26.

Onur, Oral. *1492'den Günümüze Edirne Yahudi Cemaati*. Istanbul: Oral Onur, 2005.
"Osmanlının Son Cumhuriyetin İlk Hahambaşısı Rabbi Hayim Moşe Becerano (1846–1931)." *Tiryaki* 3 (March 1998): 12–22.
Özbilge, Ahmet F. *Fener Balat Ayvansaray*. Istanbul: Bağlam Yayıncılık, 2005.
Öztuna, Yılmaz. *Büyük Türk Musikisi Ansiklopedisi*. 2 vols. Ankara: Başbakanlık Basımevi, 1990.
Özyürük, Esra. *Nostalgia for the Modern: State Secularism and Everyday Politics in Turkey*. Durham, NC: Duke University Press, 2006.
———. "Public Memory as Political Battleground." In *The Politics of Public Memory in Turkey*, edited by Esra Özyürük, 114–37. Syracuse, NY: Syracuse University Press, 2007.
Paçacı, Gönül. "Belediye Konservatuvarı." In *Dünden Bugüne İstanbul Ansiklopedisi*, 2:141–44. Istanbul: Ana Basım, 1993–1994.
Pinto, Diana. "Potsdamer Platz versus Aschenbach: Two Paradigms of Jewish Life in Europe." European Association for Jewish Culture, 2002. http://jewish-theatre.com/visitor/article_display.aspx?articleID=265 (accessed December 4, 2012).
Pioneer Women on Stage in Istanbul. *Women's Library and Information Center Foundation Diary*. Istanbul: Hanlar Matbaacılık, 2008.
Racy, Ali Jihad. "Record Industry and Egyptian Traditional Music: 1904–1932." *Ethnomusicology* 20 (1976): 22–48.
"Radyo bugün sade bir eğlence vasıtası değildir." *Cumhuriyet*, January 15, 1936.
Reinhard, Ursula. "Turkey: An Overview." In *The Garland Encyclopedia of World Music: the Middle East*, edited by Marcus and Reynolds Danielson, 759–77. New York: Routledge, 2002.
Reisman, Arnold. *Turkey's Modernization: Refugees from Nazism and Atatürk's Vision*. Washington, DC: New Academia, 2006.
Rodrigue, Aron. *French Jews, Turkish Jews: The Alliance Israélite Universelle and the Politics of Jewish Schooling in Turkey, 1860–1925*. Bloomington: Indiana University Press, 1990.
———. "From Millet to Minority: Turkish Jewry." In *Paths of Emancipation: Jews, States, and Citizenship*, edited by Pierre Birnbaum and Ira Katznelson, 238–61. Princeton, NJ: Princeton University Press, 1995.
———. *Jews and Muslims: Images of Sephardi and Eastern Jewries in Modern Times*. Seattle: University of Washington Press, 2003.
Rodrigue, Aron, and Sarah Abrevaya Stein, eds. *A Jewish Voice from Ottoman Salonica: The Ladino Memoir of Sa'adi Besalel a-Levi*. Stanford, CA: Stanford University Press, 2012.
Rozen, Minna. "The Istanbul Community between the Hatt-ı Şerif of Gülhane and the Treaty of Lausanne (1839–1923)." In *The Last Ottoman Century and Beyond: The Jews in Turkey and the Balkans, 1808–1945*, 77–130. Tel Aviv: Tel Aviv University, 2005.
Safa, Payami. "Mısır Radyosu." *Cumhuriyet*, August 6, 1936.

Şaul, Eli. *Balat'tan Bat-Yam'a*. Istanbul: İletişim, 1999.
Say, Ahmet. *Türkiye'nin Müzik Atlası*. Istanbul: Ofset Yapımevi, 1998.
Schafer, R. Murray. *The Soundscape: Our Sonic Environment and the Tuning of the World*. Rochester, VT: Destiny Books, 1994 [1977].
Schleifer, Yigal. "Bombers Kill 20 in Attacks on Synagogues." *Telegraph Media Group*, November 16, 2003.
———. "Turkish Jews Dig out after Bombs." *Jewish Telegraphic Agency/Jewishjournal.com*, November 21, 2003.
Sciaky, Leon. *Farewell to Salonica: City at the Crossroads*. Philadelphia: Paul Dry Books, 2003 [1946].
Seroussi, Edwin. "Archivists of Memory: Written Folksong Collections of Twentieth-Century Sephardi Women." In *Music and Gender: Perspectives from the Mediterranean*, edited by Tullia Magrini, 195–214. Chicago: University of Chicago Press, 2003.
———. "De-Gendering Jewish Music: The Survival of the Judeo-Spanish Folksong Revisited." *Music and Anthropology* 3 (1998). http://umbc.edu/MA/index/number3/seroussi/ser_0.htm.
———. "From the Court and Tarikat to the Synagogue: Ottoman Art Music and Hebrew Sacred Songs." In *Sufism, Music and Society in Turkey and the Middle East*, edited by Anders Hammarlund, Tord Olsson, and Özdalga Elisabeth, 81–93. Istanbul: Swedish Research Institute, 2001.
———. "Introduction." In *Maftirim*. Istanbul: Gözlem, 2009.
———. *Mizimrat Qedem: The Life and Music of R. Isaac Algazi from Turkey*. Jerusalem: Renanot Institute for Jewish Music, 1989.
———. "Musika osmanit klasit be-kerev yehudei saloniki (Ottoman Classical Music among the Jews of Saloniki)." In *Ladinar: Mehkarim ba-sifrut, ba-musika uba-historia shel dovrei ladino*, edited by Judith Dishon and Shmuel Refael, 79–92. Tel Aviv: Ha-Makhon Le-Heker Ha-Tefutsot, 1998.
———. "New Directions in the Music of the Sephardic Jews." In *Modern Jews and Their Musical Agendas*, edited by Ezra Mendelsohn, 61–77. Oxford: Oxford University Press, 1993.
———. *Ottoman Hebrew Sacred Songs*. Jerusalem: Jewish Music Research Center, 1998.
———. "The Peşrev as a Vocal Genre in Ottoman Hebrew Sources." *Turkish Music Quarterly* Summer (1991): 1–9.
———. "Reconstructing Sephardic Music in the 20th Century: Isaac Levy and His 'Chants Judeo-Espagnols.'" *World of Music* 37, no. 1 (1995): 39–58.
———. "Sephardic Music: A Bibliographical Guide with a Checklist of Notated Sources." *Jewish Folklore and Ethnology Review/Special Issue: Sephardic Folklore: Exile and Homecoming* 15, no. 2 (1993): 56–61.
Seroussi, Edwin, and Susana Welch-Shahak. "Judeo-Spanish Contrafacts and Musical Adaptations: The Oral Tradition." *Orbis Musicae* 10 (1990): 164–94.

"Seven Jailed for Turkey Bombings." *BBC*, February 17, 2007. http://news.bbc .co.uk/2/hi/europe/6370117.stm (accessed December 1, 2012).

Shelemay, Kay Kaufman. *Let Jasmine Rain Down: Song and Remembrance among Syrian Jews*. Chicago: University of Chicago Press, 1998.

———. "Musical Communities: Rethinking the Collective in Music." *Journal of the American Musicological Society* 64, no. 2 (2011): 349–90.

———. "Mythologies and Realities in the Study of Jewish Music." In *Enchanting Powers: Music in the World's Religions*, edited by Lawrence E. Sullivan, 299–318. Cambridge, MA: Harvard University Press, 1997.

———. "The Power of Silent Voices: Women in the Syrian Jewish Musical Tradition." In *Music and the Play of Power in the Middle East, North Africa and Central Asia*, edited by Laudan Nooshin, 269–88. Farnham, Surrey: Ashgate, 2009.

Shire Yisrael be-Erets ha-kedem (Songs of Israel in the Land of the East). Istanbul: Benjamin Raphael B. Joseph, circa 1921.

Signell, Karl L. *Makam: Modal Practice in Turkish Art Music*. Seattle: University of Washington/Asian Music Publications, 1977.

Simon, Rachel. "Between the Family and the Outside World: Jewish Girls in the Modern Middle East and North Africa." *Jewish Social Studies: History, Culture, Society* 7, no. 1 (2000): 81–108.

Skelton, Geoffrey, ed. *Selected Letters of Paul Hindemith*. New Haven, CT: Yale University Press, 1995.

Skolnik, Fred, and Michael Berenbaum. *Encyclopaedia Judaica*. 2nd ed. 22 vols. Farmington Hills, MI: Keter Publishing, 2007.

Sönmez, Sevengül. *İstanbul'un 100 Ailesi*. Istanbul: Istanbul Büyükşehir Belediyesi Kültür A.S. Yayınları, 2010

Stillman, Norman A. *Sephardi Religious Responses to Modernity*. Luxembourg: Harwood Academic Publishers, 1995.

Stock, Brian. *The Implications of Literacy: Written Language and Models of Interpretation in the Eleventh and Twelfth Centuries*. Princeton, NJ: Princeton University Press, 1983.

Stokes, Martin. "Sounding Out: The Culture Industries and the Globalization of Istanbul." In *Istanbul between the Global and the Local*, edited by Çağlar Keyder, 121–39. Lanham, MD: Rowman & Littlefield, 1999.

Tachau, Frank. "German Jewish Emigrés in Turkey." In *Jews, Turks, Ottomans*, edited by Avigdor Levy, 233–45. Syracuse, NY: Syracuse University Press, 2002.

Tekelioğlu, Orhan. "An Inner History of 'Turkish Music Revolution'—Demise of a Music Magazine." In *Sufism, Music and Society in Turkey and the Middle East*, edited by Anders Hammarlund, Tord Olsson, and Elisabeth Özdalga, 111–24. Istanbul: Swedish Research Institute, 2001.

———. "The Rise of a Spontaneous Synthesis: The Historical Background of

Turkish Popular Music." In *Turkey: Identity, Democracy, Politics*, edited by Sylvia Kedourie, 194–215. London: Frank Cass, 1996.

Tietze, Andreas, and Joseph Yahalom. *Ottoman Melodies Hebrew Hymns: A 16th Century Cross-Cultural Adventure*. Budapest: Akademiai Klado, 1995.

Tohumcu, Ahmed. "A Metamorphosis Story: Sema." Unpublished paper, ICTM Study Group on Music and Dance in Southeastern Europe Symposium. April 7–11, 2010. Ege University, Izmir, Turkey.

Toktaş, Şule. "The Conduct of Citizenship in the Case of Turkey's Jewish Minority: Legal Status, Identity, and Civic Virtue Aspects." *Comparative Studies of South Asia, Africa and the Middle East* 26, no. 1 (2006): 121–33.

———. "Turkey's Jews and Their Immigration to Israel." *Middle Eastern Studies* 42 (2006): 505–19.

Tokumaru, Yosihiko. *Musics, Signs and Intertextuality: Collected Papers*. Tokyo: Academia Music, 2005.

Tunçay, Mete. *T.C.'nde Tek Parti Yönetimi'nin Kurulması (1923–1931)*. Istanbul: Cem, 1989.

Türker, Orhan. *Fanari'den Fener'e: Bir Haliç Hikayesi*. Istanbul: Sel Yayıncılık, 2001.

———. *Galata'dan Karaköy'e: Bir Liman Hikayesi*. Istanbul: Sel Yayıncılık, 2000.

———. *Halki'den Heybeli'ye: Bir Ada Hikayesi*. Istanbul: Sel Yayıncılık, 2003.

———. *Mega Revma'dan Arnavutköy'e: Bir Boğaziçi Hikayesi*. Istanbul: Sel Yayıncılık, 1999.

———. *Nihori'den Yeniköy'e: Bir Boğaziçi Köyünün Hikayesi*. Istanbul: Sel Yayıncılık, 2004.

Türköz, Meltem. "Surname Narratives and the State-Society Boundary: Memories of Turkey's Family Name Law of 1934." *Middle Eastern Studies* 43, no. 6 (2007): 893–908.

Ünlü, Cemal. *Git Zaman Gel Zaman: Fonograf, Gramofon, Taş Plak*. Istanbul: Pan Yayıncılık, 2004.

Ursinas, Michael. "Millet." In *Encyclopedia of Islam*, edited by C. E. Bosworth, 61–64. Leiden: A.J. Brill, 1993.

Varol, Marie-Christine. *Balat: Faubourg juif d'Istanbul*. Istanbul: Isis, 1989.

Vernon, Paul. "Odeon Empire." *Folkroots* 19, no. 2–3 (1997): 33–37, 170–71.

———. "Sans Border Radio." *Folkroots* 130. n.d. www.bolingo.org/audio/texts/fr130radio.html (accessed August 15, 2011).

Welch-Shahak, Susana. "Adaptations and Borrowings in the Balkan Sephardic Repertoire." *Balkanista* 11 (1998): 87–125.

Wright, Owen. *Words without Songs: A Musicological Study of an Early Ottoman Anthology and Its Precursors*. London: SOAS, 1992.

Yavuz, M. Hakan, ed. *The Emergence of a New Turkey: Democracy and the AK Parti*. Utah Series in Turkish and Islamic Studies. Salt Lake City: University of Utah Press, 2006.

Zandi-Sayek, Sibel. "Orchestrating Difference, Performing Identity: Urban Space and Public Rituals in Nineteenth-Century Izmir." In *Hybrid Urbanism: On the Identity Discourse and the Built Environment*, edited by Nezar Al-Sayyad, 42–66. Westport, CT: Praeger, 2001.

———. *Ottoman Izmir: The Rise of a Cosmopolitian Port, 1840–1880*. Minneapolis: University of Minnesota Press, 2012.

Zat, Vefa. "Gazinolar." In *Dünden Bugüne İstanbul Ansiklopedisi*, 3: 379–80. Istanbul: Ana Basım, 1993–1994.

Zerubavel, Eviatar. *Ancestors and Relatives: Genealogy, Identity, and Community*. Oxford: Oxford University Press, 2011.

Zimmermann-Kalyoncu, Cornelia. *Deutsche Musiker in der Türkei im 20. Jahrhundert*. Frankfurt: Peter Lang Verlag, 1985.

Zürcher, Erik J. *Turkey: A Modern History*. London: I. B. Taurus, 1997 [1993].

Index

Abdülaziz (Sultan), 34
Abdülhamid II (Sultan), 34, 41
accordion, 77, 105
Adana, 80
adaptations (contrafacta), 31, 184n14, 207n12, 222n68; in Maftirim repertoire, 9, 23–24, 55, 112, 118–119, 155, 182n14
Adoni, Leon Yeuda, 33, 35
Adrianople. *See* Edirne
aesthetics, 43, 65–66, 109; late Ottoman musical, 18, 32, 43–44, 113
Ahrida synagogue, 35, 89, 150; map, 102, 158
AKP (Adalet ve Kalkınma Partisi or Justice and Development Party), 130, 215n37. *See also* Erdoğan, Recep Tayyip
alafranga, 38, 72, 104; versus alaturka, 52, 70, 84
alaturka, 38, 64, 67, 72, 99, 101, 110; versus alafranga, 52, 70, 84; vocal qualities, 65
Aleko Efendi, 57
Aleppo, 37
Algazi, İsak, 54–58, 63–66, 194n55, 196n64, 196n66
Alliance Israélite Universelle, 25, 64, 96, 183n17
Altıntaş, Yusuf, 146, 149, 156
Amar, Licco, 74–75
amateur musicians: 55, 191n18; Ottoman concept, 106, 201n115; in Turkish Republic, 80, 82, 84, 124. *See also* meşk, commercialization; music schools
Amiel, Judith, 171, 172–74
Ankara, 73, 130
Ankara Radio, 64, 67, 195n60
Ankara State Conservatory, 74
anti-Semitic views, 138
Apacık, Edirneli R. Hayim, 56, 60–61, 77, 112
Apollon synagogue (Knesset Israel), 54, 82, 146, 154, 159, 185n56, 191n12; map, 158
apprenticeships: master-pupil chains, 42, 45, 50; master-authenticated versions, 166; musical pedigree, 44–45, 79–80; in Ottoman music-making, 10, 12, 21, 25, 29, 143. *See also* meşk; transmission processes
Arab-Persian art-forms: Arab art music ensembles, 39; Arab-Persian suite forms, 9; Arab-Persian song-text collections, 189n90; and Turkish popular culture, 63, 69, 194n59, 197n77
Arif Gazinosu, 39
Armenians: and Ottoman court music, 8, 10, 20; in Balat, 96–99. *See also* Çulhayan; Ottoman empire; Turkish Republic
Arnavutköy (Istanbul), 39, 117; map, 40
Arsoy, Yesari Asım, 83
Artaki'nin Gazinosu, 39
Asseo, David, 80–82, 125, 202n126
Atatürk, Mustafa Kemal. *See* Turkish Republic
Austria, performing artists from, 72–76; Nazi regime and, 199nn92–96, 200n97, 200nn102–5
Avni Bey, 101, 209n58
Avtaliyon ben Mordehai, 155
ayin. *See* Mevlevi
Ayla, Safiye, 79, 202n119
Aynalı Gazinosu, 39

Bacanos, Yorgo, 57
Balat, 33, 35, 41, 70, 95–102, 203n3; Maftirim in, 122, 142, 155, 213n14; map, 40, 158. *See also* Kasturiya; soundscape
Balkan Wars (1912–1913). *See* Ottoman empire
Balkans, 7, 42, 54–55, 183n17, 191n12
baths (public). *See* performance and entertainment venues
Bebek (Istanbul), 30; map, 40
Becerano, Hayim Moşe, 23–30, 45–48, 148, 183n16, 183n18, 183n21, 183n22
Behar, David, 49–50, 61, 77–80, 82, 146, 150
Behar, Janti, 87–89, 91–92, 105–115
Behor, Papo, 54

249

Index

Bejerano, Hayyim. *See* Becerano, Hayim
Bektaş, Cengiz, 132
Belediye Konservatuarı (Istanbul Municipal Conservatory), 73, 79, 149, 166
Benaroya, İsak, 30
Benaroya, Samuel, 17–21, 23, 25, 29–32, 42–43, 46–47, 169–75
Beruhiel, Victor, 82, 151–52, 154–57
Bet Israel synagogue (Şişli synagogue), 49, 50–51, 83, 118, 159, 190n1; map, 158
Beyoğlu (Istanbul), 39, 56, 111, 154, 216n43, 216n49; map, 40
Bicerano, Salamon, 97
Birlikte Yaşamak (concert series), 126–40, 214n32
Blumenthal Brothers, 55; recording company (Orfeon), 55–57, 211n94; Columbia Records agent, 110, 211n94. *See also* recording industry; sound recordings
Böhm, Frieda Silbertknopf, 74
Bosphorus. *See* Istanbul
boys, 96; home music-making, 101; Maftirim groups, 35, 112; musical learning, 10, 30, 31, 81, 146, 154–55, 161, 220n13; and Turkish art music, 101, 156. *See also* gender
Bucharest, 25, 43
Bulgaria, 25–26
Büyükdere, 39; map, 40

café (kahve, kahvehane). *See* performance and entertainment venues
Çalgıcıyan, Nişan, 126
çalgılı kahvesi. *See* performance and entertainment venues
Capital Tax (Varlık Vergisi), 70, 197n80; public silence about, 134, 139, 216n52
Catalanes synagogue, 30
Cemil, Mes'ud, 18–19
Cemiyets. *See* music schools
Cerrahpaşa (Istanbul), 80
chief rabbinate (Hahambaşlığı), 2, 27, 96, 127, 135
Çiftehavuzlar (Istanbul), 80
"Citizen, Speak Turkish!" campaign, 62, 207n34, 218n71. *See also* Turkish Republic
civic musical friendships, in Republic, 77–85, 119, 146. *See also* ev toplantısı
coffeehouse. *See* performance and entertainment venues, café
Columbia Records (record company), 56–57, 67, 110, 196n64, 211n94
Çömlekciyan, Arşak, 57
Conquest Day (May 29), 126, 129–30. *See also* Turkish Republic
contrafacta. *See* adaptations

cosmopolitanism. *See* Ottoman empire
Çubuklu Gazino, 39, 101
Çulhayan, Kirkor, 27–28, 42–43, 54–55, 57–58, 149, 184n24. *See also* Armenians
cümbüş, 67
Cyprus, 134, 217n53
Czaczkes, Ludwig, 74

Dana, Rıfat, 141–42, 155, 213n14
Daniel, Abraham, 57
Daron, Moiz, 107
Darülelhan, 33, 71, 79, 149, 186n59, 220n21
Darüttalim-i Musıki, 149, 166, 220n21
Dede Efendi, 103, 190n4, 209n63
Derviş Abdullah Efendi, 57
Direklerarası (Istanbul), 39
dönme, 8, 180n10

Ebert, Carl, 74
Edirne (Adrianople), 2, 6, 10, 54, 61, 148; Maftirim in, 6, 9, 112, 146;
Edirneli Hayim Efendi (Apacık, Edirneli R. Hayim), 56, 60–61, 77, 112
El Kahal Grande (Edirne), 31
Eli, Izi, 141
Elmas, Bensi, 127
Erdoğan, Recep Tayyip, 130; political platform, 215n36, 215n39. *See also* AKP
Erduran, Ayla, 74
Eskenazi, Menahem, 126, 133, 141, 154
Eskenazi, Roza, 205n17
Eski Zağra (present-day Stara Zagora), 25
Etz Ahayim synagogue (Ortaköy synagogue), 58, 117, 190n1; map, 158
European Day of Jewish Culture (Yahudi Kültürü Avrupa Günü), 126, 214n28
European-style music: musical venues, 38; national music and, 63, 70–73, 76, 199n89; Ottoman patronage of, 33, 60, 193n41; republican institutionalization of, 70–72, 76–77, 171–72. *See also* alafranga; Austria; Germany
ev toplantısı, 78, 80–82, 84, 202n121. *See also* civic musical friendships
Eyüp (Istanbul), 99; map, 40
Eyyubi Ali Rıza Şengel, 79

Family Name Law (1934), 67. *See also* naming patterns; Turkish Republic
fasıl: Arab-Persian predecessors, 9; genres, 11, 37, 109, 187n71, 208n50; notated scores, 32, 220n22; performance venues, 55, 101, 103–4, 109–10. *See also* Maftirim; Ottoman court music

Favorite Record (record company), 57
Fener, 97, 99–100; map, 40, 102
Fener İskele Gazinosu, 99–101, 109; map, 102

Galata (Istanbul), 41, 54, 58, 96, 121–22, 154, 209n67; map, 40. *See also* Knesset Israel (Apollon) synagogue; Neve Şalom synagogue
gazinos: closures, 119; programs and changing tastes, 37–38, 161–62, 208n50, 210n88; in Istanbul neighborhoods, 39–40, 59, 98–102, 109, 187n72 (*see also names of specific gazinos*); Ladino and Turkish idioms for, 101, 109; negative associations, 77, 110, 201n112; ownership, 38, 58–59, 188n74; predecessors, 38, 98–99, 187n72; winter vs. summer locales, 39; women's attendance, 98, 101, 109, 115. *See also* performance and entertainment venues
gender: and class, 110; ethnomusicological debates, 13, 92–95; rabbinical views, 101, 204n9; male knowledge of Ladino song, 93; female knowledge of Turkish art music, 92–95, 104, 113–15; female knowledge of Maftirim repertoire, 112–13. *See also* boys; girls; Maftirim
Geneva, 19, 31, 70
Germany, performing artists from, 72–76; Nazi regime and, 199nn92–96, 200n97, 200nn102–5
girls, 96; "canto girls," 205n17; exclusion from in-synagogue music, 106–8, 210n79; home music-making, 95, 101, 103–4, 111; legacy as women, 113–15; knowledge of Hebrew religious song, 93–95, 112–13; knowledge of Turkish art music, 91, 94; and Ladino song, 92; and public performance, 98, 109–10. *See also* gender
Gökalp, Ziya, 72
Golden Horn, 33, 41, 70, 89, 98–99, 100; map, 40
Gözkan, Cahit, 80–81, 202n124
gramophone, 8, 57, 91, 94, 111–12. *See also* recording industry; sound recordings
Gramophone Records (record company), 56, 196n64
Greeks: and Ottoman court music, 8, 10, 20; in Balat, 96–99, 105. *See also* Ottoman empire; Turkish Republic
güfte mecmuası. *See* song-text collection
Günay, Edip, 74
'Gypsies' (Çingeneler), 37, 96–98

Hacı Arif Bey, 181n18
Hafız Yaşar, 67, 194n55

Hamidian Trade School (Hamidiye Sanayi Mektebi), 45, 188n85
Hanende İbrahim, 185n55
Haribi Avram Behor Menahem, 30
Hasköy (Istanbul), 33, 70, 78, 103, 111, 159, 186n62, 203n3; map, 40
Haydarpaşa (Istanbul), 35, 209n65; map, 158. *See also* Hemdat Israel synagogue
hazanim, 29, 32, 34, 54, 78, 173; and audience, 155–57, 161–63; and Turkish classical music, 41, 152, 161, 202n122; emigration of, 62, 69, 76; in Seattle, 169–70; training of, 42, 84, 96–97, 114–15, 128, 154, 159, 207n26
Hekimoğlu, Muzaffer, 77
Hemdat Israel synagogue (Haydarpaşa synagogue), 35; map 158
Hindemith, Paul, 73–75, 199n96, 200n99, 200n101. *See also* Austria; Germany
home. *See* ev toplantısı; performance and entertainment venues

İçeri Göksu, 39; map, 40
Ichtipol (Istanbul), 209n69
ince saz takımı, 37, 39, 100
İnönü, Ismet, 130. *See also* Turkish Republic
İptaloğos Gazinosu, 39
İsmail Hakkı Bey, 33, 118, 185n57
Istanbul: Bosphorus, 39, 104, 117, 209n65, 221n38; Jewish community, 2–3, 64, 139; migration patterns, general 11, 24–25, 45, 53–54, 70, 84, 121, 171–72; migration patterns, intraurban, 11, 41, 83, 117, 121–122, 159–160; transport networks, 39; map, 40, 102, 158. *See also* performance and entertainment venues. *See also names of specific neighborhoods*
Istanbul Belediye Konservatuarı, 73, 79, 149, 166
Istanbul Devlet Klasik Türk Müziği Korosu, 83
Istanbul Radio, 64, 81, 195n60, 202n130
İtalyan sinogog (Italian synagogue), 58, 79; map, 158
Izmir, 41, 45, 54; Maftirim in, 9, 112

Joseph, Benjamin Rafael B., 55, 148

Kadıköy (Istanbul), 104; map, 40
kahve, kahvehane. *See* performance and entertainment venues, café
Kan, Suna, 74
kanun, 79, 101, 107
Kanuni Ama Nazım Bey, 34
Kanuni Hasköylü Bohoraçi Levi, 78, 189n87
Karabaş (Istanbul), 96, 97, 99; map, 102
Karaca, Kani, 80, 82, 151, 202n129

Index

Karakaş, Avram, 34, 39, 56–60, 112
Kasturiya (Istanbul), 88–89, 95–97, 105–13, 209n69; map, 102. *See also* Kasturiya synagogue
Kasturiya synagogue, 34–35, 87, 210n75; map, 102, 158
Kemani Memduh, 37
Kemani Sabetay Sabah, 78
Kirami Efendi, 37
Knesset Israel synagogue (Apollon synagogue), 54, 82, 146, 154, 159, 185n56, 191n12; map, 158
Kohen, Aaron, 124, 128, 164
Kohen, Şemtov, 26
Kopuz, Mehmet Fahri, 34
Kordova, Moşe, 27, 54, 62, 83, 150, 191n16
Kordovero, Rafael, 77
Küledibi (Istanbul), 154
Kurtuluş (Istanbul), 122
Kuzguncuk (Istanbul), 117, 132–33, 209n65, 216n47; map, 158

La Voz de Oriente, 28, 64
Ladino, 35, 50, 70, 97, 154. *See also* gender; girls; sound recordings
Levi, Avram Hayat. *See* Mısırlı İbrahim Efendi
Living Together (concert series), 126–40, 214n32
Lonca (Istanbul), 37

Maçoro, İsak, 52, 77–80, 151–52
Maftirim: audience, 11, 31, 55, 122, 123, 135, 155–56; benefit concerts by, 109; historical development of, 8–12; intraurban migration of, 158; Maftirim project (2009), 165–68; performance practice, historical, 1–2, 9; performance practice, contemporary, 1–2, 49–50, 122–24, 135–37; as 'sacred suite,' 9; Sinagog Maftirim Korosu, 126–29, 134, 137–40, 141–42, 214n27 (*see also* Birlikte Yaşamak). *See also* adaptations; gender; Ottoman court music; *Shire Yisrael be-Erets ha-kedem*
makam, 17–18, 32, 37, 49, 152–53, 156, 222n51
Markowitz, Georg, 74
Marx, Joseph, 73
Mehmed Reşad (Sultan), 41
Mehterhane, 41, 188n83
meşk: commercialization, 32, 186n58, 209n60 (*see also* amateur musicians); conservatories and, 79–80; ethics, 44, 189n91; memory and musical ability, 25, 29, 43, 47, 151–53, 184n35, 221n35; mnemonics, 146, 151–53, 189n90, 220n12; process, 17, 35–36, 50, 146,

181n1; radio sessions, 151, 221n25; 'sanal' (virtual), 168, 224n86; venues, changing, 10, 49, 78–80, 145, 151. *See also* apprenticeships; song-text collection; transmission processes
Mevlevi: ayin, 9, 30, 45; Jewish-Mevlevi relations, 9–10, 20, 29–31, 42, 60–61, 80–81; lodge, 30–31, 60, 71; sema, 30, 61, 131. *See also* Ottoman court music; Ottoman empire; Turkish Republic
meyhane. *See* performance and entertainment venues
Mısırlı İbrahim Efendi, 32, 36–41, 66–69, 185n55, 187n67
Molla Aşkı Mosque, 33; map, 102
muezzin, 33, 97, 118
Müren, Zeki, 1
music schools: cemiyets, 49–50, 60, 191n18; palace, 10, 60, 185n57, 193n41; private schools, 32, 42, 47, 186n59. *See also* European-style music; Turkish classical music. *See also specific names of schools*
Musıki Muallim Mektebi, 71
Musıki-yi Osmani Mektebi, 33–34, 186n59

Nahum, Hayim (Chief Rabbi), 26, 103, 209n61
Najara, Israel, 10, 46, 182n14
naming patterns: Family Name Law (1934), 67–69; nicknames, 37; stage names, 67, 69, 187n67
Nazi regime, musicians and. *See* Austria; Germany
Neve Şalom synagogue, 119, 122, 155, 191n12; map, 158
Neyzen Hoca Mehmed Rakım Elkutlu, 45
Nişantışı (Istanbul), 122
Niyego, Moşe, 35
notation. *See* textual transmission; transmission processes

Odeon (record company), 56
Ongan, Emin, 82, 202n130
oral transmission: authenticity, concepts of, 166–69; gender and, 93; indirect musical exposures, 23, 36, 91, 93–95, 107, 112, 115, 170; persistence of, 11, 146–51, 171; versions, 44, 143, 166–69, 171, 223n81. *See also* meşk; textual transmission; transmission processes
Orfeon (record company), 56. *See also* Blumenthal Brothers
Ortaköy (Istanbul), 58, 117, 209n65. *See also* Etz Ahayim synagogue
Osmanbey/Şişli (Istanbul), 49

Ottoman court music: historical survey, 8–11; in Ottoman art world, 42–48. *See also* Maftirim; Ottoman empire

Ottoman empire: Balkan Wars (1912–13), 54, 148; 'cosmopolitanism,' 5–6, 22, 180n6; historiographical concerns, 5–6, 22, 74; intercommunality, 5–6, 22; Jewish communities, 2, 9; minorities, administration of, 214n26; Ottoman-Russian War (1877–78), 25; Tanzimat reforms, 96, 186n63; 206n24. *See also* Mevlevi; Ottoman court music

Ottoman Jews: historiographical concerns, 25, 133–35, 171; as identifying term, 7–8. *See also* Ottoman empire; Sephardi

Ottoman-Russian War (1877–1878). *See* Ottoman empire

Ottoman-Turkish Sephardic Culture Research Center, 11, 114

oud. *See* ud

performance and entertainment venues: baths, 91, 98, 102, 207n37; café (coffeehouse, kahve, kahvehane), 22, 39, 59, 77, 97–99, 102, 187n72, 208n43, 208n52; çalgılı kahvesi, 38, 99; home(s), 9, 37, 64, 91, 94–95, 101, 103–13, 191n18 (*see also* ev toplantısı); meyhane(s), 37, 98–99, 102, 105, 109; palace, 9, 32, 34, 40, 47, 67, 172, 189n87; picnics, 98, 207n37, 208n52; semai kahvehanesi, 39, 188n79. *See also* gazinos; synagogues; urban space

peşrev, 46, 100, 211n102

piano, 74, 104

Pierre Loti Gazinosu, 99–100

Praetorius, Ernst, 74, 200n103

radio, 64–66. *See also* Ankara Radio; Istanbul Radio; meşk, radio sessions; Turkish classical music

rebetika music, 205n17

recording industry, 38, 52, 55–59, 65, 66, 93, 196n64, 211n67. *See also* gramophone; sound recordings. *See also names of specific record companies*

Refik Bey, 45

RF (Refah Partisi or Welfare Party), 130

Rıdvah Nafiz Bey, 26

Riyaset-i Cumhur Filarmoni Orkestrası, 74

Romania, 25, 197n77

Romaniot Jews, 89

Romano, Yeuda, 61

Rosenthal, Alice, 79

Rusçuk (present-day Ruse, Bulgaria), 25

Ruşen Kam, 60

Sabah, Menteş, 77–78

Sabbath. *See* Shabbat

Salgar, Fatih, 83

Saloman Efendi, 39

Salonika, 8–10, 45, 55, 97, 191n20, 205n17

Şan Sineması, 79

Sanayi-i Nefise Mektebi, 41, 188n84

Sarıyer (Istanbul), 39; map, 40

şarkı, 11, 36–37, 100, 181n18

Şaul, Eli, 99, 101

Savaş, Taşkın, 126, 129

Seattle, 17, 31, 46, 169–70, 174. *See also* Sephardic Bikur Holim Synagogue

Şehbal Mecmuası, 34

Şehzadebaşı (Istanbul), 39; map, 40

Selahaddin Efendi, 26

Selaniko synagogue, 155, 159–60, 213n14; map, 158

Selçuk, Münir Nurettin, 65, 79, 196n67, 202n118

sema. *See* Mevlevi

semai kahvehanesi. *See* performance and entertainment venues

Sene, Emily, 112

Şengel, Ali Rıza, 79

Şenozan, Şükrü, 45

Sephardi, as identifying term, 7–8. *See also* Ottoman Jews; Turkish Jews

Sephardic Bikur Holim synagogue (Seattle), 31, 169

Seroussi, Edwin, 165, 174

Settlement Law (1934), 69. *See also* Turkish Republic

Sevi, David, 49, 122, 124, 150

Sevilya, Nesim, 32–36, 70–71, 185n56, 186n62

Shabbat (Sabbath), 26, 89, 97, 122; religious law and, 154, 167, 181n14, 224n85. *See also* Maftirim

Shire Yisrael be-Erets ha-kedem, 54, 144, 146–49; Maftirim project (2009), 165–68; notation project (1920s), 149–50; predecessors, 191n20. *See also* Maftirim; song-text collection

Şikari, Santo (Şemtov Şikari), 41, 188n85, 188n86

Sinagog Maftirim Korosu. *See* Maftirim

Şişhane (Istanbul), 41

Şişli (Istanbul), 87, 122, 159. *See also* Bet Israel synagogue

Sofia, 26, 33, 34

song-text collection (güfte mecmuası): 60, 144, 146, 148, 181n17, 189n90, 219n6, 220n15. *See also* meşk; *Shire Yisrael be-Erets ha-kedem*; textual transmission

Index

sound recordings: cassettes, 141–42, 174; commercial records, 18, 32, 36, 67, 112, 184n24, 196n65 (*see also names of specific musicians*); cylinders, 56; Ladino songs, 93, 112, 196n66; Maftirim project (2009), 165–68. *See also* gramophone; recording industry
soundscape: in Balat (1930s), 96–98, 107; as theoretical framework, 91. *See also* urban space
Sözeri, Perihan Altındağ, 67
State Classical Turkish Music Chorus of Istanbul, 83
Sulam, Yomtov, 105, 202n122
Sultan Ahmet Belediye Bahçesi (gazino), 39
synagogues, 54, 159, 190n1, 191n12; attacks upon, 118–19, 121; Mevlevi lodge, relations with, 30–31; multiple functions of, 10, 61–62, 84; map, 102, 158. *See also* specific names of synagogues

taksim, 11, 32, 41, 123, 152–53
Tanburi Cemil Bey, 18–19, 181n5, 224n86
Tanzimat reforms. *See* Ottoman empire
Taragano, Ama Pepo, 77
Taragano, Cako, 126
Tatyos Efendi, 57
textual transmission: authenticity, concepts of, 4, 166–68; discourses for and against, 44, 167, 189n94, 224n83; national music and, 72; notation (5-staff), 33, 103, 191n18; 'originals,' 166–68; scores as skeletal guides, 164, 220n24. *See also* oral transmission; song-text collection; transmission processes
Thrace, 31, 121
Thrace Incidents (Trakya Olayları), 69, 185n50. *See also* Turkish Republic
Tınışkan, Neyzen Abdurrahman Nevzat, 80
transmission processes: new technologies, late Ottoman, 11, 103; new technologies, republican, 163–68; oral-textual confluences, 14–15, 142, 164. *See also* oral transmission; textual transmission
Türk Beşleri, 72
Türk Gülşen-i Musıki Heyeti, 67–68
Türk Musıkisi İcra Heyeti, 79
Turkish Airforce March (Türk Hava Kuvvetleri Marşı), 64. *See also* Algazi, İsak
Turkish art music. *See* Turkish classical music
Turkish classical music, 26–27, 29, 84, 145, 161–62; change in performance style and aesthetics, 65–66, 80; congregants' knowledge of, 155–59; home gatherings for, 80–82; musical source for hazanim, 128, 151–53; radio ban, 61, 72, 194n59, 199n90; state funding for education, 71, 76, 201n109; Turkish art music, 1, 67, 94–95, 109, 115. *See also* Ottoman court music; Turkish Republic
Turkish Jews: historiographical concerns, 4, 12–14, 25, 53, 84, 128, 133–35, 139, 171; as identifying term, 7–8. *See also* Sephardi; Turkish Republic
Turkish Republic: anti-minority laws and events, 52, 70, 197n80, 218n71; Atatürk, 26, 61, 62, 69, 71, 130, 183n18, 217n54; Cyprus, invasion of, 134, 217n53; historiographical concerns, 6, 51, 74–76, 120, 130, 190n7; Independence Tribunals, 195n63; nationalisms, 52–53, 63, 67, 76, 133, 139; social and religious reforms, 60–63 (see also European-style music); religion, place in public life, 129–31; War of Independence (1921–22), 54. *See also* Turkish classical music. *See also names of specific laws and events*

ud (Ar, oud), 23
Udi Moşe Moiz Leon, 77
Udi Selim, 39, 77
University of Washington, 17
Unkapanı (Istanbul), 17, 99
urban space, 20, 22–23, 42, 47, 94; as theoretical framework, 5–6, 15, 21, 94; Ottoman era, 21–23, 42, 47; transformation of, 52, 59, 61. *See also* Istanbul; performance and entertainment venues; soundscape
Üsküdar Musıki Cemiyeti, 49
Üsküdarlı Bestenigar Hoca Ziya Bey, 37
usul, 10. *See also* meşk, process

Varlık Vergisi. *See* Capital Tax
Varon, İsak, 27, 45, 55, 56, 58, 192n27
von Keller, Friedrich (Ambassador), 72, 199n94

War of Independence (1921–1922). *See* Turkish Republic
Weinberg, Sigmund, 56

Yanbol synagogue, 89, 155; map, 102, 158
Yakarış Müzik Topluluğu, 126
Yaşar, Necdet, 17–21, 29, 46
Yavaşça, Alaeddin, 81–83
Yekta, Rauf, 60, 82, 149, 166
Yekta, Yavuz, 82
Yusuf Paşa, 46

Zekâizade Ahmet Efendi, 60
Zonophone (record company), 56
Zuckmayer, Eduard, 74

The authorized representative in the EU for product safety and compliance is:
Mare Nostrum Group
B.V Doelen 72
4831 GR Breda
The Netherlands

www.ingramcontent.com/pod-product-compliance
Lightning Source LLC
Chambersburg PA
CBHW022004220426
43663CB00007B/950